"MY GOD, WE'RE BLOWING UP! WE'RE COMING APART!"

The boom had failed to find its orifice. Instead the nozzle struck the bomber's longeron, the taut metal spine of the plane. In the aerodynamic stress set up by the proximity of the B-52's great wings under the tanker's soaring tail fin, the sharp, sudden contact broke the bomber's backbone and snapped it into pieces as easily as the fingers of a giant child might snap the body of a hummingbird.

Fire raced up the boom to the KC-135's vast, sloshing tanks. The flames spurted through the crumbling B-52. In an instant the cool sky was lit with the searing ball of 40,000 gallons of jet fuel burning all at once.

All four members of the tanker crew were carbonized even before the debris of their plane hit the ground 30,000 feet below. It burst apart in great hunks as it fell. When the fire burned itself out, the molten metal lay on the ground in the recognizable outline of a plane, as though poured flat from a crucible by some shaky hand.

ONE OF OUR
H-BOMBS
IS MISSING

FLORA LEWIS

BANTAM BOOKS
TORONTO • NEW YORK • LONDON • SYDNEY • AUCKLAND

*This low-priced Bantam Book
has been completely reset in a typeface
designed for easy reading, and was printed
from new plates. It contains the complete
text of the original hardcover edition.*
NOT ONE WORD HAS BEEN OMITTED.

👑

ONE OF OUR H-BOMBS IS MISSING
*A Bantam Book / published by arrangement with
McGraw-Hill Book Company*

PRINTING HISTORY
McGraw-Hill edition published January 1967
Bantam edition / April 1987

*Bantam Books are published by Bantam Books, Inc. Its trade-
mark, consisting of the words "Bantam Books" and the por-
trayal of a rooster, is registered in U.S. Patent and Trademark
Office and in other countries. Marca Registrada. Bantam
Books, Inc., 666 Fifth Avenue, New York, New York 10103.*

PRINTED IN THE UNITED STATES OF AMERICA

O   0 9 8 7 6 5 4 3 2 1

To Kerry, Sheila and Lindsey

CONTENTS

ACKNOWLEDGMENT

I wish to acknowledge with deep gratitude the kind help given me by several hundred people, both official and private, and by the organizations involved. It was their generosity which made this book possible. Though they were unstinting in cooperation and sympathy, any errors are of course my own. I also want to thank Miss Ann Thayer for her cheerful, invaluable assistance.

F.L.

1

THE CRASH

The routine had been planned, checked, rechecked, and tested down to the next-to-last detail. The last detail could never be practiced, it is nuclear war. But short of the final instruction from the President of the United States, the "go code" that would send the bombers on past four imaginary lines in the sky to their targets, the operation was as settled and familiar as driving to work. The men had done it scores of times, making sure to get a good eight hours' sleep in the last twelve hours before take off, turning out for the mission briefings with royal blue silk scarves tucked into the neck of their flying suits for smartness, switching to the black-and-white checked scarves which the 51st Bomber Squadron of the Strategic Air Command affects aloft. Still, there was a tautness, an excitement at the base. There always is when a SAC Bombardment Wing draws its turn at air alert. Even though the men had done exactly the same thing every time they flew the mission, they never knew for certain until they started back that it was just another exercise.

B-52

The 51st, flying out of Seymour Johnson Air Force base at Goldsboro, North Carolina, about 80 miles from Raleigh, had its yearly spate of air alert in January, 1966. Once every ten days or so each crew took up a B-52 Stratofortress whose eight jet engines have the power of thirty locomotives, loaded with four hydrogen bombs each having more destructive force than all the conventional bombs ever dropped anywhere. The missions last twenty-four hours, partly because that is the way the routes are mapped to get the planes to their fail-safe line and back, partly because that is as long as a crew might be expected to function alertly under anything but dire conditions. The planes could continue almost indefinitely with their regular nourishment of fuel from aerial tankers. The men, for all the apocalyptic power at their fingertips, cannot. They get tired.

Before the flight set off at dusk on Sunday, January 16, the briefing officer reminded the crews, as he always did, that fatigue was one of the problems to remember toward the end of the mission. That was just another item in the long routine of preparation, briefing, and flying. The condition of the human machine, as well as of the metal machines, was constantly watched because there is no room for mistakes in the H-bomb world. The day before, the crew of another bomber doing ground-alert duty had checked out Bomber Number 256, a part of the buddy system airmen perform for each other so that the men going up can have a few hours more at home before their long day's work. The ground-alert crews, manning half of SAC's 680 bombers at any given minute, spend four days and three nights in an enclosure close to their waiting, loaded planes and have time to spare. They must be able to scramble into the air within six or seven minutes from the instant a klaxon calls them off to war—or to another of the frequent readiness tests. They find out which it is when they have settled themselves in the cockpit. The maximum time America's radar warning system would give of a flight of enemy missiles coming in to wipe out the country is twenty minutes. But if something failed, if the split-second mechanism did not get the grounded bombers up before the base was atomized, the air-alert planes would still be ready and able to hit back.

The crew of 256, their call name at the time was Tea-16, took off with their backs to the setting sun and started on the first leg of the southern route of Chrome Dome, the code name for the four SAC air-alert missions. At every minute of every day and night since 1961, loaded bombers had been somewhere on each of the four routes. The southern flight was the most pleasant. The other three fan north, out over Alaska, up above Canada, out to Greenland. If the bombers were ever ordered to go on, they would fly over the polar regions and dip down to their targets from the Arctic. The fourth Chrome Dome mission was over the middle Atlantic, across Spain, and halfway up the Mediterranean. On, from there, would be east over friendly blue water until the time to veer up into the southern reaches of an enemy's territory. The first refueling went smoothly, as usual, and the crew settled in for the long flight.

Capt. Charles F. Wendorf, the aircraft commander, lit his corncob. The squadron leader sometimes liked to relieve the earnestness of preflight briefings with the crack that "if everything goes right, you feel like a bunch of monkeys running a lot of black boxes." The joke invariably brought a groaning laugh from the crews, because they liked to think they felt that way, and knew they never would and never could. "A sense of humor is one of the few things that makes this whole life possible," Major Earnheart, the lanky, dry commander once had said. "We're guardians of the nation and we have to get off the ground to do a dirty job." Wendorf didn't think much about implications, of missions, or machinery, as the plane raced noisily across the ocean. SAC crews seldom did. There was more than enough work to keep busy, and it was a welcome thing to have a spare pilot aboard to spell the six regular crew members from time to time. Wendorf had already logged more than 2,500 flying hours, 2,100 in B-52's. Round-faced, with a slightly pug nose and a cleft chin, his body covered with a pale but dense blond hair except on his head where he kept it cut to a bare stubble, he had a relaxed confidence of manner that added to everybody's sense of just getting on with the job. He always had a stock of corncob pipes and he wore a platinum wedding ring, but he carried no totem or good-luck piece. He never imagined it might be necessary. Like all the men, he had an established pattern of exactly what should go in each of the myriad pockets of a flying suit. One of the men on his buddy crew kept the switch-blade knife in the pocket over the left calf constantly opened to the shroud hook end, so that not even a fraction of a second would be lost if he had to cut himself out of a parachute. That precaution had not occurred to Wendorf. The need for it had never arisen and he had no reason to think it would.

The routine was undisturbed. All the crew had spent many hours studying the flight plan. They had also studied, so intensively that they could visualize the buildings, the hamlets, the hills, a further flight plan they would never follow without explicit orders from the President of the United States, decoded and understood by the agreement of at least three of them. Wendorf carried that plan in a rectangular black satchel, rather like a carpetbag but of leather with hard edges, marked with red stripes and the words Top Secret in big black letters, referred to always with an extra tightness in the throat as the CMF—Combat Mission Folder. They all knew what was in it. They had had to learn the approach to the target, the timing ordered, the decoy plan, the altitude for penetration and bombardment. But the CMF had never been opened in the air. It never would be unless the President performed the act which civilians around the world had come to call "pushing the button."

At twenty-nine Wendorf was third youngest of his crew, but he bore himself with an air of responsibility beyond his years. The team was close knit. They probably saw more of each other, as a friend at the base had said, than they did of their wives. To make up somewhat for this schedule of male seclusion, the Air Force had thoughtfully provided a rustic picnic shed and a swing and seesaw set for children just outside the alert area's wire fence. Families could have an occasional open-air meal together when the men were on ground duty. When they were away, crew wives made up a parallel team, for bridge, for gossip, for mutual support.

The youngest on the airborne, male side of the team was the navigator, First Lieut. Steven G. Montanus, twenty-three. He was dark of hair and complexion, thin-boned but tall and intensely good-looking. Everybody liked him and made affectionately crass jokes about his pretty nineteen-year-old wife Corinne. The butt of the sharpest jokes was First Lieut. Michael J. Rooney—"Mike," to his friends. Twenty-five, he was the only bachelor on the crew, and he gave as well as he took about the joys of married life versus the charms of nurses, daughters of senior officers, and belles of nearby Raleigh. Rooney was fair, nearly six feet tall, and lively, a man who yearned for combat with a tactical command and did not altogether share the views of many SAC pilots. Some liked the B-52's best, as one said, "because those eight big engines give you such a cozy feeling—if one or two or even three go out, there's still nothing serious." And some had picked the service with the ultimate weapon "because here we know we're really doing something. We're not just flapping our wings from one place to another, flying around. You heard about speaking softly and carrying a big stick? We're the big stick." That was the way Lieut. Leonard Weiner, radar-navigator on the buddy crew, put it, and it was pretty much the attitude of most B-52 men on the base. Their Southern tongues seldom flushed out the ideas with the flick of Weiner's Atlantic City-bred loquacity, but they felt no burden of discomfort at being in what Major Earnhart had called "this grim business."

Besides Wendorf, copilot Rooney, navigator Montanus, the men on the regular crew were Capt. Ivens Buchanan, thirty-four, a stocky, shy, extremely regulation-conscious man whose job was radar-navigator, the new-model name for bombardier because he has other tasks and because it is as well to have a euphemism for the man whose hand releases H-bombs; First Lieut. George J. Glesner, twenty-six, a reserved man with a fierce passion for flying who served as electronic warfare officer, the position in charge of jamming enemy radar, launching decoys and chaff; and Technical Sgt. Ronald P. Snyder, quiet and as a noncom not well known to officers on the base, in charge of the four 50-caliber guns in the bomber's tail and of helping the others when they wished. On that mission Tea-16 also carried a spare pilot, Maj. Larry G. Messinger, at forty-four the oldest man aboard and the only one who had ever dropped real bombs in real anger. He had won a string of decorations flying B-17's over Europe in World War II and B-29's over Korea, and had developed thin lines of fatigue around his eyes, a patient, wary expression on his long, soft face.

Except for Messinger, they had been flying, and playing poker, and studying, and cursing together for a year or so. In the air, nobody bothered to chatter. Crisp, regulation exchanges on the intercom were enough. They knew each other so well there was no need to say more. The noise, the constant requirement to check the hundreds of gauges and dials and switches that lined almost the entire inner surface of the cockpit, the regular reports and checks with the ground

B-17

and with the other B-52 leading the usual brace of bombers, left little opportunity for idle talk if the desire had been there.

It was dawn—the sun comes up five hours earlier over Spain than over Goldsboro—when they made the second refueling rendezvous. A tanker from the U.S. Air Force base at Torrejón, near Madrid, came up to meet them at the appointed time and place high over the sparsely populated stretch between Zaragoza and Barcelona in northern Spain. Refreshed with some 40,000 gallons of jet fuel, they flew out to the Mediterranean. The dog-leg end of the long triangle on the Chrome Dome route was a line well short of the reach of the Kremlin's warning system, SAC's mysterious counterpart. It lay across the middle of the sea east of Italy. After the sharp turn south, there was another sharp turn west. It gave the first moment of certainty that the mission was just another "indoctrination flight," after all. There was nothing more to worry about but getting home, and guzzling enough more fuel to arrive with plenty of reserves for alternate landings if the weather went soupy.

The final tanker date was over southern Spain, in an area just in from the Mediterranean coast line. SAC called it the Saddle Rock refueling zone. This time the tanker was to come up from the American base at Morón, in the southwest near

Sevilla. The KC-135, a cavernous flying gas station that seems a lumbering ugly duckling next to her sleek commercial twin, the 707, arrived to make contact as scheduled. SAC requirements provide for no more than thirty seconds' leeway, early or late, for planes flying thousands of miles to meet six miles above the earth. Both planes cruise at about 450 to 500 miles an hour, not much below the speed of sound. Making first radio contact some hundred miles apart gives them less than ten minutes to identify and approach each other in the prescribed pattern.

When they were less than five minutes apart, the bomber descended to some 2,000 feet below the tanker and the tanker banked into a sharp U-turn that would bring it out a few miles ahead of its thirsty chaser.

At that point Master Sgt. Lloyd Potolicchio, the boom operator on the tanker, strode back to the red plastic-covered mattress tucked in the bulging tail of his plane. Potolicchio was a big man, a former All-American basketball player, and it was a squeeze for him to fit into the narrow slot from which the maneuver had to be directed. He worried about his weight, eating only one meal a day to lose seven to eight pounds whenever he was on duty and he complained after every leave that his wife fed him so well that he had gained it all back. He kept himself apart from the officers on the crew, a gregarious, socializing trio. He was talkative enough, but a loner by nature, and that was all right because the crucial part of his job had to be performed alone. Potolicchio stretched out on his stomach and strapped himself down so he would not be sucked out if the inner window suddenly gave when he had lifted the outer Plexiglas shield for better visibility. For the next ten or fifteen minutes, until the operation was completed, the sergeant would in effect be commanding both planes.

The other three members of the tanker crew remained as usual in the cockpit, leaving the intimate details of the prospective coupling to the boom operator. Maj. Emil J. Chapla, the pilot, was enthused about the temporary duty in Spain. "Chap" (he hated his first name and only used the nickname) was an ardent tourist and it was one of the advantages of being on tanker crew that the men had an occasional chance to spend a few weeks in places that bomber crews only saw from six miles up. His copilot, Capt. Paul R. Lane, known by his middle name Ray, was a barrel-chested

200-pound fun lover and the navigator, Capt. Leo E. Simmons, was an enthusiast of the Spanish guitar. All four crew members were family men, but except for Potolicchio a few weeks in Spain was a lark that made up a bit for leaving their wives and children back at Bergstrom Air Force base in Texas.

The bomber men liked to argue that tanker men had it soft, because of the travel and because of the job. "It's like flying a Cadillac," the B-52 crews would say. "They go up and they're down again in a couple of hours. Nothing to it unless the boom man has such a paunch he can't bear working a few minutes on his belly."

Still, refueling was an exacting performance. Both crews had done it many hundreds of times. They had no sense of special risk or caution in approaching it once more. But there was always a sense of the need for precise control, for alertness and quick reaction, just as a driver on a long-familiar road hones an attention that had been blunted on the flat when he reaches mountainous hairpin bends.

"Tea-16, Tea-16," Potolicchio called. "This is Troubadour 14." He read off speed and altitude. The bomber crept upward, at cruising speed but gaining only slowly on the tanker, at a rate of a few miles an hour. When the distance was down to half a mile, the telescoped metal tube that was to feed the bomber pushed out into the empty air. Controlling its two stubby wings, the operator "flew" the boom to the correct position straight behind the tanker. It trailed stiffly like some vestigial tail.

Wendorf and Messinger were at the B-52's controls. Rooney was taking a rest, reading a magazine by the bunk in the narrow corridor connecting the forward part of the cockpit with its double-tiered rear. Glesner and Snyder were behind him, strapped in their seats, attending to their instruments. Below them, Montanus and Buchanan watched the pale green blip that was the tanker grow on their radar screens. Only the pilots could see out through the angled cockpit window. B-52's have so many electronic eyes and ears and brains that the crew doesn't need a panoramic view. In fact, were they to perform their ultimate mission, the pilots would draw the silver-colored blinds to block all outside vision and thus prevent themselves from being blinded by the fireball they had set off. But nuzzling up to the boom requires human direction, human judgment, human perception. "Eyeball flying," the crews called it. The pilot must

B-29

cozy in so that his bomber's lips, opening above its fuel mouth just to the rear of the cockpit, are no more than a maximum of six feet to either side of the hanging nozzle. The boom operator, watching from above like a mother guiding her suckling, operated his guidance lights—red to signal speed and course corrections, green when the pilot below had maneuvered to exactly the right approach.

They had ceased speaking, the pilot and the operator, communicating the last directions by the gesture of light and motion. But their radios remained set in communication to a common frequency. A little before they could expect the boom to drop down and lock itself in place, the operator broke the customary silence of the last two or three minutes.

"Tea-16, Tea-16," he called. "Watch your enclosure." He meant that the bomber was closing in a little too quickly. The tone of his voice was normal. There was no hint of disaster in the warning. The bomber pilot pulled back the throttles to slow himself.

It was probably not more than a minute later that it happened. The explosion, the screaming shudder of the plane's whole metal frame, the burst of flame, seemed to come simultaneously. Wendorf, in the pilot's seat to the left of the cabin, heard and felt and pulled his ejection handle. Presumably, that set off the "bail out" alarm at each of the other stations, but nobody remembered. Each man had to react on his own. Wendorf couldn't even remember afterward what he had noticed first, the noise, the fire, or the uncontrollable shivering of the cabin. It was all so fast. All that stuck in his mind was suddenly thinking to himself, "My God, we're blowing up. We're coming apart."

The boom had failed to find its orifice. Instead, the nozzle struck the bomber's longeron, the taut metal spine of the plane. In the aerodynamic stress set up by the proximity of the B-52's great wings under the tanker's soaring tail fin, the sharp, sudden contact broke the bomber's backbone and snapped it into pieces as easily as the fingers of a giant child might snap the body of a hummingbird. Fire raced up the boom to the KC-135's vast, slosing tanks. The flames spurted through the crumbling B-52. In an instant the cool sky was lit with the searing ball of 40,000 gallons of jet fuel burning all at once.

All four members of the tanker crew were carbonized even before the debris of their plane hit the ground 30,000 feet below. It burst apart in great hunks as it fell. But the main section, the wings, and most of the fuselage, simply plopped in flame. When the fire burned itself out, the molten metal lay on the ground in the recognizable outline of a plane, as though poured flat from a crucible by some shaky hand.

The bomber crew members had never practiced that emergency, but they had been lectured to instinctive reaction. Wendorf and Messinger in the forward seats, Buchanan and Montanus in the lower rear, tugged at the black-and-yellow striped handle beside each of them. A small explosive charge propelled the two pilots and their seats upward through the roof. Similar charges propelled the navigators downward through the floor. Montanus may have been hit by something, or knocked unconscious at the moment of ejection, or unlucky in some other inexplicable way. His parachute never opened. Still strapped into his heavy seat, he hit the ground with the full impact of a fall from nearly six miles. His long body was crumpled and his handsome dark face frozen in horror when he was found. A trickle of almost black blood had congealed below one corner of his mouth.

Buchanan, who had been sitting beside him, had trouble, too. But he was luckier, or more carefully mindful of the step-by-step instructions that they all had learned. He had always gone by the book, word for word. It may have saved his life. His seat, like Montanus', failed to come off and rip out his parachute. He struggled at the strap, but he was falling too fast for fingers to work with normal ease. So he bent his torso as far forward as he could and clutched at the mouth of the chute pack behind his shoulders. Handful by handful, he hauled the saving nylon out. He fed it to the wind that shrilled in his wake. Finally, the pilot canopy caught. It pulled the 24-foot white-and-orange main chute out to float. The landing was hard nonetheless. The awkward seat with the man still locked inside its arms thudded down and toppled forward, pressing his face to the ground. Buchanan was still unconscious when they found him. After a few minutes he revived. He wasn't clear whether he had passed through the big fireball, or perhaps too near a piece of flaming debris. He was badly burned and his back hurt, doubtless from the jolt of impact. But he was alive.

Glesner and Snyder, sitting with their backs to the pilots on the same level, never got out. The opening of the fuel tank was above and only a foot or so behind them. The crash may have clipped the wiring for their ejection mechanism, or shattered their part of the cockpit before anything could work.

Rooney was left stumbling, really floating, in the falling foresection. He was wearing his parachute, as always, but there were only six ejection seats and he had been taking a breather as odd man out. His path to safety, he knew from endless drill, had to be the hole left in the underside of the plane after the navigators had shot themselves into the air. He tried desperately to crawl toward it. The cabin was falling free, tumbling wildly. At one moment the force of gravity pitched him in the direction of the hole. Then the cabin careened and he was pinned to the roof, incapable of moving. Another pitch threw him not quite halfway out. But it was too brief to give him time to jump before the gravity force began to pull him back inside. The ordeal may have lasted a couple of minutes, minutes of a million seconds each. Finally, the plummeting debris turned right side up once more and Rooney dropped himself into the sky. The chute opened and jerked him short. There was still a passage of terror when a burning jet engine dropped by a few feet away from him. The heat singed the blond hair on his arms. Then the canopy billowed out beautifully and he slumped into the relief of a long descent.

Messinger bailed out a little before the pilot. There was no time to give the order on the intercom, no time for anyone to say anything to the ground. The men reacted almost instinctively as they saw an explosive flash of light and heard the deep, crushing noise of the plane breaking up. But the pilot and copilot let themselves fall until the automatic rip cord pulled out their chutes. Messinger, the instructor pilot, jerked his cord by hand soon after he left the plane. A wind roaring at 60 knots caught his chute as if it were a toy balloon and wafted him rapidly away from the rain of burning metal. It was a piercingly clear day. He watched the pink and yellow land, dotted with tiny green plots, slide behind. For a moment he could see the white wall of the surf marking an angrily frothy boundary between land and sea. Then he was over water, choppy, heaving water, drifting farther and farther east. When he touched it, he was twelve miles out from shore.

Wendorf must have left the plane a minute or two before Rooney. He knew that Messinger had ejected from the seat next to his but had no way of telling whether the others were safely out. He hit something as he fired himself into the air and it stunned him, so that he was only partly aware of what was happening as he came down. But he remembered the parachute opening, catching the wind with a gentle pull that surprised him. He had expected a shock. He looked up at the canopy. Four of the chute panels were burning. A shred of scorching cloth fell on the back of his neck, leaving a burn. He scarcely noticed, worrying about the way the canopy was streaming before the wind instead of spreading into a wide umbrella of safety. His survival kit, he saw then, was caught in the shroud lines, preventing full deployment of the chute.

"I reached up with my right arm to untangle the lines," he said later, "and it hurt. So I tried my left. That was when I felt the bone sticking out below my left shoulder. Somehow I got the shrouds untwisted. The last thing I remembered was seeing that the fire had gone out in the burning sections. I was in the water when I came to. I'm no fanatic about religion, but I knew I was going to be all right. I have faith in the Lord enough to know He was going to take care of me. I hoped my wife wouldn't worry too much. I kept thinking what a surprise it was, I was just flying along and all of a sudden here I am in the water. I counted the other chutes and saw a lot of debris still falling. I thought everybody was going to be all right."

The fate of the four H-bombs he had been shepherding did not cross Wendorf's mind. It was people he kept wondering about, and that made him wonder what was keeping him afloat. He realized he hadn't inflated his life jacket. A piece of the survival kit, he noticed then, had lodged beneath his right arm. "I saw that was all that was holding me up. So I inflated my Mae West."

Rooney and Wendorf hit the water about three miles out from shore, not far apart but not near enough to see each other over the waves.

Everything else from the two planes, worth $11,000,000 and weighing, loaded, nearly 800,000 pounds, was falling helter-skelter onto a square of land and sea more than ten miles along each side. The tanker broke into a few crushing pieces and a spray of bits. The bomber, no more really than a flying tank and bomb bay with hundreds of miles of electrical circuitry, had disintegrated into thousands of pieces. The biggest piece that fell intact was the tail section. Engines, undercarriage, cabin, hunks of wing and fuselage, electronic gadgets in their metal boxes, shreds of wire and even individual nuts and screws splattered out in a great, patternless deluge.

The explosive wrench that shattered the plane burst open the bomb bay. The package of four Quail decoys, a mock plane about 10 feet long equipped with a reflecting nose to make it look like a B-52 on radar and with pre-set instruments to make it fly like a B-52 dodging enemies, was thrown from the rear rack where it had hung. From the forward rack there had hung the four H-bombs, each built to fission enough plutonium and uranium and to fuse enough tritium to produce an explosion equal in power to about 1,000,000 tons of TNT. It would have been enough to blow up all of southern Spain. If Tea-16 had been on the way to its pre-set target, more than one of the crew members would have pressed buttons and switches to activate a series of fusing circuits in the bomb. One of the men would have had to unscrew a plate and manually shove a lever to the *on* position. Then, at the crucial moment, the bombardier's gloved hand would have clutched a duck-pin-shaped handle near him and the time of universal dread would be seconds away, a precise number of seconds while the bomb fell free, then floated on its parachute to the pre-determined detonation altitude, and then delivered atomic death, perhaps to millions. The signals had not been given; the moves had not been made. The bombs, therefore, were not cocked, "armed," as the Air Force says, so that the intricate nuclear machinery could not work. But it was there, linking the precious chunks of radioactive metal and the hydrogen fuel. The bomb rack buckled and split when the plane broke, dropping the weapons in and around the Spanish village of Palomares.

2

THE VILLAGE I

Palomares was not on the road to anywhere. Although it lay under the 10,000-mile route of Chrome Dome, it was simply the end of a rutted track that twisted four and a half miles over arid yellow hills and pinched valleys to a two-lane road of asphalt. A sturdy car with good springs, or a motor scooter, could make it. But the track was more accustomed to the toughened rims of a two-wheel donkey cart riding high above the dust with a load of alfalfa showing bright green stripes between the wooden slats. Or better, it suited the hoofs of a donkey alone, carrying two narrow-mouthed jars of water or olive oil in woven panniers slung behind the legs of a child. The village had a plaza of sorts, a baked, irregular expanse of mud where old men could lounge in front of the cantina to gossip and wait for the moment of the day when they would go in to buy a half-sized bottle of beer and relish the shade. A few low houses lined three of its sides. On the fourth side, a windowless cement building that looked like a two-story warehouse gave the square solidity. It was the movie house, built a year and a half before. There, two nights a week, it was possible to sit on a rickety folding chair and watch a 16-millimeter story of horsemen in the wild West, or Rififi in Tokyo, for the admission price of 10 pesetas—17 cents.

Most of the whitewashed adobe houses straggled down the valley or along the narrow plain that opened toward the sea, clustered in groups of three or four and almost always brightened with a clump of purple morning glories or a carefully tended row of marigolds. The movie, two shops, and three cantinas, their colored strips of plastic haphazardly

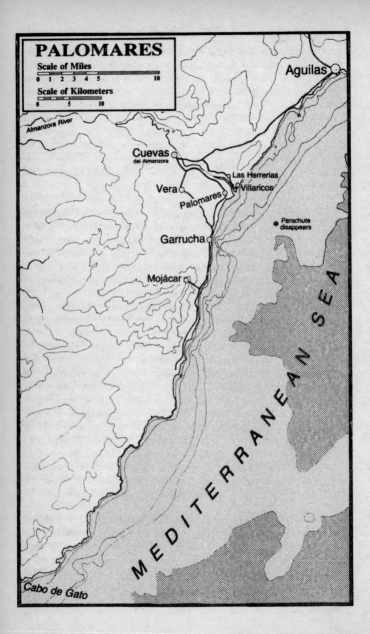

PALOMARES

Scale of Miles
0 1 2 3 4 5   10

Scale of Kilometers
0   5   10

Almanzora River

Aguilas

Cuevas
del Almanzora

Las Herrerias

Vera

Villaricos

Palomares

Parachute
disappears

Garrucha

Mojácar

MEDITERRANEAN SEA

Cabo de Gato

protecting open doorways against busily persistent flies, comprised the business district. But from outside, the way to tell a residence from a place of commerce was the open-walled extension of each house where a cow or a horse and chickens shared a roof with their masters. Here and there round concrete tanks brimmed with dull green water. Some of the houses had plumbing, an innovation requiring roof tanks, pumps, and cisterns, introduced since the export market for winter tomatoes had been discovered some fifteen years before and come to provide the basis for a cash crop. Few had bathrooms. Even fewer had hot water. All had a tree or a bush or at least a climbing hollyhock to distinguish the place of man from the braised landscape around it. Occasionally, standing by the road as though it had an independent existence, an oleander blossomed, a sign of the way nature dispersed the fruit of man's forgotten effort. Spiky tangles of cactus fenced the cultivated fields.

Monday, January 17, 1966, was just another Monday at the height of another Palomares tomato harvest. The rich red fruit hung thickly on vines held high by cane poles. They grew jumbled together on small plots, interspersed with equally small plots of beans and corn. There was more land, good growing land stretching up beyond the cemetery on the hill and down to where the fields of slag began before the beach. But it was empty, spotted with a thin bush of sage or a lonely cactus, showing everywhere the sharply shifting colors of the soil. The dry dirt went from ochre, to dull gray, to saffron except where the water came to turn it a rusty pink. Only with water, pumped and piped and coaxed into deep ditches that spread it to the thirsty plots, could the land give sustenance.

Once it had yielded treasure, copper and lead and other minerals. Nobody remembered how long ago the mines were founded but Doña Antonia Navarro Mula, the ample, smiling wife of the mayor and grandmother to his grandchildren, remembered hearing that her great-grandfather worked in the smelters on the hills and by the sea and that sometimes he took the ingots over the 320 miles to Madrid in a donkey cart. The mines had given out early in the century and were long abandoned. Crumbling pillars of the once vast buildings still stood on the edges of Palomares, and down by the sea stood the roofless walls of a warehouse lording it over a broad stretch of black slag. The open shafts were everywhere, potholes in the field they seemed, but they plunged deeper than anyone in the village could say. No sound came back when you dropped a rock down the opening.

It had been hard on Palomares when the mines were shut. The people turned to farming, but the wheat and the corn grew shorter and more scraggly as the water dwindled from the soil. They subsisted, but it was not a living. Many of the men went off to work in smelters and factories far away. They sent home money and when they returned to their families they took what savings they had brought to buy more land, some animals, to wrest a little more food from the unwilling soil.

The land was ancient to the struggle of human need. Phoenicians had roamed it, founding colonies and digging silver from its depths twelve centuries before Christ. Carthaginians had settled in the area. Later came Romans, and then Visigoths. None had left a trace on the isolated stretch where Palomares sprawls near Spain's eastern coast, some 50 miles up from the Cabo de Gata where the shoreline abruptly turns a corner and heads north. Nor was there yet much trace of Spain's newest invasion, the millions of French and German and English and American tourists who crowd the Costa del Sol on the south and covet the Costa Brava on the northeast but have somehow by-passed the province of Almería that lies between them. The Moors were there, it was one of the last regions they occupied before Ferdinand and Isabella finally completed their expulsion in 1492. Other villages in the area showed something of the heritage they had left. But not Palomares. It seemed curiously untouched by the world and by history, except the history of daily sweat and joy and sorrow beneath a sun of parching glory and an infinite sky.

There is no limit to the sky above Palomares. It expands clear and bright as far as man can see, and the people in the isolated village took a sense of scope in gazing at the vastness of the panorama stretching from their foothold on the land. Watching its emptiness, they had come to expect between the hours of ten and eleven each morning the appearance of two converging streaks of white, sharp lines slashed across the blue until the vapor trails met and two minuscule planes performed a strange and brief embrace. It had not occurred to SAC that its highly secret timetable was so well known or so widely observed from a ground that appeared only an impersonal canvas at 30,000 feet. It had not occurred to the watchers, taking pleasure in a distant spectacle, that the planes had meaning for the mightiest powers of the world and for themselves.

At 10:22 A.M. on the Monday of the accident, Eduardo Navarro Portillo, a man of sixty-eight, looked up from the jumble of his tomato vines for a moment of welcome distraction. The land was just behind the house, tightly shuttered against the sun and empty because his two daughters had married and his wife Anna had gone to visit their son in Barcelona. It gratified and yet disturbed him, the boy in Barcelona who did not like to work the land.

"He prefers to work with a pen and pencil," Navarro said later. "That is very nice. But he is not married and he is thirty."

The sepia-tinted photograph on the whitewashed wall, otherwise bare except for a few tools hanging on nails and a split-cane broom, showed a darkly handsome, soft-faced man of probable bulk, staring concentratedly at the camera as though to make sure it understood the gravity of recording an image correctly. The father was small and weathered frail, his eyes rimmed slightly red and narrowed in a permanent squint like those of all the villagers of an age to have worked that long in the sun. When he took off his frayed gray cap, the bald part beneath the wisps of hair was a delicate pink. It made a startling contrast with the creased bronze of his face. The hands were not large but heavy work had taught them where to bump with strength. He had not always worked the land. He and his Anna had been born in Palomares and they loved the muted colors, the stillness of their country, even the jagged hills where people bolted wooden doors on caves they'd cut for homes, even the bleached river bed where black goats browsed for nettled weeds. But he had left it when he was twenty-one, when there was no work and no money and not enough land for his father's sons.

"I went to the United States to the factory," he said. "To Gary, Indiana; Canton, Ohio; Buffalo, New York; Lackawanna. I don't remember where that is any more. It wasn't tourism, it was looking for work. There was a depression. I was in Texas but there's not much industry in Texas, no huge factories side by side like Indiana and Illinois. I was looking for work in West Virginia and Pennsylvania, in the coal mines. There was a strike there. It was terrible.

"What I did wrong was not go to school and learn well. That was a shame. Maybe then I wouldn't have come back. But they talked to me and I didn't understand. Sometimes they were angry and I didn't know what it was. If I could understand, I could have a better job. You're sure to get a good job if you know a language. But we didn't realize then. Now we know."

His eyes watered. He must have been thinking back on the dreams of youth, the chances lost. But his old hands stayed quietly on his knees as he talked and the few tears fell unnoticed.

"My son is learning English now. He left because there was no work here. He hoped to get work in a bank. But we couldn't give him a career. We haven't the money. Still, he has a good position. He works in a company that sells water pumps and machines from Germany."

But his son's lack of a marriage, of a home, bothered the father. It wasn't because he yearned for grandchildren. His two daughters, one married to a farmer and the other to the village shopkeeper, had already given him four. They had come to his mind quickly after what he saw in the sky.

Refueling

On that Monday he saw for a moment two planes riding together, almost piggyback. The next moment there was a violent explosion. A rain of flames began. A hunk of glowing, twisted metal was descending on the neighboring field. Navarro watched it, paralyzed with fear. Then he saw another great piece falling, he thought, in the direction of his daughter's shop so he ran to save her and her children, as though his old legs and arms could beat the force of gravity. Because he was running, he did not see the great tube fall behind him. It landed near the stone retaining wall of his tomato plot and released a deafening boom. Dirt showered in all directions. Later, he found the wall of the house had cracked. The bolt was blown off the door. The windows were broken and one of the window latches was gone, neatly sheared away as though it had been vaporized. Days later he found it blown far into the field.

At 10:22 A.M. on the Monday of the accident, Pedro Domingo Sánchez Gea was correcting arithmetic papers at his unpainted desk in the schoolroom, while 51 little boys bent their heads to the new problems he had set on the

blackboard. There were two rooms in the long white rectangle of the school building and large glass windows along one side. It was new, and the village was proud of it. But for Señor Sánchez it was a minor kind of purgatory, or at best an anteroom to the life he expected for himself and his family. The strain of patience showed a little in the tightness of his lips, the care of his bearing, the deliberate neatness of his clothes.

Sánchez had studied in Murcia, in Lorca, and in Granada, and he had taught in towns. Five years before he and his wife Milagro Jiménez Requeña had been assigned to Palomares, for teachers have to take turns at the good places and villages need teachers just as cities do. True they had a red tile floor, and potted plants, and decorative wrought-iron silhouettes of a bull and a dragonfly to enhance the house reserved for the schoolteacher, and their children Milagrito, six, and Pedro, two and a half, were thriving. They had a radio and one of the two television sets in Palomares—the other was in the cantina. They had the earnest respect of the villagers, not only for the school but for the small dispensary Sánchez ran in a room off the little kitchen. There was no doctor in the village, and although he had not been trained as a druggist, he had learned enough of pharmacology to prescribe for coughs and fevers and infections, to administer injections and vaccines. When a case was beyond his art and his cellophane-wrapped packages of drugs, someone went off to fetch the doctor from Vera or Cuevas. There were people in the village who would provide their cars for the purpose at a fee of 25 pesetas.

Still, the Sánchezes did not consider themselves a part of village life nor did they desire to be admitted. In two more years Sánchez would have enough service points to have a reasonable chance of drawing a provincial capital if he applied then for a transfer. Meanwhile, they worked and kept themselves to themselves. It was not that they disliked the villagers.

"They are hard working, the people here," Sánchez said. "They are good and amiable and the standards are high. They are generous."

But he and Milagro clearly did not consider they had much in common with the workers of the soil, many of them disliterate—in the sense that once, when they were children, they had learned to write but had forgotten after all these years when there seemed little use for writing and reading with so much other daily labor.

"Even the young people aren't used to studying," he said. "They get tired of it. They think a year or two after grade school should be enough. The fathers don't encourage them and the young ones want to earn a little money right away."

"We live very independently," said Milagro, a handsome young woman but cold in her pride. She jabbed a needle in her mending. "We don't go to others and we just want them to leave us alone. I only go out of the house if there's a funeral, or an accident or something. I go to mass, and to someone if they're really ill, but not to a little illness. I send the children for the shopping."

"If we have time to go anywhere," said her husband with a softening of pleasure in his eyes, "we go in the car, out of here. We go to Murcia or Almería. I'm so busy here, I never go to a movie or a fiesta. Then, in the town, we enjoy ourselves. I'm prepared to talk of anything gay. The best cure for illness is an injection of optimism."

He had, on the oilcloth-covered table before him which was both the family dining table and his desk at home, a pile of examination papers. They would show which of the fourth-grade boys had won promotion, and they were a very serious matter that had demanded agonies of study from the children.

On the Monday of the accident study was forgotten. First there had been a booming echo and then an angry tremor. Sánchez thought it was an earthquake and told the boys to stay still. But his wife Milagro had seen the ball of fire and the great white cloud. She ran from her house to the school across the path to tell her husband. He looked out and saw the debris falling from the sky.

"I evacuated the school," he said afterward. "We ran into the tomato patches shouting to the children to spread out as far from each other as they could. I told them to stretch out on the ground. None of them cried. You only cry for little things, not before such a terrible spectacle as this. It was too big to cry.

"When we got the boys out of the school, I turned to go back to our house. That day both our children were sick, the girl had a cold and the baby had tonsillitis. They were in bed alone. But we couldn't get back. An enormous piece of debris was falling in front of us. The trajectory was right over the house. That was terror, to stand and watch and not be able to go."

The moment was one that would stay with Sánchez all his life. Talking to his own conscience, he added, "I had over 50 boys in the school. Any other teacher would have thought of his own first."

The thing he watched shooting down was the bomb bay, several tons of twisted, livid metal. It fell in the road, 25 yards from the school and the Sánchez house, about the same distance on the other side of the road from the house of an old lady named Isabel Jordán. The shock of impact knocked her over and she complained of bad pains for months. As the chunk came down, it snipped the single line of electric wire running into the village on narrow poles of unplaned pine.

There was still wreckage falling from the sky, but the Sánchezes ran to get their children and take them to a neighbor. Then the teacher ran out again into the fields to see if he could help in the catastrophe that was something he had to share with the village.

Someone was going by on a motor scooter. He didn't notice who it was but he waved and leaped on the postilion, grabbing the driver's belt for safety.

"Take me up there," he shouted, gesturing at the great roll of flame and smoke from a hill well behind the village. Everybody was running through the fields, scouring the hills to see what had fallen. By then they realized it was a tremendous airplane accident and the common thought was for the people—the people of the village who might have been hit by one of the wildly scattered pieces of debris and the people of the planes who had gone through such disaster. Sánchez found no one who needed help. With others, he began to throw dirt at the burning wreckage of the tanker. As the flames retreated, they found bodies. They had to throw more dirt to put out the smoldering fire in human flesh.

At two-thirty in the afternoon the schoolteacher made his way home. He was trembling. So he prescribed for himself a glass of ricote, a strong wine, to revive his spirits and a tablet of passiflorine, a sedative, to calm his nerves. His wife Milagro was no longer so distracted. Her children were safe. No one in the village had been hurt, no one at all. The accident was a tragedy, of course, but not, it seemed, for Palomares. All the villagers felt sympathy for the people who had fallen so grotesquely from the sky. They couldn't help feeling excitement, too, at the extraordinary event. There were many details, many bits of news to tell, many amazing accounts to exchange of what had suddenly descended on them.

Milagro had heard some. Wide-eyed, she asked her husband, "Did you see the bomb?" He hadn't, but that was too much to miss. They took their little car and drove to Navarro Portillo's field, and there it was, a long projectile, part buried in the dirt, part broken, but still unmistakably a bomb. They inspected it. It seemed harmless enough now, its power spent. Sánchez was one of the few in Palomares who had heard of nuclear weapons but he never imagined he was looking at one. As it was, the horror of the day had exhausted him. By three he was home again, collapsing into bed for the siesta that he craved. He had barely fallen asleep when Don Juan, the doctor from Cuevas, came beating on the door to fetch him. Like people from all over the region, Dr. Juan Miguel García had heard the aerial explosion and seen the rain of metal and some parachutes. It was visible from 50 miles away. More than 500 people, all who could find any kind of transport, rushed to Palomares, propelled by an instinctive sense of service where there might be suffering and need, drawn by as irresistible a sense of curiosity.

"We have to collect the bodies," the doctor told the schoolteacher. "Come and help." Together they went back to the ashen hillside. Simple coffins had been brought. They labored to gather the remains respectfully. It was not an easy matter. Some of the cadavers were dismembered. They put what they had found into two boxes, later transferred to five coffins. It was to cause a certain bureaucratic difficulty when the U.S. Air Force came to claim its casualties. There had been but four men in the tanker. 112473

At 10:22 A.M. on the Monday of the accident, Manolo González was visiting the school where his young wife Dolores Alegría takes the girls' class. Manolo's father is Don José Manuel González Fernández, mayor of Palomares though in a somewhat loose sense of the word. Don José, a tall, lumbering man with crisp gray hair and a tanned face heavy with confidence and authority, worked for the post office in Cuevas, some 7 miles away. Cuevas was the administrative, juridical, and ecclesiastical center on which Palomares depended since it was not a village in any legal sense but only by the pragmatic fact of its existence as a collection of some 200 families. Since Don José was the senior civil servant residing

in Palomares, since he was one of the larger landowners and
therefore a man of status in the community, and since mayors
are not elected in Spain in any case but like all public officials
are chosen from above, the title of the not really established
office of mayor had fallen to him. To the extent that he had
mayoral duties to exercise, he did so from the small front
room of his house or, when the sun had eased, from the yard
before it where you could sit in a straight chair and look out
over the sea and the valleys to the hazy outline of distant
mountains. The house was a little larger than the others.
There was a central room, kept dark for coolness in the day,
in addition to the one that opened to the front and, of course,
the usual kitchen and small bedrooms. A grid of wires strung
at roof level supported a grapevine, which gave fitful shade,
and a score or so of bright plastic clothespins ready to hold up
the laundry. Two cows, two heifers, a dozen chickens, a
couple of geese, and a turkey in the enclosure built onto the
house testified to the solidity of his position. There were no
big landlords in Palomares. Most people owned more or less
of the plots they worked. But some share-cropped on extra
patches belonging to the slightly more fortunate such as Don
José, or to widows and elderly people unable to till their
patrimony.

As Don José's son, Manolo also had achieved standing,
career, and relative comfort. A sturdy man with curly dark
hair, he had a pale skin that testified to his opportunity and
decision not to work his father's fields. He had learned to be
an electrician, he had a little Citroën two horsepower
pick-up and a new house that resembled his father's on the
outside but contained two gas stoves, one of which made a
stand for a potted plant in the front room since it was new
and not required for use. There was also new furniture, a
handsome new pram for the first baby which Dolores expected
in May, and a glass-fronted armoire full of tinted crystal,
colored aluminum mugs, some best dishes, and china figures
which bespoke the dignity of a trousseau and wedding gifts.
People knew where to find him when they needed him.
Manolo was not obliged to keep formal hours for his trade.

On that Monday, when he heard the thunderous sound,
he ran to the window, like the girls in the classroom. He
pushed through them to the door to see what was going on.
In the distance, on the opposite side of the village from the
burning tanker that had drawn the attention of Sánchez, he

saw a parachute easing down to earth. Manolo jumped into the Citroën, which he drove across the cart tracks in the field with the confidence of a Thunderbird owner gunning down a superhighway, and made for the hill where it had landed. It didn't take him long. The orange-and-white canopy was strewn across the stubble like a signpost. He ran to find the man. At first Manolo thought he was dead. The bulky airplane seat in which he was still strapped rose above the limp body like a crooked roof. Gently, Manolo tipped it back and found the way to open the seat belt. The man was breathing, although his face and hands were badly burned and his clothes were seared. With other villagers, Manolo lifted him and carried him to the car. By then, radar-navigator Capt. Ivens Buchanan had regained consciousness. He was shivering as though with polar cold. Manolo drove him to Vera, the nearest town, and turned him over to a doctor's care at the clinic. Then he hurried back to Palomares to see if there was anything more that he could do.

Few people in Palomares indulged in their usual after-lunch sleep that day. When Manolo had eaten, Don José suggested they all go out again to see "the big piece," the towering tail section of the B-52 which had fallen near the bed of the dry Almanzora River. The González family happened to be swollen with visitors that day, so they were a large party crouching on the metal floor of the Citroën. There was Doña Antonia and Don José, their daughters who lived with them, and their two daughters who had married and gone away, one to Barcelona and one to Alicante, and a son-in-law. Manolo drove, but when he got to the river bed, a local policeman called on him for an urgent errand and he drove quickly away.

"So there we all were, left in the river bed," Don José said afterward. "My wife, my four daughters, and my son-in-law. We had to walk home. Well, it wasn't so bad. My wife turned to the married daughters and she said, 'You see, when my María and my Dolores come to visit, the sky can fall on us and nothing happens.'"

At 10:22 A.M. on the Monday of the accident, Roberto Puig was shaving in the bathroom of his rustic but stylishly remodeled house in Mojácar. Perched on steep terraces at the very peak of a conical mountain, Mojácar is the one clear remnant of the Moors in the region. The dazzling white houses nestle one atop the other as though they were a casbah. Until a few years earlier the women of Mojácar always draped themselves in great yellow kerchiefs, holding the ends in their teeth as they laundered in the village tank or moved silently through the yard-wide cobbled streets. Only their dark eyes showed. Some said it was a version of the Moslem veil, left as custom from Moorish ancestors half a millennium before. Some said it was a form of vanity, a protection from the sun in the belief that feminine beauty was best measured by lightness of skin. In the last few years the habit had vanished, one of the many changes come to overtake the town. Aspiring artists and writers and other people with income enough to idle, provided the living was quite cheap, had chosen it for their own. They had been attracted by its breath-taking view of the coast and the valleys, the exotic charm of its overhung streets. And they had been encouraged by the local mayor, a man who realized that Spain was beginning to thrive on tourism and wanted to make the best of it for his village as well as for his region. Nagging and arguing, he had organized funds for reconstruction, arranged investment, drawn official attention to the beauties of the spot. At the bottom of the mountain, on the beach, the government was persuaded to build a new resort hotel. The artists participated in the campaign, reviving, or creating, legends and symbols to add interest to the picturesque.

The Indalo, a toothpick silhouette of a man with legs spread and an arc stretching from hand to hand above his head, was proclaimed the ancient symbol of a prehistoric local culture, a charm that "brings success in art and love and protects against torments, rays, and the evil eye." It was selected as a totem to represent Almería at the previous year's elaborate convention of directors of tourism in Madrid. No one thought it ironic at the time that the brochure produced to vaunt Mojácar and its Indalo proclaimed that when the charm was made of Almería gold it had "a cosmic power of beneficent irradiation." Mojácar was on the maps. Palomares, 12 miles away, was not.

And Mojácar was precisely the kind of place to delight Roberto Puig, a cinematically handsome thirty-six-year-old Madrid architect with highly strained nerves, agitated feelings about the trends of civilization and the state of the world, advanced tendencies to chaotic intellectual rebellion. He made the village his vacation home, a place where he could lounge in sports shirts and dream of blueprints. On that

Monday, when he saw the accident, the fire and the falling debris out of his window, he finished shaving in a hurry and drove to Palomares for a further look at what he called the "beautiful, magnificent spectacle." Like many others, he wandered over the hills staring at metal shapes he had never seen in exhibitions of even the most tortured abstract sculptors. Far up, beyond the high walls of the cemetery, he came upon a cylinder standing in a crater. He kicked at the earth and pulled at the heavy tube, but too much of it was buried for him to haul it out.

"I was in the army, the engineer corps," Puig said afterward, "so I knew it was a bomb. It was an odd one, it didn't have any fins, but I wanted to see if it had a fuse. I got down on my knee and leaned against it but I couldn't move it. I thought it might be dangerous to force it. I never thought it might be an atomic bomb, with radioactivity. That night I felt dreadful. I couldn't sleep all night. I thought it was nothing important, just the excitement. The next day I noticed a mark below my knee where I had touched it. It was like a burn. When I learned finally about its being an A-bomb, I knew I'd gotten a radioactive burn. I actually touched it, you know. I touched the radioactivity."

At 10:22 A.M. on the Monday of the accident, Father Francisco Navarrete Serrano was going over parish records in his bare ground-floor apartment outside the courtyard of the big new school in Cuevas. As the assistant to the curate of Cuevas, Father Enrique Arriaga, he was responsible for Palomares, Las Herrerías, Las Cuñas, and other isolated villages which had no priests of their own. On Sundays he straddled his red motor scooter and bounced along the dusty back roads, scheduling mass in each little church to a timetable that would permit half an hour or so of conversation with the communicants and the trip to the next village in time for another service. The Palomares church was small, a whitewashed structure that would scarcely hold 30 people. It stood alone on the edge of the village, locked on weekdays. Even on Sundays the villagers did not usually crowd it. Their piety was far from zealous. But they showed their affection for the gangly, pale young priest who came to them with regularity, and he appreciated it.

Father Francisco was tall and already a little stooped, his black eyes bright with the gravity of his vocation and his compassion. His social conscience was as intense as his piety. A shepherd must concern himself with the well-being of his flock in body and mind as well as in soul, he felt with ardor. He and two other young priests assigned to nearby towns had graduated together the year before from the seminary at Almería and they met when they could to chat about the excitement of their first assignments, to go swimming in the sea, to discuss the problems of their poor, unlettered parishioners. They did not seem so distant to Father Francisco. He was a butcher's son from Alboz, not far away.

"We are all from modest families," he said. "It seems that all the priests of Spain are. I don't know why. God wrote it that way."

On that Monday he heard the accident but had no way of knowing what it was. Father Enrique, who was teaching a religion class in the school at the time, sent word that he was to come right away. He zipped his cassock up over his gray perlon sports shirt, not bothering about a collar, and hurried out. The car that came for him belonged to the local police chief, who had already picked up the judge. Father Enrique summoned a taxi for himself and the two seminarians and they made a caravan to Palomares. There they separated, directed by the villagers to the places where bodies had been found. With a growing sense of the miraculous as they looked at towering pieces of wreckage strewn between houses and through fields where men worked and shepherds tended animals, they learned that no one, not even a goat or a chicken, had been hit.

It was, Father Francisco reminded the people, the day of St. Anton, the patron saint of Cuevas and of agricultural workers. People crossed themselves when they thought of it. Some said perhaps the hand of God had truly shielded them. The word "miracle" passed many lips. Father Francisco was never sure whether it was being used in the holy or vernacular meaning. There was a reserve to the people of Palomares when it came to the expression of deep feelings, although they were always pleased enough to chatter about the crops and their health and the welfare of their children. It didn't matter to Father Francisco how they took what he had said. He felt that so long as they were safe and spiritually calm, it was well.

He went to the place of the burning tanker, wandering about to look for bodies in the wreckage.

"I saw a leg on one side, a hand on the other. I didn't know how many bodies there were, but I gave absolution to all who died on the hill where I was."

Later, one unmangled corpse was found. A cross hung from a chain on the dead man's neck and it had a name and the word "Catholic" inscribed on it. A wallet nearby with papers contained an identity card, a picture of a woman and two children, and a few Spanish and American banknotes.

Father Enrique, roaming other parts of the countryside where wreckage loomed, also pronounced absolution for the dead. Three other corpses had been found. There is a belief that it takes several hours for the soul to leave the body. He would not say if that or a sense of helplessness had moved him, but he did what he could. He was a man from the north, from Galicia, and he had traveled and lived long enough to have both clear and gentle notions.

"I came here for my health," he said, "but I stay because I feel sorry for them. The people here are the poorest and the last in Spain, the least educated. But they are very good people. We put off the celebration of St. Anton until the following Sunday. The day of the accident was not a day to feast. There was a gratitude that no one in the village had been hurt—it was not a question of a miracle but it was a providence of God. Still, they felt deep sadness for the Americans who died."

At 10:22 A.M. on the Monday of the accident, Capt. Isidoro Calín Velasco was thumbing with some amusement through the dossier on his desk that gave the weekend's police report. His narrow, crowded office was first off the courtyard of the buff semi-fortress of Guardia Civil headquarters in Vera. As chief, he might have had something more impressive with a long corridor as approach, but he was a man who liked to be close to things. His patent-leather hat hung at a jaunty angle from the peg of a clothes tree in the corner, looking like a slightly squashed beetle with its flat round crown and its brim pushed up in back. Once, in the Spanish wars of succession, troops had fought so literally with their backs to the wall that the brims of their sombreros had been snapped straight up above their ears. That, at least, was the story told of why the Guardia in Spain wore its distinctive hat with nothing to shade the neck, and Calín enjoyed any kind of a lively story. He ran his firm, stubby hands through his wavy hair as he read of the minor brawls inflamed by raw brandy, the bicycle accident, and the unofficial but no less interesting story of an elopement, that made up the report.

Trim, a little square but erect, proud that at forty-seven he still appeared to be in his mid-thirties, Calín took his job with all the seriousness demanded. His tough gray eyes could look as sternly official as necessary, although he preferred whenever occasion permitted to indulge their natural twinkle.

"Never think of Santa Barbara unless it thunders," he said. "We take everything as a joke. That's the Spanish character. Life is very monotonous in this area, you know. There's no industry and there's been no real rain for eight or ten years, just a few drops occasionally. There are tomatoes because that's a plant that can stand the high salinity of the irrigation water. Wherever there is a little better water, there are oranges. But the people here are very good-humored, they love to gabble. Of course, nobody believes anything they hear, but they repeat it all, every little thing. If a girl goes out with a boy, it's good for three or four days of talk. Or an elopement, that does for weeks. They like to have very fine weddings, but sometimes to avoid the expense without having to explain, they elope. It saves a wedding dress and a feast and all that. It doesn't happen so much any more, though, the standard of living is beginning to go up. A big ceremony and a party with all their friends are much better when they can afford them." His tanned face broke into a wide grin. "A little pompous they are, the people here." It was part of Captain Calín's joke to use the third person in making fun of himself.

On that Monday morning he heard the explosion and ran out of his office. From the doorstep he saw one great ball of fire and another smaller one in the sky, pieces of falling metal, some shining and some blackened, and parachutes. One man fell through the fire. His parachute had begun to open but it seemed to burn away to nothing. The fierce offshore wind dispersed the rain of objects all across the sky. Calín had a special emergency telephone line to provincial headquarters in Almería. He called. Palomares, although a dependency of Cuevas in every other official way, was under the police command of his station in Vera. He had men posted regularly in the village, but there was no telephone nearer Palomares than his own, not even at the police post.

Then he took off with 14 men, ordering them to snatch the motorcycles of the road police, using a Land Rover at his station and any other transport he could muster.

While he was on his way, provincial headquarters notified airdromes, rescue teams at Sevilla and Granada, and Guardia Civil stations throughout the area. As soon as Calín was able to report that parachutes had also been seen falling in the sea, the naval command was notified as well. In little more than an hour there were well over a hundred members of the Guardia Civil at Palomares. Calín was among the first to arrive. He found some fires still burning. When they were out, he helped arrange to send the dead to Cuevas where they were placed in the reception room, a hall of honor at the municipal building, flanked by burning candles. A priest began a service when the coffins had been laid out, and townspeople came to kneel and pay respects.

Rooting about the fields, the police chief gathered all that could be found of identification papers and valuables, such as watches, wallets, and the like. Wherever there was a large piece of wreckage or something that looked important, he posted a guard. The villagers were sternly warned not to pick up anything. The people, he knew, were honest but he preferred to leave no room for any overwhelming urge to scavenge. Then, when he had satisfied himself with his reconnaissance, Calín posted a cordon around the entire area to keep out further visitors and encourage the hundreds there to go back home. He had heard nothing of nuclear weapons or radioactive contamination, but he knew his people.

"They were very curious. They would have liked to poke into everything," he said.

Before he returned to his station to list the valuables he had collected, Calín took the trouble to test the mood and feeling of the village. A few people grumbled distress.

"You had nothing really damaged. The Americans lost the planes and the pilots, a tragedy for them. What's wrong with you?" he asked them, with the mixture of authority and gaiety that served him comfortably throughout his command.

"Well," said one villager, "the shock, all those things coming out of the sky. There was a bomb."

"You remind me," said Calín, "of the man who met his friend one morning looking pale and despairing. He asked, 'What's wrong?'

"'I had a terrible night,' said the friend. He opened his jacket and showed a round hole in his shirt.

"'Is it a cigarette burn?'

"'No. It's a bullet hole.'

"'How did it happen? That's terrible!'

"'Well, it was. But not so bad as if the shirt had been on my back instead of hanging over the chair.'"

At 10:22 A.M. on the Monday of the accident, Paquita, ninth of the thirteen children Manuel Sabiote Flores had sired, was bent over her embroidery hoop at the doorway of her house. Although she was only nine, her fingers were nimble for the delicate work and her huge gray-blue eyes, with their look of knowing all that mattered to know in the world until she would be ninety, were keen. The handwork was not a job for elderly women. It took young vision and the steadiness of young fingers.

She saw the fireball and the falling debris and before even the sound of the explosion reached the ground she had darted from her chair, dark blond pigtails flying, bangs tousled in the wind. She ran well over a mile, not bothering to follow the track but skirting the cultivated fields until she reached the hill where her father was working. A bright flush spread across the pale peach of her lovely oval face and she was almost breathless. But she did not rest before she spoke.

"Tell me, Papa," she said, "are we all going to die?"

3

THE SEA

The high wind churned the sea to a kaleidoscope of colors. There was angry gray and steel blue and turquoise and a green almost as light as lime, never blending but marking the water under the white rills of foam the way the broken hills and peaks marked the land. Where the beach sand gave way to boulders, the water stewed itself to a warning brown. It was the kind of day that forced the men of Villaricos to toil disconsolately by their boats, mending nets and splicing lines. They had no breakwater to protect their fragile 12-foot craft from the nearby rocks in such a sea, so it was too dangerous to launch. Once there had been a good dock nearby, for the ore boats, but when the mines and the smelters shut down it had been destroyed. No one knew why. That was long ago and Villaricos lived from day to day, eating and paying off some of the old debts to Don Agustín when the catch was good, scrimping by on what was left of the rice and dried peas when it was not. Don Agustín ran the only shop, a dark pile of shelves with sugar and dusty caramels and thread and a few tins. There were big jars of oil and cases of beer and vats of flour and not much more. His customers could not afford many things. Even when the sea was good, the small boats could not go far to follow the fish. And the 250 women and children of Villaricos lived entirely upon the fish brought home by their 40 able-bodied men.

It was only a mile from Palomares, but the two villages might have been separated by a desert. No one in Palomares fished. They lived off the land and were thrifty in the way of farmers. No one in Villaricos farmed. They ate from the sea, and were temperamental, improvident, in the way of sailors. Some said that the people of Villaricos were of gypsy stock, an alien, dark-minded clan that had settled on a rugged shore in stealth and mistrust for all around them. In any case, they kept to themselves.

"The poorest in Palomares is richer than the richest in Villaricos," people said, and it was true. The small children, who numbered two or three times the rest of the population, were scraggly and scrawny, often left to run about with only a brief shirt to save on clothes until they were old enough to control their bladders. At nine and ten some of the girls were beauties, golden-skinned and black-eyed with smiles of wide delight. By seventeen or eighteen, they were already drying out, their eyes pinched with worry and their hands cracked with work. By twenty-five or thirty, they were indistinguishable from the shapeless crones in stained and dusty black who sat in the dark behind the doorways waiting, waiting for the next catch.

That was why the Monday of the accident was a bad day for Villaricos, a day the men could not go out to fish. And that was why no Villaricos boats were out at 10:22 A.M. that Monday. There was a Spanish warship nearby, and a Norwegian tanker on the horizon, and a few small craft scattered off the coast. The three sturdy tugs trawling out to sea from Palomares had come down from Aguilas for the shrimp, shrimp that nestled on the edges of the underwater plateaus just before the bottom fell off in steep cliffs. Aguilas, some 18 miles up the coast, was a town of size and self-conscious worldliness. There people from the capital and the big cities came to stretch on the beach on summer days, to dance in the streets on summer nights. Many of its buildings were four and five stories high, and there were towers of ten and twelve stories going up. The Moors had built a fortress on the high point that formed one bulwark of its fine harbor. Charles III had transformed the fortress into a castle and founded a fishing village below. Now there was a fleet that put out from the town each dawn for the shrimp, or each dusk with lights for the sardines. The fishermen from Aguilas did not mind traveling for their haul.

On that Monday the *Dorita*, the *Manuela Orts*, and the *Agustín y Rosa* had gone south to the shrimp banks off Palomares. When the nets were down and the engines set to move slowly, there came the time when fishermen can stand at ease, their hands idle, their gaze sweeping in the movement of the sea and the stillness of the peaks behind the shore. The *Dorita* was closest to shore. The *Manuela Orts* moved on a parallel about five miles out, and the *Agustín y Rosa* fished farther out to sea where the underwater ravines began to smooth out once again.

They all saw the flash of the fireball and the torrent of debris driven toward them by the wind. Francisco Simo Orts, skipper of the *Manuela*, which was named for his mother, and owner as well of the *Agustín*, which was commanded by his brother Alfonso, counted six parachutes in the sky. One soon disappeared on the land. The others kept sailing toward the boats.

Although Alfonso was the elder, a burly, graying man with solid muscles, Francisco was the leader of the brothers. He had the lively curiosity, the urge for improvement that had decided him to buy the latest model depth sounder, the energetic, outgoing personality that led him to be the one whom fishermen at Aguilas called "El Catalán." Both, of course, were from Catalonia, the businesslike, independent-minded northeast part of Spain. The family had been settled in Aguilas for many years; but they retained the enterprising, more crisply self-confident style of their native province which set them a bit apart. Aguilas, in the province of Murcia, was one of the populaces that had been maligned in an ancient royal edict proclaiming "murderers, gypsies, and Murcianos" to be ineligible for recruitment to the army. The people were not sly and dastardly as that implied. They were hospitable, hard-working, and generous, but in a shy and reserved way that must have offended a vain monarch.

And Francisco Simo had the appearance to match the dash of his person—tall, square-shouldered, and square-chinned. He might have been a bronzed, dark-haired Kirk Douglas playing the romantic role of captain. But he wasn't, he was a fisherman with a fisherman's eye for sea and shoreline. The two chutes slanting toward his boat were different from those he saw in the distance, Simo noticed. One dropped smoothly, without rocking in the wind. He noticed with horror that it suspended what he thought was half a man, the upper trunk with something hanging, waving gruesomely below. It looked like entrails. It hit the water some 25 yards to shoreward of his boat and sank swiftly. There was, in any case, nothing anyone could do for half a man. He concentrated on the other chute, much larger, swinging bumpily on a course that seemed as though it might smack down atop the *Manuela*. Simo maneuvered his boat a little and watched it pass overhead. Its burden was intact. Squinting into the brightness, he couldn't make out if what appeared to be the man was alive and moving or inert. But he prepared to hurry to the rescue, only making sure not to risk an accident by running the boat too close before the chute was in the sea. He had watched it floating down somewhere between six and eight minutes, he calculated. It went into the water 75 yards to seaward of the *Manuela* and he turned to approach it. To his surprise, by the time he reached the spot, it had gone down, parachute and all, too far beneath the surface to make recovery of human service to anyone but a priest preparing rites. There were other parachutes afloat farther away.

Simo marked the spot the way he always did. The shrimp, although they sold well, were not so plentiful. A wise, successful fisherman took care each day to know exactly which part of the sea he'd harvested. That way, he could reap other rows on other days until there had been time for nature to restock the watered crop. There were no elaborate aids to navigation in the area. The shrimp fishermen had long ago devised a way to triangulate their bearings by what a man could see. Lining a distinctive mountain silhouette to one side with another peak, or one of the tall abandoned chimneys of the old smelter, to the other side, they could establish a set of coordinates to a point in the sea almost as precisely as a radio compass. Simo knew by heart each feature of the coast line. It took him a few seconds to commit to certain memory the spot where, he believed, an airman had received a sailor's burial. He noticed, too, that this airman's chute had been grayish-white, unlike the white-and-orange umbrellas which had dropped closer to the other boats. It meant nothing to him, but he noticed and remembered. He always remembered how things looked. Then he advanced the engines as much as the trailing net would allow to see if help was needed where the *Dorita* had begun its rescue effort.

Bartolomé Roldán Martínez was skipper of the *Dorita* but not its owner. Like the share croppers of the land, he split the value of the weekly catch half and half, with all expenses except labor coming out of the owner's part and the three men of his crew sharing with Roldán. The needs of his wife and two daughters, who watched from their doorway on the crowded hill overlooking the port for his return each evening, never left enough over to save for a boat of his own. Like

Simo, he was shrewd about the sea and the fish, toughened on the outside by his work and softened on the inside by the constant awareness it brought of men's need for each other's help against the whims of mighty elements. But unlike Simo, he was a reserved and quiet man, at once too proud and too humble to push himself forward in any matter that was not clearly of his business. From his lean, well-weathered face, deep-set eyes of the brightness of the sea's most placid blue absorbed all he needed of the scene around him and reflected little. He was short, sandy-haired, confident of his complex skill and his simple instincts and trusting God for the rest.

While the chutes were still high in the sky, Roldán calculated from the distance and the force of the wind where they might fall. It would have taken three-quarters of an hour to haul in the nets, too long perhaps to save a life. He ordered them drawn up a little so the boat could move more freely and decided to take his chances on a bad snag. He and his men prepared the lifesavers and moved in the direction of the closest chute. They did not dare take the boat too close in that heaving sea. The man might be wounded and unable to hold himself off. Twice in the previous year Roldán had abandoned the fishing to save the crews of stricken boats. His eyes and his arms were experienced in the dangers of rescue at sea.

Within ten minutes of the time that Captain Wendorf hit the water, Roldán was near enough to throw out the life preserver. He did not understand the words the American was shouting, but they could only have one meaning and that he knew deeply in his seaman's heart. He heard a moan of pain as the man tried to wrap one arm about the floating ring, shifting then to the other arm, and he saw the man was very pale, the bloodless color of the whitecaps.

They called to each other, Roldán and Wendorf.

"Hey, over this way," Wendorf said, more to hear himself talk and prove he was alive and being saved than with any thought of communication.

"We've got you, you'll be all right," Roldán shouted back in Spanish, more to give the stunned-looking man the reassurance of his voice than in reliance on the words.

They handed in the rope and grabbed the man's free arm to haul him over the side of the boat, riding three or four feet out of the water just then. Wendorf gasped at the explosion of pain. It was not until later that he realized the sharp tug had reset his dislocated shoulder and forced the bone back into place. The Spanish crew pulled out a mattress on the deck and skillfully took off every stitch of Wendorf's dripping clothes. He didn't remember being cold or even wet, but they saw that he was shivering uncontrollably. While the men covered the American with blankets, Roldán quickened the engines and steered the boat toward the second chute.

Wendorf watched in silence. With each roll of the boat he caught a glimpse of Mike Rooney in the water, sitting there, it seemed to him, "just dumb and happy." When Rooney caught the lifesaver and reached the edge of the boat, Roldán leaned way over to help him aboard with care. As he did, he saw the seat of the man's pants was badly torn and bloodstained. They undressed Rooney, too. The gash on his buttock looked deep and it was bleeding heavily. The Spaniards closed it as best they could and improvised a bandage, but it worried Roldán. It would take well over an hour to get him back to Aguilas and the man could lose too much blood in that amount of time. It never occurred to him to put into Garrucha, the nearby port. Fishermen go out to work and they go home. They don't go visiting.

With the gestures that accompanied their words, the Spaniards made Wendorf and Rooney understand they were asking how many men had been aboard their plane. The Americans answered with their fingers, "seven." Roldán scanned the sea. The *Agustín y Rosa* was nearing the only other parachute still visible on the water, some five miles away. It was Major Messinger's. The *Manuela*, which had a radio, was approaching. Roldán shouted to Simo that he had two survivors, in need of doctor's care, and was going to hurry them back to land. It was agreed that the remaining boats would pick up what other men could be found. Roldán asked that a radio message be sent to Aguilas to have an ambulance waiting on the dock. Then he turned full speed for home.

They put a tarpaulin over Wendorf and Rooney to keep them as dry as possible in the heavy sea and offered them food. The Americans shook their heads. The Spaniards offered mugs of coffee, which they accepted.

"I guess it was coffee," Wendorf said afterward. "It was black and it tasted terrible, bitter. But it was hot."

As they lay on their mattress gradually taking in the reality of their survival, Rooney and Wendorf began to talk. Neither one had a clear idea of what had happened, but they anxiously exchanged reports of the other chutes they'd seen and their hopes for the rest of the crew. Rooney told how he'd done his best to follow each detail of the survival drill, waiting awhile to open his chute and deciding to wait no longer when he began to tumble. It worked perfectly and so did the life belt which he inflated when he hit the water. Then he saw the boats heading toward him. There was nothing to do but wait. The only thing he felt was fierce cold in his hands after a few minutes, so he reached in his pocket for his flying gloves and put them on. It seemed terribly funny now that he was safe.

"Yeah," said Wendorf, "it's been a funny day." The surge of adrenalin was draining off and they both were feeling "lousy," in Wendorf's word. "The only thing that could complete the day," he said, "would be if this turned out to be a Russian trawler." The thought brought a moment's unreasoning panic. They had to remind themselves that they'd been over Spain when it happened and that the wind had blown them to the water. It couldn't have blown them all the way across Europe.

"Besides," Rooney said, "I had some Spanish in high school. It kind of sounds like Spanish, this stuff they're jabbering."

Wendorf thought that over. "Well," he said, "they aren't saying 'Nyet.' Haven't heard that once. I guess they aren't Russians."

The exhaustion was a swamp after the peak of fear. They let themselves sink into it and lie still. That, they had been taught in survival school, was the best thing to do when you have been injured and rescued and simply have to wait for treatment.

As they approached Aguilas, the Spaniards remembered that the men were naked under their blankets and would have to be uncovered to be taken ashore. They rummaged in the hold and found some pants and sweaters, old and not so clean as they would have wished to offer guests, but better than nothing. They dressed the Americans as gently as they would have dressed two babies.

The excitement of the day, the sense of desperate urgency to get the wounded men ashore, finally overcame the Spaniards as they approached the dock. They banged up their boat rather badly. The slip of seamanship, especially with strangers there to notice, was a source of lasting embarrassment, more upsetting than the costly damage. But the main thing had been done.

The chief of the Guardia Civil, the port captain, and an ambulance were waiting, along with the crowd of curious that always gathered when a boat came in, even if it was only an ordinary day with an ordinary catch to see. The two survivors were taken on stretchers to the hospital. A little later the *Agustín y Rosa* brought in Messinger, who joined them there. It seemed to Wendorf that he had never seen so many doctors. People kept coming in to examine their wounds, take their temperature, check their condition. They were given fresh hospital pajamas and sedatives. They did what they could to get word to the Air Force where they were, and they relaxed. For them, the ordeal seemed almost over.

Later, when he was home again and the long story of the accident and its aftermath had come to a close, Wendorf looked back on it all and found it the very opposite of a bad dream.

He was back in the routine of SAC, of planes and briefings and electronic switches, and when he considered what had happened at Palomares, he said, "Sometimes our world doesn't seem real. I guess it takes something like that to make it real."

At 10:22 A.M. on the Monday of the accident, Manuel Rodríguez Cruz was working on the report of the weekend's arrivals and departures in the port of Garrucha. There was the warship, nothing else but fishing tugs. It pleased him. Garrucha was a somnolent little port, and that was why he liked so well his assignment as Ayudante de la Marina Militar, the Spanish navy's land-based representative in the area. He was thin, pale, but as darkly intense as his straight black hair and as self-consciously official as his crisp white uniform as he went through the satisfying trivia of the documents on his desk. A year before, at thirty-seven, he had welcomed the offer of a calm and tranquil post.

"I came here from the ships looking for peace and quiet," he said afterward. "I thought I would have a couple of years' escape from the big cities, from running up and down on ships. Garrucha, I thought, was just the corner of Spain where nothing ever happens."

On that Monday he heard the windowpanes of his large, bare office rattle violently. He looked up and saw nothing. Probably something the workmen were doing in the construction of the new beach hotel, he supposed, and he dismissed the noise. But then he saw things falling from the sky, a great spray of debris dropping helter-skelter into the shallows and the coastal water and well out to sea. He stepped out onto the esplanade that faced the dock and watched for a bit with the people who had gathered.

"They're having an exercise," someone said.

"Practicing dropping things," said another. "But why here?"

Rodríguez was a navy man. He knew it was no exercise. He kept a military silence but turned swiftly back into his office. There he called his official friend, the chief of the Guardia Civil at Vera. The two men often worked together. They were affable. Rodríguez enjoyed the police chief's jokes and they had come to use the familiar "tu" in comfort. But they never addressed each other by name, only by title. Neither knew the other's name and neither would have had the discourtesy to ask.

"Jefe," said Rodríguez when he finally got through to Calín. "This is the Ayudante Militar at Garrucha. There has been some kind of bad accident. Things are falling all over into the sea. I'm going out to have a look. It may concern you."

Calín confirmed that he knew of the accident. Two planes had crashed and debris was falling on the land as well. He was on his way to see what should be done.

Satisfied that terrestrial authority had been informed, Rodríguez took a boat and raced out to perform the duties of marine authority. There were no more survivors. The Aguilas tugs had rescued them by the time he could get out, so he cruised around with a half dozen other Garrucha boats that had gone out, picking up whatever they could find afloat. There was an ejection seat with blood on it trailing from a parachute that had been Rooney's. There were life rafts, uninflated but still skittering on the surface, yellow life belts, manuals of partly burned and waterlogged paper. They gathered everything in sight. After two hours Rodríguez was certain there was nothing more. He went back to his office to collect and catalogue his own haul and what the other boats had salvaged. No one held back so much as a scrap of plastic or cloth.

It was two-thirty in the afternoon when the call came through from military headquarters at Almería. The planes that crashed, Rodríguez was told, were American bombers that regularly flew that route fully loaded with atomic bombs. This was official information, not to be repeated to the public. When he had a chance, Rodríguez mentioned it to the one man he thought should be informed and no one else. That was Captain Calín. Calín mentioned reports he had heard that one of the parachutes carried a big cylinder. It could be the bomb. But the description he gave did not sound like a bomb to the naval man. It might well have been an aerial torpedo, Rodríguez thought. In any case, neither one could see what they might do with the new information, and there had been no instructions. Calín had his guards posted. They put aside the quite imponderable question that had been raised and went about their obligations as they had understood them from experience.

4

THE WORD

The first word was received within seconds of the accident. It came to the radio tower at Morón and was immediately put through to the base Command Post. The lead bomber from Seymour Johnson, flying the Chrome Dome mission in tandem with Tea-16 but always a few miles ahead, was preparing to refuel at the same time as its companion. It had maneuvered into position and the boom was locked correctly into the tank. The copilot, who had the regular task of controlling the flow of fuel so that the rapid addition of weight would be properly distributed, concentrated on the tank gauges. Everything was going smoothly. The bomber pilot and the boom operator had nothing more to do for ten minutes or so until delivery would be completed. Then the boom would disengage with a small blast, spraying the last run of vaporized fuel harmlessly in the air. The tanker would speed forward and the bomber would hold back until the distance between the two planes was great enough for them to shift altitude and course without danger of collision.

The boom operator let his gaze wander for a moment while the operation progressed. That was how he happened to notice it. From the corner of his eye he thought he saw a flash. Turning to look, he saw a B-52 tumbling, spewing smoke. He didn't see the fireball or the other tanker. The field of vision through the tail window beyond his mattress was narrow, designed only to frame the approach of his own customer. He reported on the intercom to the tanker pilot.

"Troubadour 14, Troubadour 14," the pilot called, trying to make radio contact with the other tanker. There was no answer.

Then he radioed the tower. "This is Troubadour 10. Boom

operator reports flash in sky, possible explosion of one or both following aircraft." That was 10:22 A.M. on Monday, January 17. The tower tried to call Tea-16 and Troubadour 14, the tanker that had gone to meet it. There was no reply from either one, on any circuit. Tea-12, the lead bomber, checked in routinely. Its crew had seen nothing. The boom operator had the only eyes in the back of the airplanes' heads, so to speak. Tankers and bombers are not made for sightseeing. The other crew members could only see forward and radar does not show what is no longer there. Morón advised the Torrejón tower of the operator's report. It tried, too, to reach the missing planes, with no more success. Then 16th Air Force headquarters at Torrejón flashed to Drop-kick, code at the time for Strategic Air Command headquarters in Omaha, the news that there appeared to have been a B-52–KC-135 collision in the Saddle Rock area. There were no more details yet. Omaha relayed the report almost instantaneously to Washington.

It was 5:35 A.M. in Washington when the word came in to the National Military Command center, the most secret room in America. By comparison, entry to the vaults of Fort Knox is as simple as pushing open one's own front door. From the command center is exercised the central control over all of America's military might, the helicopters darting into the jungle of Vietnam, the Polaris submarines lurking silently beneath the seas, the missiles sunk in the empty plains, the GI's trudging off a troopship. From that room, deep in the Pentagon, come the supreme orders that send American men and machines to fight, to reconnoiter, to keep the peace, anywhere in the world. It is not a large room and it is low, the floor level raised to leave space below it for the thousands of wires which connect the room to the force awaiting command. The tweedy carpet seems to have a checkered pattern; it is laid in one-foot squares so that any piece can easily be lifted to repair the cables underneath. Rows of separate desks face, as though in a schoolroom, the large desk of authority on an elevated platform at one end. Pleasant gold curtains discreetly mask the panels on the wall where, at any time of decision or emergency, maps and charts can be projected to pinpoint the site of danger and the plan of response. Diffused lighting gives an unchanging glow, without glare or shadows. There is an appropriately awesome quality to the sounds that come muted from men's throats in that room, not because they hush their tones but because the perfection of the soundproofing kills all echoes. It is always staffed, with representatives of every action department of every service.

On that Monday Col. Charles Burtyk happened to be the officer from the Defense Department's office of public information on duty in the command center. When he heard the report from SAC, he telephoned to wake his superior, Brig. Gen. David I. Liebman.

"We have a Broken Arrow, sir," Burtyk said.

"I'll come in right away," answered Liebman.

The code had been established for several years. Any accident involving nuclear material set in motion an elaborate network. This was not the first time it had happened. The secret manuals explained at length what was to be done and who was to be notified from the instant the report of a Broken Arrow came in. The machinery began to work in a dozen places.

The lighted panel showing local time in the Command Post three levels underground at Omaha read 3:35 A.M. It was the fourth from the left of six time panels, displaying at a glance the time in Saigon, Kadena (Okinawa), Guam, Omaha, London, and Moscow. The message from 16th Air Force at Torrejón, in charge of SAC operations in Europe, was recorded, as all messages through SAC's system of multiple world-wide communications are recorded. Lights gleamed and disappeared on the long bank of control consoles as the word was received, acknowledged, and relayed. The glass-enclosed command balcony behind the five officers and five noncommissioned officers, working in pairs, was empty. The panel headed Threat Value read 000. The Bomb Alarm System showed blank. It was a map of the United States equipped to light up automatically if any of the untended radiation counters mounted unobtrusively on telephone poles near over a hundred possible military and industrial targets in this country should detect an atomic explosion. There was no rise in any of SAC's multiple danger thermometers. But Col. Thomas J. Sims, armed and on duty as the senior controller of the Command Post, did not hesitate to awaken Maj. Gen. Charles M. Eisenhart, SAC's chief of staff. A Broken Arrow required the immediate attention of top authority.

His companion sergeant, also armed, and another colonel and sergeant stood close beside him to listen as he picked up the telephone. It was their duty to eavesdrop on every word spoken over SAC communications. They were armed, because, if necessary, they also had the duty to shoot any person attempting to pass false orders or unauthorized or improper information over those communications. Noncoms as well as officers on special duty in all the SAC command posts were among the few soldiers in history ever trained and instructed to kill their superiors in certain circumstances. It was part of SAC's "two-or-more-men concept," the precaution taken in recognition that even with the most careful maintenance, men as well as machines can explode without warning. It was why there was always a nomcom alongside every colonel. Under that concept, no man but one can make a move alone at any significant stage of the atomic decision. The one lonely American with no one at his elbow, and yet answerable to all the world, is the President. Yet he is human, too. It is a problem that the philosophers of the atomic age have pondered endlessly. None has yet found a solution. It is the ultimate dilemma of maintaining ultimate power. Short of that last question of the constant sound judgment of the Commander in Chief, SAC had arranged to hedge every bet.

The colonel at the senior control console, just to the left of the center aisle dividing the bank, used a gray telephone. There were four different-colored instruments before him. Blue was the direct line to Norad, the command of the early warning system that would be the first to know of an impending attack by air. Red was the SAC system over which orders could be passed simultaneously to 45 SAC bases in the United States; to seven bases overseas; to the Thule Monitor— an elaborately equipped KC-135 always flying above Thule, Greenland, as an alternate advance station should the grounded radar center be wiped out; and to the airborne command post—an EC-135C jet circling above Omaha. During every minute that had passed since February 3, 1961, a SAC general had been high in the Midwestern air prepared with his staff to take over command of the strategic nuclear force and perhaps even of the entire nation in the event that Federal authority, underground headquarters, and alternate command posts in other parts of the country were all destroyed at once. The planes stayed aloft on eight-hour shifts, descending only when a replacement had arrived on station. There was also a gold telephone, the direct line to the National Military

Command center, to the Joint chiefs of staff, and to the President. There was a gold telephone in every room that SAC's commander and chief of staff might normally use, a fixed frequency to extend its instant range to their cars and to the walkie-talkie radios which they were obliged to carry whenever they moved out of immediate reach of a gold phone. The gray phone was for all occasions short of the primary colors of danger.

The response to the accident report was nonetheless urgent. General Eisenhart ordered the commander of the 16th Air Force to go immediately to the scene of the crash. Then he alerted the chief of the SAC disaster control team, Maj. Gen. A. J. Beck. By 4:13 A.M., Omaha time, all the members of the team had been awakened and told to be at the airfield by five o'clock ready for departure to Spain.

They were in the air at six-twenty-one that morning, Omaha time. Seventeen men, experts in communications, in nuclear weapons, in medicine, in radiation control, in information, in security, accompanied General Beck. Their equipment, always assembled on a stand-by basis, had been loaded before they reached the plane. As soon as they were airborne, briefings began on the basis of reports that had begun to pile up and they continued to receive more details as they sped toward Palomares. They knew as they left Omaha that two planes had been destroyed, that the lost B-52 was carrying four H-bombs of about one megaton each, that the other B-52 had been safely refueled and was returning to North Carolina in completion of its mission, that the other tanker had gone back to look at the scene of the crash and had sent in geographical coordinates before heading home to its base at Morón. But they knew little more. The fate of the "weapons," as SAC people refer to their bombs in delicate avoidance of the brutal word, the fate of the airmen, the atomic implications of the accident, remained open questions.

It was the Air Force Nuclear Safety directorate at Kirtland Air Force base, Albuquerque, New Mexico, that passed the word along to the small but taut organization which functions as America's nuclear fire station. Its initials are JNACC, standing for Joint Nuclear Accident Coordinating Center, its staff calls it Janac, and it works though on a world-wide basis in much the way of a hook-and-ladder headquarters. If a reactor blew its stack, if a radiation laboratory had an accident, if an atomic-weapon storage depot caught on fire, if a train carrying uranium logs to a nuclear munitions plant was derailed, if a B-52 loaded for air-alert duty crashed with its cargo, Janac would be the place to turn for emergency assistance. It is responsible jointly to the Atomic Energy Commission and the Department of Defense, and although it is scarcely known to the general public, its telephone numbers are on handy file with all kinds of officials throughout the country, just as police and hospital and fire department numbers are kept within quick reach by prudent housewives.

Janac operates from two small, ordinary-looking rooms a few blocks apart in Albuquerque. Each has a metal sideboard holding a row of telephones along one wall, a large table, metal maps of the United States and of the world on which magnetic markers show the disposition of nuclear emergency teams, and a card index listing in every detail the capabilities, the current staff strength, the deployment of people and equipment who might be called upon to deal with atomic mishaps or disasters. One room is manned by the Atomic Energy Commission and a call from anywhere to Albuquerque 264-4667 will alert a duty officer there. The other is manned by the Field Command of the Defense Atomic Support Agency, DASA, and its alarm number is Albuquerque 264-8279. An idle call to either one would be the grossly magnified equivalent of frivolously setting off an air-raid siren or sounding a false fire alarm. Until recently, with the aid of an IBM 1401 computer, the Field Command kept track of the whereabouts of every nuclear weapon in the American arsenal, from Davy Crocketts ready for battlefield use in Germany to Minutemen ready to be launched across a hemisphere. The arsenal had grown so large, the movement of weapons from one place to another so complex, however, that the task of keeping constant tab on weapons stockpiled or transported outside American territory had been shifted to the regional commands concerned. But the master file was maintained at Albuquerque. It contained the serial number of every atomic shell and bomb and missile made by the United States with precise description, and had on cross-index the serial number of every component part of every weapon. With that archive, the entire history from design to manufacture to transport to assignment of an American nuclear warhead and its projectile could be reconstructed from a single fuse or barometric sensor. Something atomic can be missing or lost. Nothing atomic is ever forgotten.

The nuclear fire station did not spring full-blown at the birth of the atomic age near Alamagordo, New Mexico, in 1945. When nuclear weapons began to be distributed to U.S. armed forces, responsibility for accidents was assigned to the agency or service "in possession" at the time of trouble. If something went wrong during manufacture or delivery to the military, the Atomic Energy Commission was called to cope with the consequences. In the same way, the Air Force, the Navy, the Army, and the Marines were expected to look after their own accidents. Inevitably, from time to time, things did go wrong although there has never been an accidental American nuclear explosion. So far as is known, no nuclear state has ever had a fission or fusion explosion except by deliberate design. The Atomic Energy Commission's handbook *The Effects of Nuclear Weapons* states honestly that despite all precautions "there is always a possibility that, as a result of accidental circumstances, an explosion will take place inadvertently." There can be no absolute, timeless guarantee so long as nuclear weapons exist. Still, as the AEC's Dr. Gordon Dunning once pointed out with a certain waspishness, "It isn't easy to set off an atomic bomb. Everything has got to be

B-47

made to work perfectly." His credentials were his personal part in development of the technique and his observation of the efforts of others to achieve it.

If the harrowing, and ineradicable, "possibility" had never taken place, the statistical likelihood of other accidents involving nuclear weapons increasing as their numbers and mobility grew had indeed been translated into fact. Before the Broken Arrow at Palomares, eleven had been announced. There had been several more. In March, 1958, Senator Clinton Anderson, a member of the Joint Congressional Committee on Atomic Energy, told the Senate that three accidents had been mentioned publicly by that time but "there more likely have been at least double that amount."

One accident, never officially disclosed, had taken place on foreign soil. A B-47 carrying atomic bombs had crashed and caught fire on take off from the U.S. base at Sidi Slimane, Morocco, in 1957. The conventional explosive in the warhead had gone off, spraying pulverized plutonium downwind. A combination of circumstances—the wind, the concrete runway, the manner of explosion—had restricted the spread of radioactive contamination to the air base so that no outsiders were affected. Nonetheless, the accident was regarded with extreme gravity because of possible political implications as well as the health hazards to American personnel on the base. It was an Air Force accident and an Air Force cleanup responsibility, but the Air Force did not have within immediate reach the experts and equipment needed to complete the job. The Navy brought assistance. That experience led to the establishment of Janac, demonstrating as it did the need for an organized, coordinated first-aid headquarters to rush in help wherever it was required from wherever it was most quickly and easily available, at home or abroad.

The lesson was not learned too soon. Nuclear accidents, although never accidental nuclear explosions, began the following year to occur in quickening succession. There were four in 1958. The first that year, on February 8, came when a B-47 collided with a fighter over the sea off Georgia. The injured bomber was able to limp home, but only by jettisoning an atomic bomb into the water. The plane was at the mouth of the Savannah River but it was night and its position was not certain. A search was made and eventually abandoned. Presumably the bomb is still there on the bottom of the sea. The second accident in 1958 taught another lesson. By some unexplained fluke the device locking a bomb to its rack in a B-47 let go. The bay opened and the bomb fell in the back yard of Walter Gregg, a thirty-seven-year-old railway brakeman, of Mars Bluff, South Carolina. The conventional high explosive went off, digging a crater 50 feet wide and 20 feet deep, blasting apart his seven-room frame house and damaging five other houses and a Baptist church nearby. Gregg, working in his garage, and his three children, playing in the yard, were knocked about by the explosion but not injured. Mrs. Gregg, sewing in her living room, was badly cut above the ear by a piece of flying debris. There was no radiation injury. Afterward, a Federal court at Charleston awarded the Greggs $54,000 damages, the Air Force tightened further its rules on the handling of airborne bombs, and the Pentagon decided on a new policy of quick and crisp public announcement of Broken Arrow incidents.

The new information policy, brought by forced awareness that everything about atomic bombs might be top secret but civilians who never went near the Pentagon could still find one in their back yard and panic if they had nothing but rumor to explain it, was for quick and crisp but not necessarily full disclosure. That became evident when the Seymour Johnson base had its first accident, on January 24, 1961. That time it happened close to home. An early model B-52, suffering from a structural defect, developed a hopeless case of aerial trembles and blew apart, of itself. One of its bombs descended by parachute. The other fell free and smashed open on landing, although there was no blast. They landed in farm land near Musgrave's Crossroads, 12 miles from Goldsboro, North Carolina. Many local people heard the accident and saw the wreckage. Announcing the crash, the Air Force said both weapons were recovered intact. Strange stories began to spread when, after collecting and carting away all the visible debris, the Air Force sent heavy earth-moving and dredging equipment into the area and began to dig more and more frantically into a swamp. "Completely unfounded," a spokesman said when local reporters asked about the rumors that a bomb was lost. But the digging went on for weeks and weeks. Finally, in March, the hunt was abandoned. Somewhat red-faced, the spokesman conceded that "a nonexplosive, nonhazardous component" of the bomb had sunk beyond recovery. It was a less than candid way of saying that a big chunk of enriched uranium, a metal far heavier than lead, had disappeared into the soggy earth although in truth there was no danger of explosion nor, at that depth, of radioactivity. Years later, when Peking began its nuclear tests, the Goldsboro incident was wryly recalled.

"Remember when you dug in the sand as a child. They used to say that if anything went down far enough it would come out in China," one atomic policy watcher said to another. "Well, it's happened. No wonder they could never find that Goldsboro uranium; it fell all the way through and now they've got it on the other side."

Maj. Burt Auckerman, on duty at Janac on the Monday of the Palomares accident, had neither time nor cause to indulge his sense of humor when the word came through. It was 4:25 A.M. by his clock. By 4:40 A.M. Air Force Nuclear Safety said they were sending a team of four to Palomares and asked whether anybody else needed a ride. At 4:45 A.M. Colonel Burtyk called from the Pentagon with further information about the crash. Major Auckerman asked if any help was needed.

"No assistance is required from JNACC at this time," was Burtyk's answer.

Still, Auckerman preferred to be prepared. A tall, bulky man with broad shoulders and an air of total, easy self-reliance, he had thoroughly absorbed the team idea on which Janac operates. He phoned his superiors, and then the members of what would be the first-aid squad if one were sent. The proper composition of a Janac group had been well established and there was always someone on call for each position: radiation monitor, explosive ordnance disposal specialist, weapons expert, physician or health physicist, public information specialist, command representative. Waking up one of each, he told them to ready the clothing and equipment they would need for a Broken Arrow trip to Spain. He always kept a good supply of cash in his safe for sudden departures. When he checked with Walter White, a rangy, long-faced man who was his AEC opposite number, and found that the same word had come through from the Atomic Energy Commission in Washington. Similar preparations had been made. The messages poured in with mounting frequency. By six-thirty-five local time, Auckerman learned that a jet transport from Travis Air Force base near San Francisco had been diverted in the air and was on its way to Albuquerque to pick up passengers for Spain. Although there had been no request for help and everything seemed to be in hand, it was decided to send a collection of experts from Janac, the Air Force, Los Alamos, and the Sandia Corporation, which does research for the AEC in Albuquerque, to the accident scene as observers.

Douglass Evans had been alerted at Los Alamos at six that morning. A short, jolly man with slightly yellowing white hair, he had worked on America's nuclear development since its secretive beginning during World War II and was about to retire. His appearance and his bubbly manner might have led a stranger to guess his expertise was in popping champagne corks. Evans' specialty was high explosives. The call rather pleased him. It would probably be his last field trip, he thought, before settling down to pasture, and he had hugely enjoyed what he considered his adventurous but not dangerous profession. He was told to be at the airport in forty-five minutes. When he had packed and was ready to leave, he called the laboratory director for a last-minute check on transportation.

"You said," he asked, "that I'm to get an Air Force plane at Albuquerque for the flight to Maine?"

The director groaned. "No, not Maine. Spain! Get your passport. You're not going to Maine."

Evans took time out to roar with laughter at himself. Then he tossed all the warm underwear and heavy sweaters out of his bag and shifted his imagination from sparkling snowdrifts to palm trees waving in the sun. It was something of a mistake, he realized later. The early mornings and the winter nights were piercing cold in Palomares. Repacked by seven-thirty, he was on the four-passenger plane that is the largest able to land on Los Alamos' mesa-top air strip.

The Air Force transport was supposed to leave at eight-thirty. Not everything went smoothly. It was eleven in the morning by the time it was refueled, loaded, and airborne. Crossing the continent, it developed engine trouble. Everything and everyone had to be unloaded and transferred to another jet for the trip across the Atlantic.

Long before they left Albuquerque the experts knew the precise identity of the bombs they were setting off to recover. The serial numbers of the four H-bombs loaded aboard the lost B-52 came in from the Seymour Johnson base at 8 A.M. local time. Half an hour later their index cards had been pulled out for continuing special attention and their individual descriptions and life histories had been delivered to Washington. So far as they knew, the people who stayed behind at Albuquerque had nothing further to do but await the reports that would close the incident.

It was nearly six o'clock that Monday morning when Col. Vernon Cammack, deputy commander of the Seymour Johnson base, was called at home by his Command Post. "My socks dropped," he said later. He had already pulled on his socks because the working day started early and ended late when a SAC base was on air alert. An urbane man with softly waving dark gray hair and Air Force blue eyes, he had learned long before to relax at attention, to be ready to spring at any moment without winding up his nerves. He hurried to the Command Post, a few steps down the corridor from his office at Seymour Johnson headquarters.

Despite his position, he went through the procedure of anyone entering that well-guarded room. He rang the doorbell. Then he stood in front of the one-way mirror which filled the top half of the door and served as a large peephole for the guard inside. The windowless room was not so big as the Command Post at Omaha, but in a similar way it had all quickly needed information displayed graphically on its walls. A diagram of the base on one side showed the position at that moment of every parked Seymour Johnson plane and special equipment such as fire trucks and fuel trucks. It looked like a child's game. Simple plastic planes with red wings represented tankers, planes with blue wings represented bombers, the model fire trucks and fuel trucks were red and yellow. On the other side a chart gave the latest information on the weather and the state of the nation's security. Under air-defense condition, listed as yellow, red, or all clear, a check mark showed all clear. In the box by Defcon, the number 4 was written in chalk. Except for the period of the Cuban missile crisis in 1962, when the national defense condition, Defcon for short, was posted as number two, it had been at four for nearly a decade. It had never gone to number one—all-out war—since the system was established. But neither, for a long time, had it ever eased to number five—all-out peace.

For Cammack and the men at his base the normalcy of the chart was misleading. There was little they could do, but they waited tensely for each new report, looking for names of survivors. It would be his duty to tell the next of kin the good or bad news. It was also his duty to dispatch the next set of air-alert crews. The other bomber had come home safely and two more had departed on Chrome Dome by the time they knew who lived and who had died.

It was 7:05 A.M. Washington time, an hour and a half after the accident, when the messenger from the White House Situation Room brought the note into the President's bedroom. He was eating a breakfast of melon, chipped beef, and hot tea. The White House press secretary, Bill Moyers, had already been advised by telephone. President Johnson read the text rapidly. It said:

> A B-52 and a KC-135 tanker collided while conducting a refueling operation 180 miles from Gibraltar. The B-52 crashed on the shore in Spain and the tanker went down in the sea. Four survivors have been picked up and three additional life rafts have been sighted. The B-52 was carrying four thermonuclear weapons. The 16th Nuclear Disaster team has been dispatched to the area.

The President reached for the phone and called his Secretary of Defense.

"Is there any danger of an explosion?" he asked Robert McNamara.

"We doubt it," was the answer. McNamara explained that the search for the weapons would start as soon as the Air Force could get to the scene.

"Do everything possible to find them."

The President hung up. The conversation lasted less than fifty seconds. There were more reports through the day as corrections and further information arrived. At nine o'clock that night another written summary of the incident was delivered to the President. After that, the latest word on Palomares was brought to him each morning at seven along with reports on all other critical developments since the day before.

Joseph L. Smith, Second Secretary of the United States Embassy in Madrid in charge of liaison with the military—everything from dealing with parking tickets hung on some testy American colonel's car to preparing for negotiations on

U.S. bases in Spain—walked down the fifth-floor corridor to the Ambassador's office. The door was open and he could see no one there. So he popped his head into the small room across the reception hall where Timothy Towell, the Ambassador's personal aide, sat flicking through the morning's cables, his feet on a cluttered desk.

"Where is the Ambassador?" asked Smith.

"Not here, Joe," said Towell, a friendly thirty-two-year-old with a pug nose, a thatch of straw hair, and a deadly earnest devotion to his job of making his chief's life easier. Whether that meant passing martinis and affable platitudes to a boring dowager at an official cocktail party, rushing through urgent messages when the Ambassador had found some new place to swim up in the mountains and was incommunicado, or simply fending off the constant parade of people who wanted something, Towell performed with dedication.

Smith sat down. "I think we should get in touch with the Ambassador right away," he said quietly. It was a little after ten-thirty on that Monday morning. Smith held a scrap of paper on which he'd scribbled notes during the telephone call he had just received from Torrejón. "Two Air Force planes have crashed in midair over southern Spain. I think he ought to know about it. One of them was a bomber."

Towell screwed up his ruddy face. Smith said nothing about H-bombs and the young diplomat's mind did not make the frightening leap. "Is this really the kind of thing we should bother the Ambassador about?" Towell asked. "He's making a speech. Can't it wait until twelve-thirty?"

The political officer said he thought not, without going into details. With his handsome open face, his smooth dark hair, his undramatic calm, Smith was impressive and Towell thought it over carefully. He might have felt differently if Smith were excitable and given to bursts of self-importance like some of the people he dealt with, but there was a quality of measured judgment in the Second Secretary, Towell decided, which really should be taken seriously. He agreed that the Ambassador should be told without delay.

"Well, where is he?" asked Smith. That was embarrassing. On Towell's desk there was the program of the businessmen's convention that the Ambassador was addressing and the place where the morning session would be held. But neither of them had a notion where it was, or how to reach it. Towell called the commercial section of the Embassy, but of course no one was there. They were all at the convention, and their secretaries couldn't help. Finally, one of the Embassy chauffeurs said he thought he knew the address. Smith decided to jump in the car and try to find it, although there was a risk that the speech would be finished and the Ambassador headed back to the office by the time he got there. Towell said he would wait in the Embassy in case anything more came in.

The speech was over by the time Smith sidled into the hall where the American Management Association was meeting, but the Ambassador was still on the platform managing a diplomatically fascinated expression as someone else droned on.

"Are you with the convention? Right over this way, there are still some seats," said an enthusiastic greeter at the door, propelling Smith with a firm elbow grip and a smile as wide as his plastic convention badge.

"No, no. I have to see Ambassador Duke."

"Well, you've missed the speech, but just sit down anyway. There he is. Great fellow. Tobacco, isn't it?"

Smith tried to be both definitive and unobtrusive. He explained that he was from the Embassy and he had an important message to deliver.

"You're not going to take him away from us, are you?" boomed the greeter.

"I don't know." The reply was coolly businesslike enough to work at last. Smith was taken to a side room where a number of people were standing chatting. Glass doors led to the platform and he could see the row of notables on the dais. He posted himself in the doorway and stared fixedly at the Ambassador, trying to force attention by the silent power of his wish. Duke saw him, noticed nothing, and glanced away. It was agonizing. But it turned out to be a double-take. The Ambassador turned again, noticed a discreet beckon, and mumbled excuses to the people on each side of him. Then he stood up and tiptoed off the platform. Smith had typed out the first information on an Embassy memo sheet in case he hadn't been able to extricate the Ambassador and would have to pass him a note, so he handed it over as the quickest way of breaking the news. He added that there had been nuclear weapons on the bomber and gave further details that had come in since the first call.

"I ought to phone and see if they have anything more," Duke whispered. Smith said it was too early, he had the last report just before he left the office. Duke retrieved his coat without explanation to his hosts. They went downstairs, dismissed the car that Smith had come in, and headed back together to the Embassy. After half a block the Ambassador changed his mind and ordered his driver to take them straight to the Foreign Office. It was housed in a vastly magnificent old palace in the center of the city, an acute disadvantage to anyone too hurried to appreciate the scenery while waiting for traffic to crawl through the clogged streets. They bore the irritating delays in tactful silence.

Angier Biddle Duke was a man born to tact. He need never have done a day's work in his life. Yet no man embraced his job, every conceivable aspect of it, with more enjoyment. Tall, handsome, bred to be dashing on a polo pony, charming at a debut, suave in a salon, never intended to shuffle papers unless it be notes involving a Wall Street deal or a Philadelphia case involving millions, he had entered the United States Foreign Service in 1949 and loved it ever since. It was not, of course, sheer luck that he had made Ambassador—to El Salvador, in 1952—as the youngest man ever appointed to that rank in the country's history. His grandfather was the tobacco and University Duke, and his mother was Cordelia Drexel Biddle, all resounding names in American society and economy. But he was not one for resting on his riches. Duke liked to move, if necessary, within the walls of a room. He had a habit of pacing off any restricted space with his long lope. But whenever possible he was on the run, "from El Morocco to El Salvador," as a socialite chum once put it, and when he got there "he dedicated more sewers, slaughterhouses, and clinics than a half-dozen politicians," an astonished Salvadorean remarked. He had been Chief of Protocol in the Kennedy administration, distributing his smiling sympathy to a hundred embassies in Washington with enthusiastic concentration on the ones whose countries were too young to have made the atlas. In Spain, where he presented his credentials on April 1, 1965, he ranged an uneasy nation with the same zeal and a shrewd sense of the hard-headed pressures beneath the foam of diplomatic niceties.

It was clear enough to Duke what might be the implications of this Broken Arrow. The United States had acquired three air bases in Spain in 1953 in return for economic and military assistance that had reached more than a billion dollars. The domestic opposition to Generalissimo Francisco Franco blamed the United States for what it claimed had been the vital bolster to a teetering dictator. The opposition was fragmented, inchoate, bewildered. But some among them were bound to find useful political ammunition in a charge that the Franco regime had wantonly delivered the nation to possible nuclear disaster in a cynical deal for dollars to keep itself in power. The United States had closed down one air base in the thirteen years since the agreement, and missile technology had made the other two much less important, but there was also now the key Polaris submarine base at Rota to consider. The existing base agreement was to run out in 1968. Both sides had already begun the subtle jockeying for position when the time would come to begin to talk renewal. There was no way of foreseeing what the wake of the accident would bring, but it seemed clear enough that in one way or another Spanish-American relations would be affected. Duke's concern was to minimize whatever troubles lay ahead and the first step, he felt, had to be a gesture of consideration, making sure that the Spanish government was informed.

With Smith ambling behind him, the Ambassador strode through the pillared halls into the musty back corridors where the unceremonious work of diplomacy was done. There was no one in the outer office of Angel Sagaz Zubelzu, the head of the American section, and no one inside either. A flunky shook his head in contented ignorance. He didn't know where anybody in the section might be found, he told them. If nobody was there, then they must all be out. The Americans hurried back down the corridor and climbed the enormous staircase to the office of the Foreign Minister. His reception room was deserted, too. A phone rang insistently on a secretary's desk but no one came to answer. Finally, Smith found an usher who told them the Ministry had gone to a funeral. He reeled off a list of other officials. Each time the usher nodded sadly, "Also at the funeral." Finally, the Spaniard had an idea.

"Would you like to see the assistant chief of protocol?"

It was not what the Ambassador had had in mind, but Duke was almost ready to deliver his message to the porter at that point. "Fine, fine," he said. "We'd like to see him right away."

The usher was not prepared to leapfrog the routine of courtesy, nonetheless. He showed the Americans into the formal waiting room, an ornate salon with tapestried couches and ormolu vases meant to clothe any toughness in the business to be done with a soothing grace. They were left to wait alone. When at last the assistant chief of protocol arrived, Duke spent no more time on formality.

"We have some unpleasant news," he said. "There has been a crash of two Strategic Air Command planes over southern Spain. I don't know the details yet, but I wanted to inform the Minister."

It was, the assistant chief agreed, clearly not an issue of protocol. Eventually they were shown to the Under-secretary's office and the message was delivered in detail. Duke relayed all that he had heard about the crash, repeating clearly that nuclear weapons were involved but no one yet knew what had happened to them.

"Four kilometers from Cartagena?" the Under-secretary interrupted. He gawped in distress when Duke tried to fix the place of the crash. It sounded as though a major population center might be involved. That could mean mass evacuations, panic, an overwhelming disaster. It was a misunderstanding.

"No, no," Duke reassured him. "About 40 kilometers from Cartagena, not near any city." Neither of them had ever heard of Palomares.

"But still I feel it's a terribly serious, important event, far beyond the lives that have been lost," Duke said. "I don't know what the aftermath will be, but we have to establish an immediate close working relationship. There is going to be a lot of cooperation needed on all sides." It was a discreet way of asking the Spanish government not to use the incident against the United States, but to ease the unavoidable resulting strains as best it could. Pedro Cortina Mauri, the Under-secretary, caught the underlying message deftly.

"Will this refueling operation continue over Spain?" he asked.

"I don't know." Duke's was an honest answer to a question with its own undertones, and he understood them.

Cortina did not press the point. He closed the interview, saying smoothly, "Yes, we'll work together."

The meaning was not clear. But it sounded auspicious. So far, at least, the collision of the planes had not entrained a collision of the governments. Spain made no protest.

It was one o'clock by the time the Ambassador and

Smith got back to the big modern embassy building on Serrano, a broad street in the newer section of Madrid where wide, shady avenues made city life an unstrained pleasure. Duke called a meeting of his top aides. Representatives of the 16th Air Force and JUSMAG—the tongue-twisting acronym of the American mission in charge of all military relations with Spain, including military aid—were present. They got out the *Black Book,* a loose-leaf folder of secret contingency instructions alphabetized according to the type of trouble that might happen. Under A, for accidents, there were several pages outlining precisely the chain of command responsibility and the first procedures to be followed in case of a Broken Arrow. There was even a precooked public statement, ready for release when the blanks for date and place and type of planes involved had been filled in. It said that a small amount of radioactive contamination had resulted from the accident but that there was no danger to the populace. That part could, of course, be stricken out before release if it should be inapplicable, but the disaster was taken for granted and the balm offered sight unseen. The form was neatly prepared. It just did not fit the situation.

The military, Duke learned, had already begun to move. After a phone call to the State Department, he decided that his job was to stay on in Madrid and man the lines to the Spanish government. That seemed to take care of everything for the moment. The meeting ended and they all went to lunch. It was after two, but lunchtime in Madrid is two to four, so no one minded.

The Air Force issued the only announcement later in the afternoon. It said merely that a B-52 and a KC-135 had crashed over southern Spain. The names of survivors and casualties would be released when next of kin had been notified. There was no mention of H-bombs or air-alert missions. It sounded routine, a sadness as at any accident, but no more. Scarcely anyone not yet drawn into the increasingly frenzied pace of official response paid the least attention. But Harry Stathos, the alert UPI bureau chief in Madrid, remembered instantly what B-52's were doing over Spain when he got the word. He pressed the Air Force spokesman to say whether there had been atomic bombs aboard the plane. His urgent queries brought no answer. He filed a short story reporting the crash and saying that H-bombs might have been involved but that there was no official

confirmation. It made a brief item in American papers.
Spanish censorship limited what was published there to the
Air Force announcement. That caused no stir at all.

The Command Post "hot line" on the desk rang at 10:23
A.M., the General noted. He listened to the brief report and
shot back questions. "What kind of fire? An engine fire? Call
Morón right back and get clarification." Then Maj. Gen.
Delmar Wilson cradled the receiver and headed for the
Command Post, 150 feet down the hall from his office at the
Torrejón Air Force base. Long but not quite so lanky as he
had been as a bomber pilot during World War II, especially
around the waistline, Wilson was nonetheless still the trim,
clean-cut, poised officer and gentleman of the better military
manuals. "A Hollywood producer's dream general," a scientist
said of him later, "the kind that listens to everything, decides
without hesitation, and never flaps. You've seen them in lots
of movies, the good-looking boss of the good guys." His hair
was a light, unstreaked gray and his position as commander of
the 16th Air Force was his last post before retirement, but his
tanned skin was taut under his square jaw, his reflexes steady.
He didn't bother to look at himself in the one-way mirror. The
Command Post door opened to him quickly.

As soon as he had gotten a better version of the lead
tanker's report relayed from Morón, he called General Eisenhart
in Omaha. It was agreed that he would leave for the scene of
the accident as soon as possible, in about an hour, he told
SAC. The men on duty began to make the calls as soon as he
hung up. Within fifteen minutes some 45 people, the members of the accident control team and the aircraft accident
investigation board, had been assembled in the Command
Post. When all were there, they were told why they had been
summoned and instructed to get together all the equipment
they would need for departure in an hour. Wilson did not
take the time to pack a bag. He took the head of the accident
board, Col. George Payne, his personal interpreter-liaison
man-major domo, Angel Corujedo, and Col. Barnett "Skip"
Young of his staff and flew off in a T-39, a small "businessman's
jet." The nearest airfield to the Saddle Rock area was at San
Javier, the Spanish air academy, and word was sent ahead that
they were coming. But first Wilson flew to the coordinates
reported by the tanker as the approximate area of the crash.
Descending to 1,500 and then to 1,000 feet, they circled the

speckled mountains just behind the coast looking for something that would pinpoint the spot. On a pass down what appeared to be a valley—it was the bed of the dry Almanzora River—they found what they were seeking. The tail section of the B-52, no longer burning, sat neatly upright on an empty sweep of sand. From the air it looked intact, as though someone had put it there waiting to assemble a bomber. Wilson surveyed the area a little further but noticed nothing else distinctive. Now, at least, he knew exactly where to go and he ordered the pilot to hurry to the airfield. The transport from Torrejón was just taxiing off the runway as they came in to land. It was nearly two in the afternoon.

The Command Post at Torrejón had been in touch with San Javier in the meantime, begging for buses, staff cars, taxis, anything that could be rounded up to get the men the rest of the way to Palomares. They had some equipment—a radio, some radiation monitors, some rations—not much. The lucky ones whose wives had been at home when the summons went out had overnight cases with shaving things and a change of underwear. Many had nothing but what was in their pockets when the word came. Wilson gave the destination as best he could and ordered everybody to meet at the tail section of the smashed B-52. They had only ordinary touring maps to guide them, maps that did not mention Palomares or the tracks that led to it. But the tail section dominated the landscape where it had fallen. If they could get to the general area, they couldn't miss it.

The Spanish commander of San Javier had further news. Three crew members had been rescued and were in the hospital at Aguilas. Wilson took a car to see them first. He told his men he would meet them at the tail of the plane.

Just after they left the airfield "Moose" Donovan arrived. Maj. Gen. Stanley J. Donovan was head of JUSMAG—Joint United States Military Advisory Group—commander of all American forces in Spain as well as senior U.S. representative to the Spanish military. He had a row of offices in a wing of the Air Ministry in Madrid and he made it his business to be on easy, man-to-man terms with the ranking generals. They, after all, more or less ran the country. It wasn't hard for him. A bluff, beery-faced Irishman with a rough-edged tongue and a hearty sense of humor, Donovan had properly earned the nickname of a bulky, overwhelming, but not really aggressive animal. The Spaniards liked him and he learned to deal with them in comfort. His wife Peggy had written a breezy, warmly affectionate tourist guide to Spain. They planned to stay there when the time came for retirement. Meanwhile, his position and his friendships had brought Donovan ready access to the top officials. Torrejón had sent him word of the accident and of Wilson's decision to fly to the site. Donovan called on the Air Minister and on General Agustín Muñoz Grandes, chief of the Spanish General Staff and number-two authority in the country, after Franco, to tell them personally of the accident. He learned from them that a Spanish marine helicopter had seen a midair collision and an officer at the San Javier base had reported an explosion in the sky. He, too, decided to have a look at the scene and flew down.

By the time the straggling caravan of American officers set out from San Javier that Monday afternoon the word had been widely spread. No one knew yet what cleaning up after the accident would mean, but the operation was launched. From halfway around the world, people were converging on Palomares.

5

THE ARRIVAL

The first Americans to reach Palomares, probably the first ever to set foot in the isolated village, came in a helicopter from Morón bringing a doctor. When he learned no one was injured in the village but that a survivor of the crash had been taken to the clinic, the flight surgeon hurried off to Vera to see the airman. The helicopter went off again. It was the first the villagers had ever seen and it caused almost as much excitement as the terrifying rain of flames and metal. Nobody imagined that it was the vanguard of an invasion.

The landing in force, so to speak, began toward dusk on that Monday. Colonel Young and Col. Carl Payne, a rangy Texan who had absorbed a bit of Spanish from his native San Antonio, secured the beachhead. They went first to the tail section parked on its river bed. Excited villagers clustered around, pointing in all directions and jabbering at once about the many strange things that had descended on them. The Guardia man posted at the big hunk of plane told them that his officers were gathered on the distant hill, up by the cemetery, so they went there to hear reports. Captain Calín, the jaunty police chief from Vera, had the situation in hand, he felt, and he delivered his information proudly. From him, and from the others who pressed forward, "Skip" Young found out with relief that there had been no civilian casualties, no damage. The survivors had been taken away. Satisfied that their first concern, for people, imposed no further requirements, they began a hasty survey of the wreckage.

"We immediately decided we needed a place to operate, a command post," Young said later. "It was getting dark. And then we learned that the town's electricity had been cut. That happened when the bomb bay sheared the power line. It gets

67

dark fast there in the desert. There wasn't any moon. The mayor offered to let us use the schoolhouse, but there was no light there. Then somebody told us the local bartender had a couple of kerosene lanterns and a room above the bar where we could set up."

By the time that was arranged, 49 Americans had arrived in Palomares. None of them imagined that there might have been a nuclear explosion. The AEC and SAC had always said that was virtually impossible. But they took quick radiation readings as a matter of course. There was no sign of danger. It was good to be certain, and to discover no villager had been hurt. It seemed almost as impossible as an accidental nuclear explosion that so much wreckage could have fallen on a village without injuring anyone.

"We're in luck," they told one another. There was no further concern for the people, still running excitedly all over the place so each could see with his own eyes all there was to be seen. That caused some resentment later when the people began to realize what they had innocently breathed and touched that could not be seen. From the Air Force view, all that remained was to find and recover the four bombs and cart away the debris. It obviously was going to be a big job, but no one supposed it would take more than two or three days. Despite the dark, they split up to get it started right away.

Capt. Joe Ramirez, a twenty-nine-year-old lawyer from Corpus Christi, Texas, was sent down on Wilson's disaster control team as its legal member. In all his time on duty in Spain he had never before been called to the Torrejón Command Post. When the sergeant summoned him from his office on the base at ten thirty that morning, he picked up a little packet of forms and instructions about handling claims in the event of an aircraft accident and hurried to the assembly point to show that he was prompt at drill. But he did not doubt for a moment that it was an exercise. He was still unclear about what was going on when he was told to be ready to fly to the south of Spain in an hour. A bomber had gone down, he realized, but he understood that it had fallen in the sea. There weren't likely to be complicated damage claims from fish. He checked out a flying suit and a pair of overshoes, dropped in at the PX for a toothbrush, shaving gear, and a pair of pajamas just in case, and told his boss he'd probably be back in the office at the end of the afternoon. A sturdy, compact man, with the dark hair, dark eyes, and soft tongue of the border, he was fluent in Spanish and pleased enough at the thought of a jaunt into the countryside.

His first shock came when the car in which he was riding from San Javier stopped for gasoline. He got out to sample the local gossip.

"Someone said they heard the tail section of the plane had dropped in the middle of a town called Vera. I nearly fell over backward," he said afterward. "I could picture the damage, the claims we'd have, with debris like that in a town." Vera was on the road to Palomares and it eased him, when they arrived, to find the first rumor of the hundreds he was to hear had been quite wrong. They got directions, took a series of wrong turns on the back roads, and finally reached a fork in the dirt track that was the entrance to Palomares. On the other side of the fork he saw a lot of people on a mountainside, with cars and buses sitting in the fields. That, he figured, must be where the meeting place was fixed. It wasn't easy to reach. As they passed through the village, they had to detour around an engine pod in the middle of the road, just in front of a house. General Wilson had already arrived on the hillside, above the cemetery, when Ramirez got there. There were no other Americans around with fluent Spanish and no Spaniards who could communicate in English, so he was pressed into service as interpreter. There was a row of hand-carved, dark wooden caskets laid out by a water tank.

When they realized that an American who could understand them had arrived, the villagers turned their attention on Ramirez. Mayor González was primarily worried about the bodies of the dead. It had not been easy for him to arrange for transportation of the caskets to Cuevas where there could be proper services. Everyone had a story to tell.

"I ducked under an olive tree when I saw this big thing chasing me across the sky," the mayor told him sheepishly. "Kind of silly, I know, but you can't think what it was like to have a ton of flaming metal headed for you."

"How many planes were there?" asked another. Ramirez said there had been two. "Only two, and all this fell from them?" The villager's amazement was on the brink of disbelief.

"The poor men, they were totally roasted," said another. "We feel sorry for you. It was a terrible accident."

A woman crossed herself before she spoke. "At least they

died quickly. God would not have let them suffer. But what of their families? Did they have children?" She crossed herself again.

Everybody wanted to tell, to help, to run an errand, serve as a guide. It didn't surprise Ramirez. He felt the people he knew in Corpus Christi would have behaved much the same. But it was comforting news to the senior American officers. They hadn't known whether to expect the people to be hostile, bitter, even menacing. The outpouring of sympathy and the eagerness to do anything that might be useful made the hard day a little easier.

A Guardia came up and told Ramirez that besides the man who landed in a parachute, some kind of a projectile with a parachute attached had fallen in the town. The Air Force lawyer had no idea what that might be. There was so much to hear, to see, barely time even to translate. But when he had a chance to mention that report to Colonel Payne, the Colonel realized quickly that it must be a bomb. Ramirez looked for the Guardia to get more details but he had gone off. Another one said yes, he had seen something like a torpedo in the mountains. There was a parachute all rolled up on one side of it and it had made a crater. Payne, Ramirez, and the Spaniard set off to look for it.

The high wintry sky was crowded with too many stars to count, the nightly company of lonely places that is denied to city dwellers whose own electric glow curtains off the universe. But it was very dark afoot. The Guardia had a feeble flashlight in what looked like a cigarette case. Payne had another, but it could only illuminate the rocks and underbrush for a yard or two ahead. They stumbled over the hills for more than an hour. All the little valleys, the cliffs, the crevices they passed began to look alike. The Guardia was growing morose in embarrassment.

"It was by a tomato patch," he kept repeating. "I saw it this afternoon. It must be right by here because it looked like this. There was a plowed area nearby and I remember an old barrel in the corner of the field." But they kept trudging on in useless circles. They decided it was hopeless in the dark and headed back to the cemetery where the road ran down to the village. On the way they saw a barrel. That revived their spirits and they moved off behind the Guardia to search again. Still, there was no luck.

Increasingly worried, the Guardia, who was a private,

whispered to Ramirez, "Tell me, what's the rank of this man with us?"

"He's a colonel," Ramirez answered.

"A full colonel?" There was awe in the blurred peasant voice.

"Yes, a full colonel."

The Guardia sighed unhappily. Then the cheering thought occurred. "He's got patience that one, thanks to God. If he was one of ours, he'd have booted me all over the place by now for running him in circles and getting nowhere."

Ramirez grinned in the dark. But it had to be admitted they were getting nowhere. They gave up and went back to the village.

Colonel Young, a husky man with heavy brows, a rugged square-cut face, and the warmly happy eyes of one who had grown up as the favorite of the family ("I was the first male child on either side and my grandpa thought I was the greatest thing since sliced bread," he said later with a laugh), had been stumbling over neighboring hills to look for another airman. He had heard a report that only six bodies had been found and thought there might be one more survivor lying injured, unconscious perhaps. But his search that night was no more successful.

He went back to the bar where there were lanterns and witnesses. Ramirez and a few other Americans gathered there. It seemed the whole village had tried to push into the little room to steam off its excitement.

"I heard there was a woman on the plane," explained one villager. "She got the pilot drunk and that's why there was a crash."

"No," said another, "it was deliberate. One plane rammed the other one. I saw it. The pilots must have had a fearful feud about something. I wonder what it was."

"I'm sure it was an accident. They have all that gasoline, you know, and maybe the flier tossed a lighted match out the window and it made everything blow up," said a third. "That happened once in a garage near where my cousin lives in Barcelona. There was a tremendous fire. Not so big as here, though."

The stories tumbled out as recklessly, as wildly as the burning bolts had fallen from the sky that morning. Some bits were helpful, about all the places where the wreckage fell. But mostly they grew in gorgeous fancy. Young chuckled as he listened, grateful for the villagers' good humor after what might so easily have been a disaster for them. He stood a round of beer for everybody. There were 30, maybe 40, maybe more people in the bar. He didn't count but he couldn't help chuckling again when he figured out the bill had come to exactly $1.87. There were olives and bits of pale cheese and smoked raw ham available to nibble with the beer, but no real food. A supply of Air Force in-flight lunches had been put aboard the transport at Torrejón along with a few radiation monitors and other equipment. Someone brought the paper boxes into the bar. There was no such thing as a restaurant in Palomares and the Americans were getting hungry. The Spaniards watched, astonished but politely hiding their distaste, as the Americans wolfed cold corned beef, crackers, canned peaches, and cookies for their dinner.

Like the other Americans in the first team to arrive, Sgt. Raymond Howe found himself racing in confusion from one mountainside to another trying to check the jumble of reports. A thirty-eight-year-old professional, bantam-size and bantam-tough with bright blue tattoos on his arms, Howe was a member of Wilson's battle staff assigned to what was called the bio-environmental engineering services of the medical department. He had brought with him from Torrejón a PAC-1S, the standard armed forces radiation monitor for alpha rays, a ANPDR-39, which is similar to a Geiger counter, and a 27-C monitor for beta and gamma rays. His first immediate checks showed negative on all the equipment and all three types of radiation. In the absence of a nuclear explosion, virtually no beta or gamma rays were to be expected although the uranium in a bomb does give off a minuscule amount of gamma radiation. It is fission that produces a large amount of these highly penetrating and therefore most dangerous rays. Alpha radiation is of such short range that it cannot penetrate a sheet of tissue paper, or unbroken human skin. It can, therefore, cause damage only if the radioactive metal is absorbed into the body. Assured by his preliminary survey that there had been no vast release of nuclear energy requiring a mass evacuation and immediate, stringent measures, Howe turned his main attention to finding the bombs. He started by making radiation checks on the wreckage of the bomber. It was all over town. The big piece of fuselage on the hill by the cemetery showed nothing. Neither did the tail section in the river.

Howe made inquiries for other major pieces of debris. He heard that one of the Guardia Civil men had seen something that he called "a kind of weapon." It was almost dark but Howe quickly got his team together and they followed the men down the river bed. There, lying innocently on the soft sand, was the long aluminum tube of an H-bomb, on the outside a simple cylinder that looked like an old-fashioned water boiler or perhaps an overlarge tank of cooking gas, on the inside one of the most intricate mechanisms in the world. It had apparently landed sideways on a steep but spongy bank and rolled harmlessly to rest. Applying his instruments, Howe made sure there was no radioactive leakage although it looked intact. The EOD men—explosive ordnance disposal— also looked it over thoroughly for damage. There was none. They were trained to handle damaged weapons, to disassemble them in any state so that no further accident was possible, either through detonation of the high explosive or any kind of tampering. It was called the render-safe procedure and involved disconnecting components of the bomb so that, while they remained together in its shell, there could no longer be a sequence of reactions. It was too dark for the delicate task by the time the bomb was found. The main concern for it at that point was security, in any case. If the high explosive had not already gone off, it wouldn't blow up sitting still. But the United States does not like to display its H-bombs.

Howe posted Air Force guards by the bomb, deciding that disposal would have to wait until dawn. He explained that there was no danger of explosion or radioactive leakage, arranged to send them some in-flight lunches, and promised to send relief guards in the middle of the night. To prevent any conceivable mishap, he fixed a password. No one was to be allowed near the spot without giving it. The pass was simple: two flashes of light and the word Guss, Howe's nickname which emblazoned his tattoo.

No word of weapons, of H-bombs, of radioactivity was mentioned to the villagers. The crash itself had been a tragedy. Men had died. The Americans, the Spaniards thought, had come only to collect their own and clean up the debris.

The Air Force called the site where Howe had placed his guards Number One—the place the first bomb had been found. He knew there were three more to go.

* * *

General Wilson took Angel Corujedo, for the language and whatever complexities might arise with the local officials, and drove directly to the port of Aguilas. Corujedo was a unique figure at Torrejón, a kind of community middleman. He was a Spaniard from a large and struggling family who had accepted the offer of an emigrant uncle to go and live in New York, and thus to ease by one the number of children dependent on his widowed mother. That had been many years ago and he had stayed long enough in the United States to adjust to the manners and habits as well as the language of another country. He went home from time to time on visits. He happened to be in Spain in 1936, when the Civil War began. Conscription ended his travels abroad. But he felt semi-American and yearned for the chance to use "Hi" and "Okay" and drink Coca-Cola again as a matter of course. When the Air Force came to Spain in 1953, he offered himself and was taken on. By the time of Palomares he had been at the Torrejón base longer than anyone. He was sixty-six years old and his long service as arranger of formalities with local authorities, greeter at formal occasions, interpreter for men in command, had given him the stature of dignitary in his own right. The military bearing never rubbed off on him. There was gray stubble around the pink pate of his head and a ring of softness around his middle. But he had acquired, and proudly, the military sense of hierarchy. Wilson found him invaluable in buffering local problems.

Corujedo cleared a quick way for the General to the hospital room where the survivors had been taken in Aguilas. They were in reassuring condition, shaken up but well enough to tell about the accident. None of them could explain more than that they had come in a little fast upon the tanker and could see it above the cockpit, rather than ahead. Their main comment was on how it had upset them to bail out over land and find the high wind carrying them out to sea. Wilson asked how many other chutes they had seen in the sky. Two, said one. Three, said another. There was nothing definite to go on about the others in the two crews. Before leaving San Javier, Wilson had arranged for an air-sea rescue helicopter to come down with a flight surgeon. It landed on the Aguilas high-school soccer field. Wendorf was still dazed as he was carried out. He thought it was a bull ring. Crowds turned out to watch as the three airmen, in new pajamas someone from the hospital had hurried out to buy, were flown away. They were taken back to the base hospital at Torrejón. After two weeks, a period set more by the accident board's need for detailed interrogation than by the requirements of their health, they were flown home to North Carolina for leave and eventually a return to duty. Buchanan, who had fallen on land and suffered serious burns, was taken from his hospital at Vera to Torrejón on the same day but had to be treated for a month before he was released.

Wilson felt his first responsibility was to his men. When he had sent on the ones at Aguilas, he drove to Palomares. "The danger of contamination crossed my mind," he said later, "but I wanted to see about the survivors and the casualties." He quickly inspected pieces of wreckage in the failing light, gathered the first reports, and then went on to Cuevas where the dead had been taken. The caskets had been laid out in state, services were being performed. It was necessary in the circumstances to secure a formal release for return of the bodies. The Mayor of Cuevas drew up a series of documents, but he was uncertain about the proprieties. There were definite regulations about the procedure to be followed in handling the corpse of a Spaniard who died outside the administrative authority of his residence. But the rules were not so clear for foreigners, and for military foreigners at that. The military governor, the civil governor, the coroner, the judge, all had to be consulted. The local doctor had to verify and certify. The question of whether Wilson should sign for seven or eight bodies distressed them all. There were, he insisted, no more than 11 men on the two planes. Four survivors were already on their way to the Air Force hospital. The Spaniards insisted they had eight corpses and could not release them if Wilson signed for only seven. The combination of haste and morbid awe in collecting the parts of the corpses which had been dismembered had led to the false count. And the Spanish officials' honest sympathy for the loss of life only made the argument more unpleasant. When at last the bureaucratic problem was resolved, it turned out that there was no vehicle available to take the caskets to San Javier, where a plane was waiting to transfer them to the American base, and then back to the United States for burial. Scrounging turned up a baker's delivery van, and that was used. The Air Force had to buy the baker a new truck soon afterward. He complained that no one would buy bread from a van that had served as a hearse.

It was after eleven by the time Wilson got back to Palomares. The crowd in the bar was still dense. General Donovan was there and a new tremor of excitement pulsed through the village. Simultaneously and in the flesh, two major generals were on display, in a community that had never played host to an authority so high as official of the province. Wilson had his gratitude and appreciation for their sympathetic help translated to the people, but decided that for the work ahead he'd best set up Command Post in the field. He ordered it to be established first thing in the morning by the tail section, still the central Air Force landmark. Collection of debris and the search for three more bombs would, he realized, take manpower and clean-cut organization. He had only an ordinary field transmitter to communicate with Torrejón, a radio that any receiving set could overhear, and he was by nature wary of information leaks. An officer was sent to Vera, a drive of three-quarters of an hour, to telephone Madrid, a connection that seldom could be made in less than half an hour and often took as long as two or three. The discovery of the first bomb was reported and reinforcements ordered. It was after midnight when the men at Torrejón were routed out of bed and told to report at once to base. They left, six busloads of 40 men each, by two-thirty that morning, most of them with nothing but their uniforms and a blanket and box lunch issued as they started. It was not, perhaps, the quickest way to get them down to Palomares but Wilson had already realized that he would need ground transport as badly as he needed troops.

The only thing left to be done on that long Monday was to find a place for the Americans already on the scene to spend the night. Some were sent to Cuevas, where they had been told the Guardia Civil had made arrangements. Ramirez was in that group. They pounded on the police headquarters door. A lieutenant, tugging his suspenders into place as he finally shuffled sleepily to open, gazed at them in bewilderment. He had heard nothing of Americans needing beds. And at that hour? And in the winter, when even the few tourist hostels were closed? But they persuaded him. The one plentiful amenity of the area was good will. By 3 A.M. Ramirez was asleep in his flying suit on a soggy bed with a U-shaped mattress in an ancient boardinghouse. Others were bedded no better in Vera and the fishing port of Garrucha. Some slept in the cars and in the cold fields, wrapped in whatever they could find. Corujedo, with his flair for managing, arranged a senior officers' quarters. There was a seaside hotel, the Maricielo, not far from Garrucha. He found the woman and her nephew who had stayed there as winter caretakers about to close it up for a few weeks' holiday in Madrid. They had packed and planned to leave early the next morning. Captain Calín of the Guardia Civil had mentioned to Corujedo that the hotel belonged to Lieut. Gen. Rafael Cavanillas. That general, it happened, had been commander of Corujedo's unit in the Civil War. When Anita, the caretaker, refused to change her mind, Corujedo wheedled and argued and talked of his acquaintance with the owner. It settled nothing.

"Then I'll call him and you'll see." By some quirk of the otherwise reliably sluggish telephone, Corujedo actually got through. The hotel was kept open, put in fact at the exclusive disposal of the U.S. Air Force. Anita and her fourteen-year-old nephew Marcos cooked and cleaned and served and tended bar and made the beds for some 40 men from that day until the Americans departed. They never got their fortnight in Madrid, but they met and made friends with an extraordinary assortment of people. By Tuesday the newcomers were streaming in. On Tuesday the operation began to take shape.

6

THE CAMP

First light at that time of year broke a little before eight. Wilson ordered everybody to be at the tail section, ready to start at dawn. There was no reveille, no alarm clocks, but no one was relaxed enough to oversleep. The men swallowed bitter coffee and white bread, the Spanish breakfast bought wherever they could find it, and gathered in the river bed. The sky faded near the sea, tinting slowly at first and then bursting into brilliant red and orange as the sun lifted itself above the Mediterranean. They were the colors of flame, but it took time to cook the chill off the air. The high wind, swirling dust off the eroded land, had a bite.

Col. Carl Payne was in charge of the search. He was a Texan with a quiet sense of humor, thin-rimmed spectacles, a clear-cut sense of organization, and fortunately, as the frightened Guardia had noted, great patience. There was confusion to try the soul even of a man who disliked order. It did not help that the leader of the accident board, the group whose duty it was to find all the pieces and try to figure out just what had happened, was also a Colonel Payne, Col. George Payne. Payne teams were running everywhere. Carl Payne surveyed the scene from the river bed and divided the panorama into three rough sections. Every pair of eyes not urgently at other work was drafted to his groups—doctors, bomb technicians, public relations officers, lawyers, everyone— and sent off to find the three missing bombs. Two helicopters came in to join the search.

Within an hour one radioed success to the Command Post, which was still nothing but a communications kit, a hodgepodge of borrowed cars, and a few men poring over illustrated but vague tourist maps of the area. The helicopter had seen a wad of parachute and a metal tube protruding from the ground. It lay on a hill well behind the cemetery, a great square of adobe walls and weathered crosses cramped askew. Ramirez found his guide of the previous night. They had no trouble going straight to the spot where the bomb nestled at the junction of three ridges. They must have passed it half-a-dozen times the night before, he realized. It was named Number Two.

"I wouldn't have known what an H-bomb looked like if it hit me in the face," Ramirez said later. "I just went up to see what the thing was and I shouted to the others on the hill, 'Hey, over here. There's a crater.' I was standing right on the edge of the hole it dug, about eight feet wide and two or three feet deep. They shouted not to go too close. Then someone came up with a Geiger counter. That was the first I heard about radioactivity. Except for the crater, there wasn't anything to show there'd been an explosion. I saw what looked like the front end of a torpedo. There weren't any cracks or anything oozing out or strewn around. It didn't look messy."

It was the bomb that Puig, the architect, had knelt against. He had not understood the crater since the great chunk of half-buried metal looked solid, like an ordinary bomb. But it was solid uranium, so heavy and tough that it had scarcely been affected by the explosion. The bio-environmental and weapons experts knew very well what the crater signified. It meant that at least part or, as it turned out, all of the high explosive had detonated. The conventional powder in an H-bomb is powerful, an explosive devised to provide a brief but intensely concentrated blast. It is not TNT. It is an improvement that gives more yield for its weight and bulk, although it is measured in terms of TNT, the yardstick for blasting force as horsepower is the measure for driving force. Since its development the same explosive had been used for conventional American weapons because it is more efficient than TNT. Its job in an armed H-bomb is to drive a mass of plutonium wedges into a solid sphere. Neutrons are knocked off some of the atoms. If one happens to hit another plutonium nucleus, it splits that atom, releasing more neutrons. Up to the point of critical mass, they zing off into surrounding space. When enough are packed together to assure that ever more nuclear targets are bound to be hit, a chain reaction is established. It can be slowed, as in an atomic power plant, to produce a steady source of energy. Uncontrolled, the chain reaction releases all of its tremendous force in a fraction of a second. The elemental power that binds an atom together is loosed in an explosion of blast, heat, and radioactivity. To press the plutonium in a bomb into a critical mass, the conventional explosive must all go off at the same instant with the same amount of force.

That does not happen when a bomb is not armed and the detonation has been caused by fire or impact, never distributed with precise evenness in space and time. Then, instead of causing nuclear fission in the plutonium, the heat and pressure of the blast pulverize the radioactive metal. The plutonium sprays out in the form of almost infinitesimal grains of powder, too fine to see or feel. It burns easily, fusing with the dust in the air and any dirt thrown up by the explosion. The conventional detonation of such a bomb inevitably causes a plutonium cloud. The amount of contamination that results depends on the wind and the amount of dirt which captures the plutonium powder. The uranium log is not likely to be much affected. It is, in any event, far less radioactive than plutonium and therefore far less dangerous, although it gives off energy forty times as long.

The hydrogen atoms, which are the "H" in an H-bomb, are blown off by the blast. They create no danger. The AEC has explained in its manual that an H-bomb can be made with deuterium, a double form of hydrogen, or with tritium, a triple form. Both are natural substances, found in minute quantities in water. Their release by a broken H-bomb makes no meaningful change in the level of radioactivity in an area. So long as the hydrogen simply escapes, it is insignificant. But when it undergoes fusion, combining two light nuclei into a single heavier one, it provides the strongest force known in the world. So much mass is left over from the merger of nuclei and converted into energy that the very small amount of hydrogen in a bomb provides half of its destructive power. Fusion of light atoms is what makes an H-bomb from five to fifty times as devastating as an A-bomb of similar size. If it could be set off by itself, the most powerful nuclear bombs could be carried in handbags as the first era of nuclear fiction suggested. But the fusion reaction which is the principle of the sun's radiant energy requires the extremes of heat and pressure only achieved on earth at the instant of nuclear fission. All H-bombs have to incorporate the A-bomb reaction of splitting heavy atoms into two or more lighter elements. Half of the bombs' energy, therefore, comes from the fission of plutonium and uranium. As one bright-tongued physicist explained it, the conventional high explosive is the match, the uranium is the paper, the plutonium is the kindling, and the heavy hydrogen is the roaring wood fire. But the energy potential of the different elements multiplies so vastly that the amount of each in a bomb goes in opposite proportion to their power. It is as though a boxload of matches, a carload of paper, and a pile of twigs were used to light a toothpick which burned as hot as everything else combined.

The nuclear reaction potential and the radioactivity of the bomb's ingredients have no special relation to each other. Because its nuclei disintegrate steadily under normal conditions, giving off radiation, it is the man-made element plutonium that is the meaningful danger in an atomic accident where there has been no atomic explosion, either fission or fusion. The design of the bomb and the readiness with which plutonium powders and burns cause the problem. It was self-evident to the experts as soon as they saw there had been a conventional detonation that there must be some degree of plutonium contamination in the area. The questions remaining were how much and how far it had spread. At that point the orders were given to cordon off the surrounding fields and bar all entry until painstaking measurements could be made. No one gave any explanations. No one except the American officials who had to know and the highest ranking Spaniards had yet been told that H-bombs had been involved in the accident.

The search for the two other bombs was hastened. The airmen were still looking haphazardly since they had neither the manpower nor the equipment yet for a methodical hunt. Only five of the Americans—which included Corujedo since both sides presumed his U.S. nationality though he was still a Spanish citizen—could speak enough Spanish to make sense of the jumbled reports brought in. They tried to check on everything they heard. Another story from the Guardia Civil about a torpedo in a tomato patch sounded, at first, like a garbled direction to Number Two. But the guide led them to the opposite side of the village. There, just below the garden wall of Eduardo Navarro Portillo, they found Number Three.

The parachute was also partially strung out behind the tube. Sergeant Howe, who had just supervised performance of the render-safe procedure on Number One, was one of the first to see it. He realized immediately that there had been a detonation, although in that case a partial one. Chunks of partly burned explosive were lying about, along with pieces of the casing. The critical connections inside the bomb had been broken by the blast. There was no need for render-safe on that one. The bomb seemed to have fallen free and hit at a slight slant just below the wall. There was a gap of a yard or two where the stones had been blown loose. That was another bit of luck. The wall had served to muffle both the force of the explosion in the direction of the house and to limit the upwind spread of the plutonium cloud. Had the field been open where it fell, the house some 25 yards away would have been far more severely damaged. Perhaps it would have collapsed. Certainly it would have collected a good deal of plutonium fall-out. The strong offshore wind, still blowing, had carried most of the plutonium dust in the other direction. Navarro's house was on the northern tip of the village. Beyond it were tomato patches, empty fields and gullies, and the sea.

It was a little after 10 A.M. on Tuesday that Number Three was found. The time jolted "Skip" Young's memory. Although it seemed years, it had only been twenty-four hours since the accident. He studied the sky for a moment. At first he saw no planes, but then his eye caught the straight thin lines of vapor trails. Following them until they met, he watched another bomber and another tanker refueling. Only then could he really believe that it was possible to see aircraft from five miles below. Some of the villagers watched, too, and shuddered. They said nothing to the Americans. But they grumbled to each other.

"More planes, more and more on top of our heads," one complained to Mayor González. "It's getting dangerous now that the Americans have come." He pointed to the helicopters hovering close above the ground. Other aircraft had been coming to inspect the site. After the moment of intense relief when they discovered 200,000 pounds of wreckage had not touched them, the villagers began to feel a new uneasiness.

The Guardia Civil chased them from the immediate area of the bomb sites. The people perched on nearby ridges and dirt parapets separating plots to watch as the Americans worked. Only slowly did word spread that not all of the debris was pieces of aircraft. But there was no panicky distress. The bombs had not caused any real damage, the villagers reasoned. The explosions had been minor blasts, so there was nothing more to worry about. Few, if any, would have understood the difference if someone mentioned H-bombs. No one did.

Still they watched as Howe's men, wearing gloves, picked up bits of things and collected them in plastic bags. The chunks of high explosive were carried up the hill to Number Two site, an isolated spot, and thrown in a bonfire. In the open air, with no added heat generated by compression, the explosive burned harmlessly to ash. And they watched Howe moving to each piece of broken metal with his PAC-1S, a machine the shape and size of a cigar box, with a short boom like that of a portable vacuum cleaner. The sensitive face on a disc at the end of the boom detected alpha rays. He found some when he pressed the face on the shreds of metal casing. An inch away from the metal the reading was negative. There was little danger, he decided. The main part of the bomb had broken in three pieces. He picked them up, with ordinary gloves as sole protection, and put them in wooden boxes to be carried to the dump established near Number Two. It was important not to raise dust which would spread the contamination. But that was not a risk with the unbroken bomb. It was put in a sling. A helicopter came to fetch it, hauling the dangling bomb to where it could be loaded on a truck. In a perverse way the scene reminded one of the Americans of the opening sequence in the film La Dolce Vita, a sequence where a helicopter is shown carrying a statue of Christ across the skies of Rome. There was something of absurd human mockery about the sight of a helicopter trailing a divine, or demonic, cargo through the air.

By the next day packaging had arrived. Someone had calculated that the metal boxes used in shipping spare jet engines would be about the right size. The three bombs, two in pieces and one whole, were trucked to San Javier, flown to Torrejón, and then, after inspection and repacking, flown back to the United States. The fissile material from the whole bomb was recovered. More important, thorough post-mortems were performed on each to discover in as precise detail as possible how their components had been affected.

That left Number Four.

Captain Ramirez roamed the sprawling village and the fields asking people what they had seen falling from the skies. He was, he explained, particularly interested in something long and round. An old woman who he thought looked like a gypsy pointed to something 100 yards from her house. She was reluctant to speak to the Americans, whether from shyness or fright he couldn't tell. They followed her gesture and found the boom from the tanker. Another heavy piece of metal had fallen on the other side of her house. More and more, Ramirez noticed, the villagers were coming to speak of the "projectiles" when he asked them for information.

"Skip" Young stopped to speak to a farmer gathering tomatoes. Had he, by any chance, noticed a cylinder? The American made a circle with his arms to suggest the circumference of what he sought. The farmer shook his head. His wife, straddling a donkey at his side, said eagerly that she had seen something of the sort. Young followed her across the fields. That time the clue led only to a tubular starter cartridge from the bomber. It was typical of the way things went. Later, Young recalled that incident more vividly than the rest because he found it had been nearly reproduced in the sharp strokes of a distant artist's pen. Herblock, the Washington *Post*'s brilliantly sensitive cartoonist, had caught just the flavor of the beginning of the search. His drawing showed a perplexed peasant at ease upon his burro, confronting a stiffly embarrassed American officer, his arm rigid in salute. The caption read, *"Perdóneme. Ha Usted Visto Un . . . Uh . . . H-Bomb?"*

The accident board people inspected and registered and measured, and when they had recorded every detail, gave word to the removal teams to cart each piece of wreckage to a dump site selected on the empty beach. The junk pile, as they called it, grew rapidly. There was a shortage of everything needed for the work. To haul away the engine nacelle in a road, Ramirez persuaded a farmer to abandon his plowing for an hour and drag the wreckage behind his antiquated tractor. The American paid 300 pesetas, five dollars, and got a receipt. It was the start of what was to become a staggering Palomares bill. The bigger pieces of debris had to be left where they had fallen until heavier equipment arrived. The tail section was cut up with acetylene torches before it could be added to the pile.

The Combat Mission Folder, the most sensitive cargo on the B-52 apart from the bombs themselves, was also found on Tuesday morning. The black leather satchel was lying near the wreckage of the cockpit. It had been badly burned but there was no sign that anything had been removed or touched. Remains of the innermost secrets of SAC—codes and target— were quietly retrieved and returned by safe hand. Talk that mounted long after about a frantic hunt for the "black box" never disturbed the Air Force. That part of the search had been quickly, and satisfactorily, completed.

But it was becoming clear that the rest of the job could not be accomplished so easily. It was time to introduce some military method.

The team from Omaha had arrived at the site by dawn. They had reached Torrejón late Monday afternoon, local time, spent a few hours at the base for detailed briefing, and gone on to Palomares through the night. The experts from Albuquerque and Los Alamos arrived soon after. With the additional radiation counters they brought in, the task of plotting and marking out the areas of contamination was begun. The crater sites were the starting point. From there, stooping foot by foot along the rough terrain, the men had to measure radioactivity of the soil until they found the "zero line," the line beyond which the monitors gave only zero readings. The fragile faces of the counters were always breaking. A sharp edge of rock, even a prickly piece of stubble could puncture them. But the range of alpha rays is so short that a monitor face held even a few inches away from a contaminated object might fail to register. Some of the technicians wore orange flight suits and pinned on their chests the radiation badges— strips of film to record the dosage of radioactivity they received—which they used routinely in their work. The villagers noticed and wondered. But so much of what the Americans were doing was strange.

The big blue Air Force buses set out in convoys from Morón and Torrejón about 2 A.M. on Tuesday. The men were told they'd be in the field about three days, but few of them had time to collect anything more than a pair of boots and a toothbrush before they left.

It was not so long a drive from Morón. The airmen stumbled out of the crowded buses and stretched their legs on Palomares fields at lunchtime. They had not had a chance to sleep, but Colonel Payne decided they could see well enough to help search while the light remained. He changed his tactics from the morning's skeltering activity. There were almost 200 men available by then. Payne ordered them to draw up abreast in one long line, close enough to touch fingertips. The first man on the right carried a guidon, hastily made from a scrap of cloth and a cane pole, to keep the line straight and mark the limit of the ground covered. Then they marched, looking for an H-bomb or a crater that a falling bomb might have made. They worked out from the spots where major pieces of wreckage had landed. There were ridges, tall clumps of cactus, short but steep cliffs, boulders, ditches, in the way. The order was not to break the line. No matter what the obstacle, if it was humanly possible the men had to go over it, not around. Payne was taking no chance that an H-bomb might slip through a momentary gap in the advancing human tide. They covered several miles before it started to get dark. It was becoming obvious that the tall, thick growth of the tomato patches would have to be cut for a thorough search. The vines were too dense to see through. The tomatoes were vermilion ripe and lusciously juicy to dust-parched gullets. The farmers went on harvesting where they were left in peace. The Guardia Civil kept them away from the fields that the Americans were working, and the airmen helped themselves from time to time as they passed the heavily laden vines.

The Torrejón buses straggled in at the end of the afternoon. They had also brought some flat-bed trucks and an ambulance with medical supplies. It had been a hard drive over the narrow, twisting roads. Not all the men could be seated. Some had had to sit on duffel bags and suitcases in the aisles. They were not proud of themselves as a smart Air Force unit when they made their first appearance at Palomares that day, unshaven, unwashed, unpressed. Lieut. Ralph Meyer, a twenty-six-year-old hospital administrative officer, was in the last bus which pulled up to the Command Post at five-thirty Tuesday evening. It had broken down on the way. The driver had almost collapsed with exhaustion, and it was discovered that all the relief drivers were riding in the front bus, which had gone on.

As commander of his busload, Meyer straightened himself as best he could and reported in. Then, showing first concern for his men as an officer is schooled to do, he asked, "Where do we sleep?"

The answer was a pointing finger. It pointed at their own blue buses where they had just spent fifteen jouncing hours. There was nothing else. Some men had sleeping bags and spread them in the fields. Some curled up in the buses and trucks. The Morón convoy had brought extra rations so they did not have to go to sleep hungry, but there was no chance for a wash or a hot meal. They were tired enough not to care so long as they could sleep.

The first camp was set up the next morning. They pitched tents in the river bed by the tail section. Supplies were beginning to come in from Air Force bases in Germany, in Libya, and the United States.

The villagers sat on a hill above the newly named Camp Wilson and watched the men plunk down to eat a meal from cans. They had baked beans, hot dogs, peach and apricot juice that day. Captain Calín of the Guardia Civil tasted some and wrinkled his nose. "Terrible," he confided later. "Americans don't know how to eat. It's all so sweet. And they gobble it so fast. Maybe that helps not to notice how it tastes."

The tent city was finished in a day. Neat stone borders were made to line the entrance paths to the khaki canvas homes. Huge litter bins were posted at appropriate spots. The Spaniards gasped when, later, they saw Americans toss brand-new plates and forks into the bins with garbage when they had finished eating. It was a while before they learned the dishes thrown away so wastefully were only made of paper and not meant to be washed and treasured. The villagers shook their heads in amazement at how hard the Americans worked and how foolishly they sometimes went about it. It looked as though they meant to live in the river bed, the dustiest, most uncomfortable, most exposed place in the area. True, the Almanzora was completely dry. But sudden thunderstorms in the mountains could send flash floods hurtling down its bottom. Sometimes there had been walls of water four or five feet deep, sweeping away everything in their path. Animals had been lost that way, drowned in the churning torrent. People knew better than to stay in the river bed. Two days later the Americans realized their mistake. They moved the camp a mile and a half to a small plain on the edge of the beach. An old mine building stood there. It was roofless but at least it had four walls to give some respite from the wind and it could serve as mess hall and recreation room. A hard-packed slag field nearby became the heliport. Someone scrawled a sign on a board and posted it, announcing Welcome to Wilson International Airport.

From Wheclus Air Force base in Libya, Gray Eagle packets arrived. They were huge crates, pre-packed with everything a field unit might require to operate without normal civilian support. There were generators, stoves, refrigerators, shovels, tents, tools, blankets, and cots. The one thing overlooked was laundries. The prime precaution necessary against alpha radiation was to wash away the plutonium dust before it could be breathed or eaten. On the first day the men who had been out on the search were sent to bathe in the sea before they settled in for dinner. The water was a little more than 50 degrees, and it seemed even colder coming out into the sharp wind with dripping clothes. Nor were there enough spare clothes to go around. Everything seemed to be extra large or extra small. The unused supplies left on the stock shelves at Torrejón had been dumped in the buses at the last minute. Complete mobile laundries, with washing machines, were flown in from Germany. They occupied two tents and, when they were established, consumed 20 pounds of detergent every day. Portable showers were dispatched to avoid the shivering daily dip. By two weeks after the accident there was a solidly based community of 64 tents, 747 people, a motor pool, a kitchen with 22 cooks who baked 100 loaves of bread a day, a PX, and a nightly open-air movie in the abandoned mine building featuring films "ten years older than the ones you see on the late-late show," as Captain Byrum put it.

Capt. Fritz Byrum, a husky flight surgeon with a soft, round face and a Mississippi drawl, had gone down with the first team from Torrejón as the medical officer. There had been no casualties to attend, so at first he was drafted into a search team. As more men arrived, he turned his attention to caring for their health. Supplies of potable water were a problem. The water in the irrigation ditches would do for showers and laundry, but not, he ruled, for drinking. The Navy turned out to have a 2,000-gallon tank truck in Cartagena. It was the only one in Spain. But after a day or two Byrum realized it was too risky to send the truck to Cartagena for fresh water every day. If the vehicle broke down on the long trip, the camp would be left dry. He dashed around the countryside until he found another, closer, source of good water and a smaller tank truck that could be filled as a reserve while the big one was away fetching the daily supply. He set up an air-evacuation system for anyone seriously ill and a field dispensary that was soon busy treating pulled muscles, sore feet, all manner of cuts and scratches. The latrines were of necessity open ditches, but neither typhoid nor dysentery, which he most feared, nor any other epidemic, plagued the camp. The only medical evacuation that became necessary was of a man who got appendicitis.

The officers and men trudged the parched hills together. They did not have enough canteens. The high point of the search for one colonel came when a corporal unknotted the string that held an old whisky bottle to his belt and offered to share the last of his orangeade.

By the middle of the week Camp Wilson was a going concern. And General Wilson began to know by then that there was a great deal to be concerned about. A Spanish officer, Gen. Ramiro Pascual, had come in from Sevilla to coordinate the military problems. They were developing a scope that required direct communication with the top echelon in Madrid. Communications were one of the worst headaches.

As more and more people came, the switchboard at Vera could not handle the traffic. The Spanish government was persuaded to install a new and larger one, the Air Force paid $2,500 a month for a leased line to Madrid and laid its own line from Camp Wilson to Vera. Wilson felt better when at last he had securely coded telex and telephone communications to his base.

The judge from Vera hurried down to Palomares with a special question. There were not yet many Americans there who could speak Spanish. He found Captain Ramirez and explained what he had to know. In his hand was a small piece of simple machinery.

"I've got a man in court waiting to be charged," he said. "He stole this. But how can I tell if it's petty theft, or felony, or grand larceny?"

It was an engine starter, worth perhaps $20 new. Waiting for the rest of the story, Ramirez said it was from one of the planes, a tool of no great worth.

"The thing is," the judge said, "this fellow picked it up somewhere around here. Then he got drunk last night. He was running all around Vera waving this thing. He said it was a dangerous weapon that the Americans were looking for, but he had it and he was going to blow up the whole town. The Guardia hustled him off to jail and now I have to charge him. The crime depends on the value of the stolen goods."

Ramirez named a small figure, under five dollars. He turned to listen to some other visitors, hoping always for the tip that would lead to the highly valuable object of the search, the real weapon.

They were naval officers from the *Juan de la Cosa*, the Spanish warship that had been off Garrucha on the day of the accident, making new maps. They had seen the crash and were bringing the debris they had picked up at sea. Ramirez asked if they could provide some details of just where the pieces had fallen, to help in establishing the pattern of everything that dropped from the two planes. Wilson's men had started making charts of the wreckage to figure out where the fourth bomb might have landed. The navy officers offered to mark a map of what they'd found. But there had been lots more, they said, picked up by fishermen who were out that day. They had also heard stories that the fishermen saw parachutes drop in the water and sink.

"Where can I find them?" asked Ramirez. He had learned by then to look for a bomb at the end of a parachute.

"I think they were from Aguilas," said the officer.

The judge gave him a lift into Vera to telephone the port captain at Aguilas. It was arranged that he would go to interview the fishermen that night when they returned from the sea. Wilson had ordered that nothing, not the slightest clue, should be overlooked. "A keen competitor and believes in going first class (in undertaking any project)," said the General's official Air Force biography. His men did their best to put the principle into practice.

The first full report on the situation was made by "Moose" Donovan. At the end of the third day, when the organization was shaping up, he flew back to Madrid. In Washington, in Omaha, in Albuquerque, teams had been established to follow every detail of the operation. Donovan outlined the plans, the problems, the requirements, informed Ambassador

Duke, and called on General Muñoz Grandes to fulfill the promise of close coordination with the government of Spain.

"There is some radioactivity spread around," he told the Spanish Chief of Staff, "but there's no reason to be concerned about the health of anybody in the area."

Muñoz Grandes made soldierly acknowledgment of the report and made some plans of his own. It was time, he felt, for the Spanish government to have a more immediate role in the operation. And he inquired about U.S. intentions for continuance of the Chrome Dome mission over Spain.

Later, officials gave conflicting versions of who made the first decision. At its next meeting the Spanish cabinet demanded that flights over Spanish territory be suspended. The Department of Defense came to the conclusion at about the same time that it could not risk the disastrous embarrassment of another accident in Spain, at least so long as the consequences of the first had not been cleared away. In any case, the change in the Spanish-American agreement was made without dispute. The flights were canceled "temporarily." No one sought to make the decision more precise, but it was understood that unless some international emergency arose, no further H-bomb missions would fly that route.

From the strategists' point of view it was a blow. The air-alert route to southern Russia was ruled out, leaving only the polar route approaching targets from the north. But Secretary of Defense Robert McNamara made the diplomatic decision firm. He had long doubted the worth of the number of costly air-alert missions SAC was performing. Seizing the opportunity, he ordered a reduction of the sorties by half. The announcement was made many weeks later, with no reference to Palomares or to Spain's demand. The ruling was the first international fall-out of the Palomares affair. A few months later the air bases in Spain were transferred as previously planned from SAC command to the U.S. Tactical Air Command in Europe, headquartered at Wiesbaden, Germany.

The interview with Muñoz Grandes also launched another set of machinery. Donovan's report on the existence of radioactive contamination had been dry but vague. It sounded like a minor mishap requiring attention but no reason for distress. Muñoz felt the Spanish government should have its own information on just how great the danger was. He had a chat with Gen. Arturo Montel of the general staff and asked about the problem. And he arranged to alert the JEN—Junta de Energía Nuclear—which is Spain's atomic energy commission.

Neither Spain nor the United States had yet officially admitted that H-bombs had landed with the wreckage. It was only on January 20, the fourth day, that the Air Force issued a brief statement confirming that there had been "nuclear weapons" aboard the bomber. But the word was spreading around the world, and a few reporters had gone down to Palomares in an attempt to puncture tight-lipped official silence. They saw the astonishing build-up of Air Force personnel and equipment, the rows of tents clearly meant to sustain a bigger, longer operation than merely picking up the wreckage and the dead. Questioning the villagers and those few local authorities who were disposed to talk, newsmen heard that the Air Force was still looking for a bomb. André del Amo of the UPI's bureau in Madrid was the first foreign reporter on the scene. He collected a bewildering crop of rumors and an endless, frustrating series of "No comment" from the Air Force. Then one afternoon, as he stood alone by the edge of a field trying to figure out what on earth was going on, an American sergeant shouted to him.

"Hey, buddy, can you speak Spanish?"

"Sure."

"Well, tell that peasant over there to get out of that field, for God's sake. I can't make him understand a damned thing. There's radioactivity there and we've got to keep the people cleared out."

The news went out around the world. Still, nothing was said in the censored Spanish press and radio. Communist stations in eastern Europe seized upon the report and elaborated excitedly. Radio España Independiente, broadcasting in Spanish from Prague, issued frightening reports of widespread *"radioactividad"* in southern Spain. The villagers learned nothing about the odd spectacles they witnessed from their own radio stations and they began to tune in to foreign stations for more information. That was how they first heard of *"radioactividad,"* a word that was to become a menace surpassing understanding. They did not know what it was, but they knew it had something to do with the strict instructions to stay away from certain places, something to do with the strange instruments some of the airmen carried, something to do with the taut, worried look in some of the Americans' eyes. Both Americans and villagers were beginning to be quite sure that the danger of the accident had not ended when the last piece of blazing metal hit the earth.

7

THE DANGER

The talk about *"radioactividad"* spread quickly through the village. Some people said it was like the plague. You couldn't see it or smell it or taste it, but if you got it, it would kill you. And yet nothing had happened since the accident except the American invasion. Nobody had fallen ill. The mysterious machines the Americans were using were unsettling. There must, the villagers felt, be something unpleasant behind the orders to keep out of certain fields. But nobody had an explanation.

Eager to keep up good relations and yet distinctly ill at ease, Mayor González asked General Wilson's liaison man, Corujedo, to tell people whether there was danger, to explain the incomprehensible reports. The Spanish and American governments had been consulting regularly since the first day on just what should and should not be told the public. There were fears of provoking uncontrollable panic. The Spaniards insisted that silence was the best possible preventive. It was not hard to win the sympathy of American generals to a policy of saying nothing at all so as to be sure nothing damaging was said. Corujedo found a way to comply with those orders without refusing the Mayor's appeal. He climbed on top of a box in the middle of the village and addressed the people who pressed around.

"I and my general and all the Americans love life as much as you do," he told them. "We're walking around the village and the fields as much as you are. I'm an old, homely-looking man and I'm not afraid. I don't think you should be the least bit worried either."

They listened and nodded. It made sense. But still . . .

As Corujedo started away, grinning and joking to cheer

them, a shriveled old man tugged at his arm and whispered something he had heard. Could it possibly be true? What was it really about? There must be something in it with so many strange things going on. The questions were pressed with urgency.

Corujedo burst out laughing.

"How many children have you, Grandpa?" he asked jovially. The man replied. "And you're still *macho*?" The man's smile was at once proud and sly. "Well," Corujedo boomed, "I can see you're a real man, and you'll be making babies for another twenty years. Don't you fret about that. I bet you'll be having sons when your grandson has the baptismal feast for his first-born." He clapped the man on the shoulder and went back to the camp.

By late afternoon on the day the broken bombs were found, it was becoming evident to the experts that contamination was going to be much more of a problem than their first measurements had indicated. Each time they checked for the zero line they found that it had shifted, sometimes two to three feet, sometimes 10 feet and more. The wind kept moving, expanding the pattern of radioactivity. The more the plutonium dust was spread, the less concentrated was the danger in any one spot but the greater was the number of people likely to be exposed. Sergeant Howe had worn an Air Force gas mask when he made his first measurements. A great supply of sea-green surgical masks and caps and gloves was ordered from the Torrejón hospital for the airmen who had to comb the fields. The gauze triangles that covered nose and mouth were simply to keep the dust out of the men's lungs, but they looked like some science-fiction gadget and added to the atmosphere of mysterious menace.

By midweek Navarro, who lived closest to Number Three site, and a few of his neighbors were told to move out of their houses. Contamination had been found settling on the walls and roofs. Some of them sneaked back at night to feed their animals. In the daytime, they lolled unhappily in the village. More and more fields were ordered closed to the peasants. Both for purposes of search and for decontamination, teams of airmen were sent out to hack down the thick tomato vines. They used machetes, pocket knives, scythes, anything they could find, working from dawn to sundown. Fire trucks were brought in to wet down the roads, the fields, the mounds of cut vegetation to prevent the dust from spreading farther.

Bulldozers cut a road where there had been a narrow cart track so that the equipment pouring to the camp could be moved in faster. General Wilson sent to the provincial capital, then to Madrid, for good detail maps to chart precisely the area affected. But there were no maps. Air Force officers hastily drew some until photo-reconnaissance planes could complete an air mosaic for the planners' work.

The Spanish government said nothing, but it acted promptly when General Donovan brought back word of radioactive contamination in Palomares. At six o'clock on Wednesday evening Dr. Eduardo Ramos Rodríguez received a call from his chief, the head of Spain's atomic-energy commission, JEN.

"Hurry, hurry," he was told. "I've something urgent for you."

Ramos rushed out of his laboratory without bothering to change from his white smock. He had read about the plane crash and thought nothing of it. Then, the next day, he had heard from a young relative who was in the Spanish forces that such planes carried nuclear weapons, but there still seemed no likely connection between the news of the day and his work in the bio-environmental section of the JEN. Dr. José María Otero Navascues, the president of JEN, made the link clear to Ramos in a word the moment they met. There was contamination from the accident, Otero said. No more was needed. Ramos immediately collected a team, including his American-educated assistant Dr. Emilio Iranzo, and they took off for Palomares in less than an hour. They flew to San Javier and went on in the JEN's mobile laboratory, a Volkswagen Minibus converted into a remarkably complete traveling atomic monitor station.

They reached the village at dawn on January 20. The Minibus was equipped to test samples of air and water. They found nothing at first. It was puzzling. They proceeded to Camp Wilson to find out from the Americans what the problem was. The General received them and turned them over to "Doc" Norcross and Captain Pizzuto, experts who had arrived from the Air Force Nuclear Safety directorate at Albuquerque. When the Spaniards said they were physicists, the Americans went straight to the technicalities. Col. John A. Norcross was a bulky man with a maelstrom of red hair and a luxuriant, costume-party red mustache, a man too eager and able to enjoy his life to waste minutes of it fitting unforeseen circumstances to inapplicable rules. In theory, the American experts were not supposed to reveal that there had been plutonium in the bombs. But it would have been absurd, Norcross decided, to fall back on the "No comment" routine when Ramos and Iranzo asked, "What are we looking for?" They were expecting beta and gamma radiation, and had found none.

"That's right," Norcross boomed in his hearty, cheering voice. "There isn't any. It's alpha, from the plutonium dust."

The measuring had begun but it was still uncertain how big a task lay ahead. The Spaniards and the Americans set up joint teams of prospectors to creep across the hillsides and establish exactly the size of the problem. They worked comfortably together. Most of the Spaniards had studied in American universities. The whole survey took two weeks. But within a day or two it was clear both that the intensity of radiation was well below the level of immediate hazard to the population and that the cleanup job would be enormous because of the large area involved.

The moment of greatest danger was at the passage of the plutonium cloud when the two broken bombs exploded. A person or animal breathing the cloud as it moved could have absorbed a pernicious amount of plutonium in his lungs. After that, the danger was one of slow accumulation, of breathing in tiny amounts day after day. The easiest way to check the gravity of exposure was to monitor the outside of the body. The quantity of contaminated dust on an exposed person's hands, hair, shoes would obviously be immensely greater than what might have filtered through his nose and mouth into his body. The JEN team borrowed the empty movie house and set up equipment there. They wore white overalls and looked medical. Alongside the blue-gray and the orange flight suits of the Air Force, the green nose masks and the peculiar field probes, the JEN physicists completed the surreal cast on strange location. It was an awesome sight to the villagers. Still, they were docile when they were summoned to be tested, standing willingly in line for their turn to be scanned with the monitor's boom. Some of the children cried at first, scared that the machine would pinch or sting or cut, and they were surprised that they felt nothing. Older people looked with fascination at the needle oscillating nervously on the dial. They did not understand, but they accepted. Some, particularly members of the Guardia Civil who had stood guard near the bombs on the first day, gave off high readings. They were told to wash their bodies, their clothes, their hair, their shoes, and a few were ordered to burn their clothes. Other people watched and copied.

"How could I wash my suit?" the Mayor said. "It would be ruined anyway. So I burned it."

The pigs, the donkeys, the goats, the rabbits were monitored, and some were ordered washed. Navarro's wife Anna returned to the village five days after the accident to find her husband staying with their daughter. Their pig, she heard, had "radioactividad." It seemed inconceivable that anything so intangible could be washed away with water. "I couldn't take a chance," she said. They slaughtered the pig. The meat was tested and pronounced safe but Anna still could not believe. Secretly, she burned the whole carcass.

The medical team at Camp Wilson checked the Americans each day. The JEN people checked the Spaniards. From those whose clothes or bodies showed traces of contamination, urine samples were taken to figure out how much plutonium they had absorbed internally. A few of the samples tested remarkably high, so high that it meant serious danger for those lives. There were none of the radiation-disease symptoms of lassitude, nausea, and diarrhea, falling hair and peeling skin, but those only appeared when there had been a tremendous dosage including gamma rays released by fission. The readings seemed to indicate future cancers.

Dr. Wright Langham was attending a conference in Washington that week. When he got back to his hotel on Friday night there was a handful of messages in his box. The calls had been coming in all afternoon. The last message said "Telephone Commander Hedrick as soon as possible. Urgent. Call whenever you get in. No matter how late."

Hedrick was in the military applications office of the Atomic Energy Commission. Langham finally reached him at 11 P.M. The first question sounded ludicrous after such an insistent, cryptic command from a man whose job dealt with the nation's most sensitive secrets.

"Have you read the newspapers?" he asked Langham.

"Yes, more or less. What about?"

"Didn't you read anything that might affect the Los Alamos product?"

Langham understood.

"Orders are for you to proceed immediately to New York City. You'll be met by two colleagues. They'll have your tickets and further information."

That was all. Langham called his wife at home in Los Alamos and asked her to pack a bag for him for a long trip. He told her the names of two colleagues who would be joining him and who could bring it along. But he wouldn't give his destination.

"How can I pack if I don't know where you're going?" Julia Langham said with a mock scold in her voice. "You might need winter underwear, or a bathing suit, or evening clothes, or overalls. How can I tell?"

At last he relented. Swearing her to secrecy, he said his destination was Spain. There was a reason for secrecy. Word that the world's foremost expert on plutonium and the health hazards of radiation was on his way to Palomares might easily have loosed an avalanche of terror.

Langham was a small, urbane man, given to dashing sports jackets and lively talk. His bright, easy humor and his disarming modesty belied his passionate dedication to his subject. But then his chosen field in science was not one that led to an insulated, test-tube existence or attracted meek, professorial types. His childhood and youth had toughened him inside, although he had too much grace to let his manner ever show it. Brought up on the Texas panhandle in the worst of the dust-bowl days, he was driven to his first experiment by necessity, trying to feed the cattle. Nothing could be wasted, and he tried tumbleweed. Then he discovered that grinding and adding bonemeal to the tumbleweed fodder kept it from having such a painfully laxative effect. As a boy, Langham dreamed of becoming a doctor and he worked in a shoeshine parlor to save money for medical school. But he couldn't make it. Eventually, scrabbling his way through college, he was inspired by a chemistry professor and after that he was destined for the laboratory. But his laboratory had only fed his sense of high adventure and his one regret, at fifty-four after twenty-three years of atomic pioneering, was that he was no longer eligible to volunteer for the first trip to the moon. "I assure you I have no fascination for being a dead hero; I much prefer to be a live coward," he once said of himself in an attempt to ward off admiration for his courage. Nonetheless, he had always seized the chance to be at the frontier.

It was like Langham to have found the challenge irresistible when, with the ink fresh on his Ph.D., he was offered a job and told that no single, simple question about the conditions of his work could be answered unless he first accepted. "That intrigued me," he said later, "and there was no way to find out what it was but to say yes." "It" was the Manhattan Project, the secret, frenetic wartime effort to make an atom bomb before the Nazis could. He moved out to Los Alamos when it was a non-place, no more than a Santa Fe post-office box number to the rest of the world. Every word of his mail was censored. Unlike the censorship for soldiers in World War II, the supervision of communications to the Santa Fe box number was itself a secret. Langham was one of the scientists who sat in a bunker near Alamagordo on the day called Trinity and watched their handiwork go up in the world's first monstrous mushroom cloud. And he was the man disguised in a war correspondent's uniform who showed such peculiar concern for his duffel bag on the California Limited to Oakland in early 1946.

Inside that duffel bag, packed in an aluminum container, was far more plutonium than all that fell on Palomares. It was to provide the core for a bomb to be tested at Bikini, and atomic design at that stage was not efficient enough to consume much of the fuel. Langham slung it over his shoulder going in and out of the railroad stations, held it close beside him as the train joggled over the desert and the mountains. Seven armed FBI men kept guard. It had been decided that the risk of flying the plutonium to its destination was too great, not because an accident might be dangerous but because the value of the duffel bag was put at $50 million. At the Oakland station a convoy met Langham and drove him to the dock where two destroyers were waiting. Each destroyer was to take one plutonium core such as was carried to the South Pacific. The cores were not sent on a single ship as a precaution against its going down at sea with a duffel bag worth more than a destroyer. A watchman stopped the unmarked convoy as it approached the dock. It was well after midnight.

Langham watched with mounting delight as the frail old man argued with the FBI and the Secret Service. "My orders are nobody gets on the dock after 11 P.M.," the watchman told them stubbornly. The business part of an atom bomb sat on the car seat beside him in the middle of the road for an hour while an individual with a strict sense of duty held off the pomp of authority. Of course the plutonium, and Langham, finally got aboard and made it to Bikini, but the watchman's refusal to be impressed was what stuck in his mind. "I don't know who that man was," Langham said years later. "He was little and he had a tobacco-stained mustache, king of seedy. But he's my hero."

It wasn't that Langham lacked a sense of danger, but that he had measured the danger of plutonium more precisely than anyone else. Once, after a long series of laboratory tests and tests on animals, he had decided that there was still one question that could be answered in only one way. The question was whether plutonium might be more hazardous to the human body than the experiments on other creatures indicated. It was not something Langham liked to discuss. His colleagues talked about it. "He sprinkled plutonium on a sandwich and ate it," said one. "Knowing Wright," said another, "I doubt it. I bet he drank it in a martini."

Reluctantly, complaining that the fuss he had stirred by being his own guinea pig was quite unreasonable, Langham set the record straight when he was asked. "I did two simple little tests," he said. One was to place enough plutonium on his skin to show whether people absorbed it more readily than animals. The other was to drink "an extremely tiny amount of plutonium in a glass of water. I would have preferred a martini, but the laboratory has a rule against drinking on the job, and I am very conscientious about obeying rules." Both tests proved his calculation that the hazard was negligible up to a certain point.

That had been more than a decade earlier. Ramos and Iranzo, the JEN experts in Palomares, knew about it and about the rest of Langham's work. He reached Camp Wilson just a week after the accident, a week in which the secret evaluation of the gravity of the affair had changed from bad to very much worse. The highly disturbing urinalysis results were shown to Langham soon after he arrived. He asked for details of the way the samples had been taken.

Plutonium is a bone seeker and when it enters the body, all but a small proportion remains in the lymph nodes, in the kidneys and liver, and eventually the bones where it causes various kinds of cancer. It is practically insoluble, over twice as dense as iron, and far more poisonous than cyanide. A thin button of solid plutonium three inches across weighs three-quarters of a pound. A pound has the explosive energy of 16,000,000 pounds of TNT. The "maximum permissible body burden," the level worked out by health physicists as the limit up to which there is a certainty of no danger to a person, is six-tenths of one-millionth of a gram, equal in weight to an ordinary particle of dust and in size to a sphere about nine times the diameter of a red blood cell. The comparable AEC standard for "maximum permissible air concentration" is 0.00003 millionths of a gram per cubic meter of air. Although plutonium was invented by man only a quarter of a century ago, research has been so intense that much is known about its properties.

Experiments had shown that except for open wounds, it does not pass through the outside of the body to any appreciable degree. Nor does it enter significantly through the stomach if it is swallowed. "Gut absorption," Dr. Langham wrote in a paper for the International Atomic Energy Agency, "is about 0.002 per cent of the ingested dose." Almost all of what is swallowed is excreted. The significant danger comes from breathing plutonium dust. Even then the filters in the nose and throat trap a considerable amount and eventually expel it. What does get into the lungs, however, stays in the body and makes it somewhat like a walking atomic-energy plant, no danger to those outside since the body itself is a shield but, beyond a certain quantity, lethal from inside. Of the quantity absorbed by the body, about one-tenth of one per cent is passed on through the urine in each twenty-four-hour period during the first ten days after exposure. After that, the rate of excretion drops to a hundredth of one per cent in twenty-four hours. It has been calculated that fifty years after a person absorbed a dose of plutonium, 80 per cent of the dose would still be in his body.

Since the traces in the urine represent so small a fraction of the dosage remaining, the most minute particles entering a test sample from external sources give wildly distorted projection results. Langham had discovered this twenty-three years before, making tests on twelve soldiers who worked with plutonium at Los Alamos. He had a hunch, when the urinalysis showed imminent danger, that something must be wrong. So he had the men sent on three-day passes to Albuquerque with orders to do anything they liked as long as they took no personal possessions of any kind and only clothes fresh from the laundry. On their return to Los Alamos they were sent straight to the hospital and kept there until fresh twenty-four-hour urine samples had been collected. They were made to wear clean gloves each time they used the lavatory. Langham's suspicions turned out to be correct. The high radioactivity reading of the previous samples was due to specks of plutonium dust from clothing, from particles of dried skin peeling off the hands or from under the fingernails. They had fallen into the sample bottles from outside the body, where they were no danger. As soon as he saw how the samples had been collected in Palomares, he was certain the answer must be the same. New samples, taken under more stringent conditions, showed quite different results. The absence of dreadful symptoms was easily explained. Dust had dropped into the test bottles. Samples perfectly free of external contamination could be collected only in a place far removed from plutonium dust, and then only after three days, Langham had found. That was because it takes three days for the human skin which is constantly renewing itself to shed dead cells to which plutonium might cling. Even the small amount of contamination that would fall into a urine sample as a result would grossly distort the test reading.

The good news did not surprise him. As soon as he arrived at Palomares, he went to look at the two craters and studied the measurements and radiation readings that had been taken. There had never before been an accident like the one at Palomares. And yet everything looked familiar to Langham and the men from Albuquerque. It wasn't only because the landscape was so much like the New Mexico desert with its pale yellow soil and gray vegetation, its jagged hills and lucid sky. It was because they had been through the same situation, uncannily the same, they began to realize, as they gathered more and more details. Palomares was a twin of one of the four tests in Operation Roller Coaster. The other accidents on which the experts already had full information have not yet taken place. "Palomares," Langham said later, "was the type of accident we had anticipated for over ten years but hoped would never happen. It was the classic case."

In 1955, when the idea of putting SAC on air alert was first proposed, the question was secretly debated of whether plutonium might be too dangerous to carry around in planes. Some experts argued that even normal transport of atom bombs and fissile material should be made by air because the risk of accident was less than by truck or rail. A plane crash is most likely on take off and landing, two points and usually two points fairly well removed from population centers. Trucks and trains can crash at any place along their route, and they cannot always be routed away from the places in which people live. Besides, a large part of the U.S. nuclear stockpile consisted of plutonium weapons by then. Was there any use in having the arsenal if it could not be carried to delivery bases? The furore in Washington led to an urgent request to Langham's group for a study on the hazards involved. In two months they produced two papers, "sort of seat of your pants research," Langham called it. Both documents remain secret, but when he saw the Palomares situation, Langham arranged to have at least sections of one of them declassified so he could give the information to the Spanish experts. The radiation levels predicted in the studies became such a burning issue among U.S. experts in the fifties, however, that it was finally decided to test them by simulating various possible accidents in the Nevada desert.

There was TG 57—tests made in 1957—and then Operation Roller Coaster. They cost many millions of dollars. The TG 57 tests included subsequent decontamination operations by removing topsoil and plowing. They proved that no danger remained for a person spending the rest of his lifetime on the site.

Operation Roller Coaster was a series of tests made jointly by Britain and the United States in 1963, at Goldfield and Tonopah, Nevada. They showed, first of all, that dropping, burning, bashing, or otherwise mauling an unarmed atom bomb in the worst crash conditions imaginable failed to produce any nuclear explosion. In this, the results confirmed tests that had been made in 1955 and 1956. Further, Operation Roller Coaster showed what to expect of the plutonium when the conventional high explosive in a bomb went off by accident.

The few people in Nevada who were aware of the elaborate preparations being made in the desert at the time asked in amazement, "What on earth do they want to build a roller coaster out here for?" They were right. It wasn't for fun. One part of the series was called Clean Slate, in which one test simulated what would happen in the worst possible train or truck accident, and two tests simulated what would happen if accidents occurred in different types of the earth- and concrete-covered igloos in which nuclear weapons are stored. The fourth test of the series, called Double Tracks, was a preview of Palomares, although deliberately contrived to produce the maximum danger of the circumstances. There were two parts to the experiment. One was to measure radiation in air and soil samples at varying distances from the point of impact and at successive points of time. The other was to measure the effect on living creatures, the amount of plutonium that entered their lungs in relation to the amount in the air in front of their noses, the way it moved through their bodies, and the harm it did them. One hundred beagles, 100 burros, and 100 sheep were exposed, in mixed groups, at a series of points where large air concentrations of the radioactive dust were predicted. Some of the animals were sacrificed immediately after the explosion, to determine how much they had absorbed from the passage of the plutonium cloud alone. Others were killed and dissected at regular subsequent periods. The last ones were slaughtered for autopsy two and a half years later.

The lessons of Roller Coaster led to refinement of AEC guidelines on how to handle nuclear weapons. No reason was found to change the occasional practice of hitching a car with an H-bomb to an ordinary freight train, but rules were set about the speed limit to be imposed on such a train, the special couplings required, the special design of the car to be used. The question of the best design for storage igloos was reopened. A moving-picture camera caught in color exactly what happens to plutonium and uranium when high explosive crushes them by implosion. The metals, it was discovered, were not vaporized but ejected by the blast in crumbs or at the most in liquid drops, which then burned to vapor.

"It looked like the Fourth of July," said Dr. James Shreve, the lanky Westerner who ran Roller Coaster for the AEC and who raises goats and horses at his New Mexico ranch on the side. "There was an umbrella of incandescent streamers. You could see the plutonium and uranium burning. They got so hot they were luminous, bright enough to expose film without any other light. If the Palomares bombs had gone off at night, they would have lit up the neighborhood. It all happens in a fraction of a second, but the streamers persist and the plutonium jets along them into the air, burning like a sparkler. The chemical reaction is so violent that once the burning starts, you can't put it out."

Whenever there is an explosion, a hot gaseous fireball is produced. A firecracker or an ordinary bomb makes a small one which disappears so quickly it is seldom noticed. A nuclear explosion makes such a huge fireball and resulting mushroom cloud that the shape has become the symbol of holocaust. Even when there has been no nuclear explosion in a bomb, the gases reach thousands of degrees Centigrade right away and the ball rushes upward in a couple of seconds. If there is hydrogen fuel present, it is dissipated long before instruments could possibly be brought to measure it in the air.

As a result of Roller Coaster and TG 57, the experts learned to forecast from air samples the amount of plutonium deposited in a being's lungs, and to calculate the hazards to man. They learned the results of various decontamination techniques in great detail—plowing, wetting, scraping the top of the ground. And they learned that the greatest danger of plutonium contamination comes when an accident takes place in a dead calm, when the atomic cloud goes up and down again, depositing a high-noon shadow of dust at ground zero.

Palomares had been in luck, not only in surviving the debris and two conventional blasts without a single casualty, but in the way the plutonium sprayed out. The ground wind was 30 knots, a turbulence that rapidly diluted the airborne particles and moved the plutonium cloud quickly away from the village. And the wind blew offshore, carrying the cloud over uninhabited fields and out to sea where the dust scattered in too thin a fall-out to be measured. "The major plutonium hazard was over before anyone knew what had happened," Langham said later. A final stroke of luck came in the fact that the bombs were falling so fast they buried their noses deep in dirt before the blast went off. The glowing metal particles "scavange" dirt, clinging to it and falling near the point of impact. Some burn their way into the granules of earth so that the metal is completely covered and the alpha radiation effectively shielded. From the measurements and the readings, Langham concluded that well over half of the total amount of plutonium in the two bombs was in the soil scraped away and removed from Palomares. What remained was so widely diluted that the likelihood of anyone's absorbing a harmful amount was nil, according to his calculations.

Altogether, the circumstances at the moment of the accident were so fortuitous that Iranzo said to Langham,

"God must have had His hand out." Langham put it another way. "The laws of probability occasionally, but not often, let a gambler fill an inside straight."

Langham never really saw Palomares. For nearly a week he worked from dawn until late at night a mile away in one of Camp Wilson's guarded tents. When the charts were completed showing exactly how much contamination remained in exactly which areas, he began to negotiate with the Spaniards on the formula for the decontamination task. Working from his own studies, the results of TG 57 and Roller Coaster, and applying the AEC "factor of ten"—a rule that sets the safety guidelines at ten times below the experimentally established minimum requirements for safety—he drew up a proposal for the cleanup. The Spaniards drew up a counterproposal that would have imposed at least fifty times more work and expenses on the Air Force. They were at a deadlock. Wilson reported the situation to General Donovan in Madrid.

The blunt Irishman shot back a command.

"Tell this man Langham and the Spaniards to get together."

Wryly, General Wilson showed it to the expert and asked for advice.

"Who's this Donovan?" snapped Langham. "Do you have to answer him?"

Wilson ignored the *quid pro quo* of pique. In a quiet voice he said only, "Yes, we have to answer him."

Later, Langham came to enjoy the waspish humor and the warmth beneath Donovan's gruff way of flashing his stars. At the moment he was peeved. There was, he felt certain, no health problem in Palomares requiring his presence as a health physicist. After his patient exposition of his findings to the JEN people, also acting under instructions from nontechnical higher-ups, they had told him, "That may well be. But think of the psychological problems. And what they mean economically. The tourists won't come. Real-estate values will plummet. What will happen to tomato exports next year? And after that?"

Those, Langham answered in firm but gentle tones, were not problems in physics. He decided to go home. It was not a quarrel but a professional impasse. "They killed me with kindness," he said of the JEN people later. "They were competent, knowledgeable, courteous, understanding, and practical. I really came to love them. But they were tough at the bargaining table."

Caught in the middle, Wilson simply started his airmen on the task of decontamination. The dispute, after all, was not on how to go about it but how enormous it had to be. The roofs and walls of a few houses were washed and, in some cases, repainted. A layer of paint was enough to shield any alpha radiation that might possibly have remained after the washing. The vast amount of water spraying that was done was to hold down the dust so as to prevent further spread of plutonium-laden particles, and to dilute them in the areas of lowest contamination. The tomato plants and other vegetation that had been cut down were all carted to a big ditch, wetted, and covered with a plastic sheet until final disposal could be arranged. Teams of Spanish and American experts kept checking and measuring. When a field showed clean on several checks, red flags were put up at the corners and it was released to the farmer who was also given an elaborate certificate pronouncing it completely safe. "With respect to the condition of the fertility and safety of the land in question in this document, at this moment, the same conditions exist as were present prior to the 17th of January, 1966, and such land should be returned at this time to its owners for normal use," the document read. Another paper certified precisely how the decontamination had been carried out on each plot and that repeated checks showed it free of radioactivity. They were in English and Spanish, signed by every authority involved, and so ponderously official that the people who received them were at least as much bewildered as reassured.

There was so little exchange between the villagers and the outsiders—General Wilson had forbidden any airmen to leave the camp except on official business so there was little chance for fraternization—that it was weeks before the impact of the red flags was understood. Then the Americans were red-faced. An officer was sent to scour the neighboring towns for all the bolts of bright green cotton he could find. After that green and not the age-old sign for danger festooned the boundaries of the fields found clear of radiation.

But the American responsibility was to the Spanish government, and it was essential that the definition of the task be made in complete agreement. That had to be settled in Madrid. The outlines of the job were worked out between Otero, the head of JEN, and John Hall, the AEC's man for international liaison. They had worked together often before, Hall knew Otero's thirteen children, whom the Spanish scientist liked to call "much more of a problem to cope with than atomic energy," and he knew the developments of Spain's atomic program. The United States had provided considerable aid to the Spanish program under a bilateral agreement and, apart from Palomares, much future cooperation was envisaged. Spain had already begun to produce uranium, just as the Congolese supplies and others were running out. Otero was convinced that before the end of another decade Spain could be the world's prime supplier of uranium ore. The personal relations between the two countries' atomic experts were warm and easy. Still, specific orders had to be drawn up.

Langham had spent a day in Madrid on his way back from Palomares, not sight-seeing, though, because he had a ferocious cold. "If anybody sees me," he joked, "they'll think it's some kind of radiation sickness from the coast. I'd better stay out of circulation." He flew to Washington, briefed the Atomic Energy Commission, the Defense Department, the Joint Congressional Committee on Atomic Energy, and the State Department, and got home to Los Alamos ten days after he had left to tell his wife she had no idea of how to pack for Spain in winter. He barely had time to complain before word came that he must fly straight back. That time Julia Langham, a lively Minnesota blonde pretty enough for a chorus line but actually a microbiologist, packed warmly for them both and went along.

There was a hurry because, despite Air Force efforts, the dust continued to spread, lowering the concentration of radioactivity and thus the danger in any one spot but enlarging the area to be treated. The longer it took to get Spanish-American agreement, the more work would have to be done. The Spanish cleanup proposal would have required Wilson to haul away the topsoil from well over one hundred acres, replace it with soil from untouched land, and deep-plow about a square mile of slightly contaminated land. The Air Force went to work while it waited for the bargainers, starting from the bomb sites and going on with the cleanup as fast as it could. But Langham felt that was vastly exaggerated, far beyond the most austere safety standards.

On his return, he was given an office in the Madrid Embassy, next door to Joe Smith. The name plate on the door was left empty because Langham's presence was still a secret. Ambassador Duke cautioned him not to speak to anyone but

Embassy officials and the JEN experts with whom he had to work. Then negotiating on the cleanup formula began once more in earnest. Langham proposed soil removal in areas showing 1,000 or more micrograms (one-millionth of a gram) of plutonium per square meter. That was equivalent to 135,000 radiation counts per minute, meant testing every square inch, and would have affected two acres of Palomares land. Where the plutonium content was 100 to 1,000 micrograms per square meter, he suggested plowing to a depth of 10 inches. A content of 10 to 100 could be handled by simply sprinkling, to settle and dilute the dust, and nothing was needed where the content was 0 to 10, he suggested. The total area to be treated by such a formula would have been 550 acres. The Spaniards balked. After weeks of discussions a compromise was reached on February 14, nearly a month after the accident. Wilson had already cleaned more than the new agreed formula required. In the end, 604 acres (nearly a square mile) were treated either by soil removal or by plowing, with topsoil carried away wherever the reading showed anything above 400 micrograms of plutonium per square meter, or 60,000 counts. The formula was far more strict than would have been applied after an accident on American soil.

A new crisis broke when Wilson reported that a large part of the neat pattern on the charts marked for plowing was in fact steep, rock-strewn hillside. "Not even a Missouri farmer could plow that," the Americans complained. Besides, they pointed out, furrowing the barren hills could cause a dust-bowl problem much worse than the plutonium menace. It took a fresh round of bargaining in Madrid. This led to another Air Force stone-root operation. Readings were taken at each corner of each square meter of the area and airmen turned the unyielding ground by hand, with picks and shovels and rakes, until the radiation count dropped below the possibility of detection. The plutonium was, of course, still there, but well dispersed.

The decontamination job took eight weeks. As one of the Air Force officers said, it might have been done in three or four days in their home states of Texas or Oklahoma. But the cultivated Palomares plots were tiny, some no bigger than a house. Cactus fences, mounds of dirt, irrigation channels, and old stones marked the boundaries. Eight hundred and fifty-four separate plots had to be treated. The only cadastral maps were crude and out of date. People did not bother with land surveys and deeds, they knew by the old landmarks what belonged to them and what belonged to their neighbor. It was a serious problem. The big earth-moving equipment started to obliterate the only proof the villagers had of the borders of their property. Immediate and loud complaints obliged the Air Force to agree to work between and around the little plot lines. On one of the first days a team shoved aside a boulder lying in the path of the plow. The old man watching the metal teeth cut deeper into his field than anything had ever reached before sat down beside the stone and wept. Col. Alton E. White, the head of the team, asked him what was wrong.

"That is my marker," the farmer said through his tears. "My grandfather put it there. That was the end of my land, my father's land, my grandfather's land. Now my neighbor will say that piece of land is his. How can I prove it is mine?"

"Bud" White, a freckled, towheaded Texas farmer before he went in the Air Force, bent down and picked up the boulder in his big, powerful hands. He cradled it back in the hole where it had lain for three generations.

"It's not the same," the farmer mourned. "It has been moved. Things are not the same here any more."

But if Palomares could never be restored exactly as it had been before the bombs fell, the American aim was to leave it as nearly the same as possible. The delicate monitors kept breaking down. Wilson organized a shuttle service to take them back to Torrejón at the end of each day's work for overnight repair and return to the camp at dawn. Later, the maintenance shop was moved to Camp Wilson where it was set up for all-night work in a tent completely lined with plastic to make it free of dust. A deadline of April 1 had been set for the return of all the arable fields to the farmers so that they could prepare to sow the next season's crop. The last piece of land was handed back on March 15. The Air Force bought three huge tree-mulching machines and flew them from the United States to chew up the crops that had had to be cleared from 319 acres so that the soil could be treated. Ripe tomatoes and sweet alfalfa poured into the machines along with cactus and sage and came out a kind of sticky bran. A total of 3,728 dump truck loads of vegetation was hauled away to the river bed where a trench had been dug.

While the decontamination formula was being worked

it in Madrid, the Spanish and American experts also began to plan for disposal of the topsoil. Langham arranged for geologists to make a survey of the area, to determine the solidity of the ground and the likelihood of earthquakes. Digging began for a pit that would be lined with concrete and asphalt to bury the contaminated earth. Colonel White figured it might have to be the size of the Empire State Building lying down, although no one yet knew for sure how many acres of topsoil it would need to hold.

The Spanish negotiators agreed. "The one thing you can be sure about is that the Spaniards weren't afraid to have it buried here," Otero said later. "Do you know our story about Spanish courage? Six men were in a plane learning how to parachute for the first time. They were all afraid. The sergeant told the Englishman to set an example and jump first. The sergeant told the Englishman to set an example and jump first. The Englishman refused, but he pushed out a Pole. When the Frenchman's turn came, he refused at first, but the sergeant said it was for the glory of France, so he jumped. The German agreed to jump when the sergeant said it was an order. The Italian refused, and kept right on refusing, no matter what the sergeant said. The Spaniard refused, too. The sergeant told him he had no courage. That made the Spaniard furious. 'What,' he said, 'you say I have no courage? I'll show you.' And the Spaniard threw away his parachute and jumped."

But the JEN said that, of course, the atomic burial plot would have to be fenced off and the United States would have to take a lease on the land and maintain responsibility for it until radioactive decay had become totally insignificant. Langham calculated quickly. The standard physicists' measure of decay to insignificance is five half lives. A half life is the time it takes a given amount of radioactive material to lose half its energy. For plutonium it is 24,360 years. A burial in Spain would have committed the United States to care for a corner of that country for 125,000 years, longer than even such a futuristic minded man as Langham chose to contemplate. In any case, one of the other Americans suggested, it would be a poor idea for the United States to leave behind a kind of monument to the accident. It became obvious that the soil would have to be taken out of the country. Someone suggested dumping it in a Mediterranean deep. The radioactive content was low enough for that not to present an appreciable hazard.

Then Otero spoke up. "My American friends," he said, "I advise you not to do this without the permission of Jacques Cousteau. You think of Cousteau as merely a famous French underwater explorer. But he holds himself king of the Mediterranean. I've had my experience of what happens when anyone wants to touch the Mediterranean without first asking Cousteau." He told of the time he had been host at a conference of European nuclear experts in Mallorca. They were discussing what to do with low-level wastes from their countries' atomic programs. The French delegate proposed a dump well out to sea. When word reached Cousteau in Monaco, he organized a protest from the mayors of all the Mediterranean coastal towns. In the middle of the outcry General de Gaulle recalled the French delegate from the conference and he never appeared at another. "So," Otero concluded, "you should know what to expect if you use the sea without asking Cousteau."

Eventually, the decision was to ship all the contaminated dirt back to the United States for burial. Colonel White, in charge of the decontamination operation then, was told he would be given 55-gallon oil drums to load for shipment.

"I thought it could never be accomplished," he said later. "With the amount of dirt we had to move, those drums seemed much too small. Then I realized that one cubic yard of soil would weigh 600 to 700 pounds, and that would fill one drum. After all, it was a very smart idea. We could never have managed anything heavier." The airmen who had cut the vines and cane poles by hand, raked the hillsides by hand, built the camp, and watered the fields, had to fill the barrels by hand and load them on barges. The officers remembered only one direct complaint. A corporal came up to the communications tent and asked to be allowed to telephone to Torrejón.

"What for?" asked Colonel Payne.

"I'm not doing my job," the young man said. "I'm a flight engineer and they've got me out here farming. My staff sergeant ought to know about it."

"You're doing what your country needs, son," the Colonel told him. The lecture on the importance of the operation lasted two or three minutes. Payne gave him a friendly thump on the back then, and he went away smiling. The hours were long, the work was hard, and not at all what the men were accustomed and trained to do. But they did it, and thought up ingenious ways to make it go faster and quicker. When the barrels came, they worked through sixteen-hour days in shifts, with team races to lighten the drudgery of shoveling.

Colonel White calculated that it would take 5,500 barrels to hold the dirt he had to load for shipment. An urgent order went out to find them. There were no handy stockpiles. The request came in to the Navy support service in Naples, and the rigid specifications made clear that the drums would have to be specially made. A Naples firm was approached. There was a strike of metallurgical workers, it explained, and besides the job was not worth while because it would require adapting the machines to meet the unusual standards. The Navy was not allowed to say why it had to have the steel barrels. The supply officers pleaded with the Italian businessmen to take the order without asking questions. They finally succeeded, and the empty drums were on their way by sea to Palomares twelve days later. They cost $27,000. When they arrived, White took three of them to test. One was filled with clean soil, one with two-thirds soil and one-third mulch, one with half vegetation and half soil. The lids were bolted and one-inch metal bands welded on as seals. All three were dropped from a helicopter hovering 15 feet above the ground. When they did not break, or crack, or split, the frenetic days of the drums began. A new road was built for the operation so that the loaded barrels would not have to be carted through the village.

In the end, 4,879 of the blue metal drums were filled, loaded on barges that came up on the beach, and transferred at sea to the U.S.N.S. *Boyce*. Radiation checks were made at each stage of the operation to make sure no one involved in transporting them would be exposed to danger. The *Boyce* arrived in Charleston, South Carolina, on April 8. That was a date to remember in Palomares for a different reason. Much more had happened by then.

The removal or dispersion of the last of the three bombs with the end of decontamination put Palomares completely off the danger list, physically speaking. But little had been explained to the people and the information had trickled out slowly. Their uncertainties and sense of helplessness grew as the days of crisis lengthened. And there was still a fourth bomb missing. The search became visibly frantic. The suspense moved toward despair.

"That, too, was fortunate in a sense," Langham said afterward. "The drama of contamination attracted little attention. Everybody was thinking about the lost bomb. The two that broke were much more serious. The other one could have stayed in the sea and nobody but a few fish would ever have noticed."

Nobody else felt that way at the time. After the plutonium cloud had passed, there was a far greater fall-out of fear.

8

THE FEAR

Like the bombs, fear came to Palomares from abroad. But there was no sudden explosion. The worries crept in gradually, shyly at first in the form of guileless questions, then more and more openly, urgently. Sergeant Howe, the dryly determined Air Force expert whose grave mien had earned him the sobriquet of "the undertaker," said later that it was not until the third day after the crash that he came to be aware of the villagers. The Air Force was so busy, so preoccupied with its tangle of problems that it did not quickly notice all the problems that it brought.

General Wilson anticipated from the start the standard military nightmare of involvement with civilians. "We always have a few who get too much of that cheap vino and make fools of themselves," he said afterward. "From the very first day I decided to confine all our men to camp. I didn't want anything to undermine what I was attempting—to build up the people's confidence and show them we had come strictly for business." It worked beautifully on one level. There was not a single nasty incident, a single international brawl, a single blustering father and whimpering daughter as a result of the American invasion. But on another level the mutely sober dedication of the airmen to their duty aroused an uneasiness that soon expanded to a quiet terror.

"The Americans are still looking for something, but they won't say what," an official of a neighboring town told the foreign press. It had to be something immensely important, the villagers told each other as they saw more and more high-ranking officers, more and more airmen and police, more and more strange and gigantic equipment collected in their midst. No one remembered who was the first to say it, whether one of the Guardia Civil whispered it in confidence, or somehow the Mayor wormed it out of the Americans, or someone happened to catch the Spanish-language broadcast of the BBC or Moscow.

The ancient radio, installed on its own high shelf beyond the reach of smaller children, was the great pride of Manuel Sabiote Flores, the way he kept up with the world. It wasn't that he had never learned to read, but he never got accustomed to the habit. Besides, the papers never seemed to say things clearly. They said only what the government allowed, and he remembered very well how the government had come, what could no longer be said, and what began to be said when the terrible fighting had stopped. The Republicans had held out the longest in the area around Palomares; the bitter taste of civil war had faded slowly there. Sabiote did not pretend to understand politics but he knew there were other numbers on the radio dial which would bring news that the Spanish stations did not broadcast. When he heard they were talking about the village, his own village that was not even on the big maps, he began to make a point of tuning in to those other stations. So did everybody else. They did not like to discuss with each other that they had listened to the Communist broadcast from Prague or East Berlin or Algiers, where a secret transmitter served the Peking faction of the outlawed Spanish Communist party. Instead, the men gossiped in the square and the women bent their heads together over the laundry trough and mumbled.

"There's supposed to be mortal radiation. Have you seen anything?"

"You know the Guardia Civil has closed off the village. Nobody from Vera or Cuevas or anywhere can come in unless they have a special permit."

"It's a special kind of bomb the Americans have lost. It's very dangerous. That's why they wear the masks and carry the little boxes with a tube."

Toward the end of the week the foreign broadcasts were speaking openly of the search for a missing H-bomb. They spoke of radioactivity. But the Americans and the Spanish officials said nothing. Eventually, it was announced that a "military artifact" had disappeared after the crash and had to be found. The broadcasts began to speak of "possible tragic consequences of nuclear contamination," of the danger of "cancer, as occurred in Hiroshima with the bomb dropped by the Americans in World War II."

Still the officials said nothing. But the Spanish doctors came on the heels of the Americans and they began to examine the fields and the houses with the same odd instruments. They wore white, and they washed very carefully, the way doctors do when they examine someone who is seriously ill. The broadcasts said that the Americans and the Spaniards were keeping terrible dangers secret and foreigners began to come asking all sorts of questions, the questions the villagers were asking. Perhaps they were not such foolish questions if the foreigners asked the same things. The broadcasts said one of the British newsmen reported that dynamite in two bombs had exploded and drenched thousands of people with invisible *"radioactividad."* The Spanish and American officials said it was an "absurd and completely unfounded rumor." But there had been explosions, everybody heard them, and the Spanish doctors were asking the people to come and be tested with their machines.

The broadcasts also began to talk of widespread panic and mass evacuation of everybody in the region. But the Americans and the officials were pouring in, not running away, and few of the villagers had any place else to go. The broadcasts said there was a big demonstration in Cuevas with people shouting "Down with American bases" and "Yankees, go home." But the few children who went to the high school in Cuevas in the bus and the priest who came every day from Cuevas on his motor scooter said there had been nothing of the kind. Nobody but the radio had heard of such a thing and a demonstration was not like radioactivity. If it was there, it would be seen. There were lies on the radio too, then. Who could tell what to believe?

Along with the bewilderment came a sense of growing helplessness. Navarro, whose house was closest to Number Three site, was told to move out for a few days. Orange flags flew from poles planted where things had fallen from the sky. Lines of Americans stomped across the hills like toy soldiers, leaving fluttering strips of paper on the cactus as they passed. (It was toilet paper, a stroke of ingenuity that came to the search leaders trying to think of how to mark each strip of ground as it was covered. After the first week there were so. many ribbons of white issue waving from the plants that an urgent request was sent to Torrejón for a big supply of toilet paper in assorted colors. With soft pinks and greens and yellows assigned to different squads working parallel to each other, the confusion was diminished.) Pigs and goats and burrows were herded into their pens and thoroughly showered. Farmers were ordered out of their fields, whether the harvest was ready or not. Tall vines and alfalfa were chopped and dumped in mounds with worthless scrub and cactus. The people were told not to touch anything strange, not to go near the places cordoned off with flags. They obeyed. It was their habit to respect and accept authority. But they did not understand and they worried.

A villager, an elderly man proud enough of his achievements in having bred and fed so many children that he could afford to humble himself before a young compatriot, managed a quiet conversation with Dr. Iranzo a day or two after the JEN team had arrived.

"Tell me," he begged. "What is the secret? You can see I'm a grown man, a man of family. You can rely on me. Please let me in on it. What are you looking for?"

Iranzo saw no reason to evade. In full candor, he answered, "I'm looking for alpha radiation."

The older man's face sagged at the wound to dignity. "You shouldn't make fun of me," he said. "I asked an honest question." Then he walked away.

As he spoke to one after another, Iranzo tried his best to explain. He had studied at the University of Rochester, he had visited Los Alamos, he had taken part in scientific conferences. He was as much a Spaniard as the people of Palomares, but his everyday tongue was the language of advanced research. It was not the same idiom as theirs. They asked him about Hiroshima, Nagasaki, dim words of the past whose terror had been revived on the radio.

"It's absolutely different here," he told them. "There has been no nuclear explosion. The kind of radioactivity we have here can only hurt by entering the organism, through the blood stream or inhalation. We are examining everybody to make absolutely sure that hasn't happened. We can tell by the tests if there's anything to worry about, and we can tell you there's not."

They nodded. It sounded reassuring. But when they walked away and talked it over once again, someone reminded,

"He said it. Don't you realize, he said it. He said we have radioactivity here."

"Well, he said there wasn't any danger. The machine showed it. That's what the machines are for."

"Maybe there is and maybe there isn't. How do I know? Would they bring machines and close the fields if there wasn't any danger?"

That sort of talk was just beginning when Joe Smith and Tim Towell dropped in at the bar four nights after the accident. The cryptic reports reaching Madrid had also begun to worry "Angie" Duke. After the first call on the Foreign Office, the Ambassador had relaxed about the accident. The Air Force reported progress. Then came reports of "minor contamination." The newspapermen were beginning to press more and more insistently for information. Duke decided he needed some firsthand Embassy reports. Just before they were leaving the office late Thursday afternoon he called in the two young diplomats and told them to go down to Palomares for a look. They drove most of that night, slept in a small town on the way, and arrived before lunch the next day. It wasn't easy to get into Camp Wilson. By then the Guardia Civil had closed the road to strangers. Smith took out his diplomatic pass and waved it vigorously. They had to argue. Finally they talked their way through and reported in to an Air Force Command Post which seemed to wish the Guardia Civil had been more strict. The operation was under control, they were told. There were no particular problems that required State Department help. If there was anything they needed, they could ask Colonel Young.

"Well," said Smith, "we need a place to sleep."

Young told them about the Maricielo at Garrucha. When the new road was cut through, that became a fifteen-minute drive. At that time it took a good hour from the camp. When they arrived, the hotel seemed as insulated an Air Force preserve as Camp Wilson. No one was there but Marcos, the young bartender, and he told them they could not stay. Señor Corujedo had reserved all the rooms. No one could be admitted to the hotel without Corujedo's express permission. The atmosphere seemed stiff with emergency. Towell and Smith had thought they were going to observe a kind of Civil Aeronautics Board accident investigation. They had not yet heard anything about radioactivity, about a lost bomb. They had to argue again, this time with a boy. It was unusual. By the time they drove up to Palomares to have a look at the village, it was evening. The little bar was crowded. But the villagers stared silently at their coffee with cognac, sneaking an occasional glance at the newcomers. Smith and Towell moved apart to launch some conversations.

"How are things going?" Smith asked, the classic investigative opening, carefully drained of any hint that courtesy could seize upon to make the answer fit the question's wish.

"So so," said one man.

"You can call it a chance," said another. "Changed is the one thing I know it is."

Little by little the uneasiness came out. The men spoke of the surprising things going on in the fields, the way that the Americans were working and they were forced to idle. Someone said, "It's a kind of plague. It's a thing you catch without knowing it, without even knowing you have it. Then suddenly it hits you. And finished. That's what's in the fields. We have to stay away."

Nothing was clear in the patchy stories but a dull fear, a sense of ominous mystery. The diplomats knew no more than the villagers. They went back to Camp Wilson to inquire. The officers told them for the first time about the complications that had arisen. Smith and Towell reported the unhappy atmosphere in Palomares. Colonel Young thanked them and said nothing more.

All through the first week the people in uniform went on with their peculiar farming. The people in the village sank into unaccustomed idleness. An order was given not to move the crops. The reason was to prevent the further spread of radioactive dust until the contamination measurements had been completed and the zero line firmly fixed. But that was hard to understand and no special effort was made to explain. The word "*radioactividad*" was on everybody's tongue by then but it was still forbidden by the two governments for official public use.

The Air Force officers began to realize they saw no old people about, no women. There were always clusters of villagers staring as they plodded through their search patterns, as they dropped to the rough ground for their box lunch and twenty minutes' midday rest, as they queued for the PX truck and mail call in camp. But the Spaniards seemed to be from a village of only young men and children.

Someone thought to ask Iranzo about it. He shrugged unhappily.

"They are there all right, the old people and the women. They are sitting in the houses waiting to die."

"Doc" Norcross happened to be working the fields with Iranzo the day one of the Guardia Civil men came up. He approached the two officials respectfully, taut with distress. He was one of the first on the spot after the accident, he explained, he had stood many hours on guard in the places now forbidden. After a few days he had developed a severe chill, then fevers, ferocious headaches. He had heard of the radioactivity. It had made him deperately ill. What, he pleaded, should he do?

Iranzo spoke gently to the young man. If he had absorbed enough radioactivity in Palomares to kill him, the scientist said, he still would not conceivably be showing such symptoms for a year. And there was simply not enough around for him to have absorbed a fatal dose. Iranzo went on for ten minutes with his explanation. When he was done, the Guardia walked off with a healthy stride, swinging his arms to show his fitness, the joy of relief on his face. The chills and fevers and headaches vanished. The cure was complete.

But that was one young man. There were 1,200 villagers, another 700 to 800 people from neighboring towns who had rushed to see what happened on the day of the accident, many tens of thousands in the region which the broadcasts called the danger zone. Palomares people, trudging to market in Vera, had been used to hailing rides in passing carts. The wife of Bienvenido Flores Gil, a farmer, came home one day trembling with anger and fear, not sure which afflicted her worse.

"I climbed on the cart," she told her family, "and of course we began to talk. When I said I was from Palomares, the woman screamed at me and cursed. She said, 'Get down, get down. We don't want to be infected, too.' They're all scared of us, scared to be near us. And nobody will buy anything from us."

A dead whale was washed up on the beach, down toward Garrucha. It was 18 feet long, a titan in a sea of sardines and shrimp.

"If the lost bomb is in the sea," people said, "it's not only killing the fish. It killed a whale." Nobody dared to touch it. It lay on the shore for days.

"Can the bomb kill a whale?" one of the Guardia Civil finally asked Norcross.

"Doc" laughed heartily. "Certainly," he said. "If it fell on the whale's head it could kill him, or if the whale tried to swallow it. It definitely wasn't radiation that killed him. But that whale's downwind from here. If it stays on the hot beach much longer, what the smell will do to us will be worse." Eventually the dead animal was towed well out to sea. The mystery of its appearance lingered.

By the second week everybody was talking about the lost bomb. The JEN people and the Air Force radiation experts had a day of severe fright when the zero-line measurements indicated a third zone of contamination. It was possible, they reasoned, that the lost bomb had totally disintegrated, that they were about to discover another large area covered with radioactive dust where no precautions had yet been taken. But that was a false alarm. Further measurements showed that the new zone was small, an overlap where dust from the two broken bombs had been blown erratically by the wind. The U.S. Navy had begun to arrive by then. Scores of frogmen camped on the beach at night and combed the shallows in the daytime, working in the same tight formation that the airmen used on land. Mine sweepers started a patterned sonar search of the sea bottom. The land had been tainted by the bombs people had seen. Had the sea been tainted by the missing bomb? people asked. The mystery of the fourth bomb magnified the fears to giant screen proportions. It could be anywhere. No one could be sure of being safe.

Don Enrique, the senior priest from Cuevas, talked with Joe Smith about the mounting terror.

"The people are suffering," the *cura* said. "They are living in ignorance. They have an intimate part in the tragedy, they are the object of a tremendous secret. It is not a reason to leave them in panic. I believe in sincerity and clarity.

"Let your experts explain what it is all about to me. I am no scientist but I have studied and traveled. I will do my best to learn and then I will explain to them so they can understand."

The offer was relayed to ranking American and Spanish officials. Don Enrique received no reply. In Madrid, the Spanish government refused to say anything and the American spokesman was told to answer questioners, "We do not discuss the movement of atomic weapons."

But the highest authorities were beginning to realize they had far more trouble on their hands than they had imagined even in the first bad week after the accident. There was constant argument, and no agreement, between the two governments on what the public should be told. As a result, nothing was said to settle the rumors. They did agree, however, that more official Spanish-American coordination was needed on the spot. Madrid designated Brig. Gen. Arturo Montel, a good-natured, roly-poly man who headed the material section of the chiefs of staff and had often dealt with the Americans, to be its representative as the senior Spanish officer in Camp Wilson. That was on January 26, nine days after the accident. By then Duke had received the upsetting report from the diplomats he had sent down and he hurried to Palomares to have a look at the problems for himself.

Until then it was the impact on government relations that had concerned him. When a week had gone by since the accident, an agonizing week that ended looking worse than it began, he had suggested a soothing message from President Johnson to Generalissimo Franco, the Spanish Chief of State. That idea was rejected when some people argued it would make the accident look even more serious than the public realized; and some people argued that with further developments uncertain, it was better to keep the voice of the summit in reserve. Instead, Secretary of State Dean Rusk sent Foreign Minister Fernando Castiella a telegram which read:

> AMBASSADOR DUKE AND MYSELF HAVE BEEN IN CLOSE CONTACT ON THE UNFORTUNATE ACCIDENT IN SPAIN OF TWO UNITED STATES PLANES. WE WANT TO ASSURE YOU THAT WE ARE DECIDED TO DO EVERYTHING NECESSARY TO MINIMIZE THE EFFECTS OF THE ACCIDENT. I HAVE ASKED AMBASSADOR DUKE TO REPORT TO ME DAILY ON THE MATTER AND TO SEND ME ANY SUGGESTIONS YOU MAY WANT TO MAKE. MEANWHILE, I WISH TO EXPRESS TO YOU HOW DEEPLY WE APPRECIATE YOUR COOPERATION.

The U.S. Chief of Staff, General Earle G. Wheeler, sent a similar message to Gen. Muñoz Grandes, his Spanish opposite number. The messages were not made public. Duke did not object. The policy of withholding information to prevent a spread of panic was advanced with earnest explanation and he felt, he said, that "they were the dentists saying the tooth has to be pulled. I'm not the one to say, 'No. I know better.'"

But when he reached Camp Wilson he felt differently. The situation seemed unbearable with rumors settling thicker than the dust and nothing but "No comment" to filter truth from fearful fancy. He was not, he considered, in a position to leak information that had been specifically classified. But he called a press conference when he returned to Madrid to explain something of what had happened. He drew a diagram showing how the planes had come in over the coast and collided, how the wreckage had scattered, where the big pieces of debris were found. He never mentioned H-bombs. He described the great cleanup operation without mentioning radioactivity, as though it were only to collect the parts of shattered aircraft. Even that raised a huge behind-scenes row.

In his report to the State Department he was candid and pessimistic. There were no longer any grounds, the Ambassador said, to expect an early end to the Palomares operation. Decontamination was going to be a long job. The prospect of soon finding the missing H-bomb was very small. Everything pointed to a long, painful affair, he said, and he did not need to make the obvious point that every day it lasted multiplied the pain.

The Spanish government showed no such alarm. "You will find it," Spanish officials told American counterparts. "You are doing so much, you have such a lot of equipment. The less said to disturb the people, the better." But Madrid sent Montel to make his own assessment.

General Montel lunched with Wilson and Donovan, who had returned to Palomares immediately after he arrived. That went very well. Montel was a professional soldier, born in Cuba where his father had been an expatriate engineer, but educated in Spain. At seventeen he entered the military academy. When the Air Force was formed, he switched from infantry to aviation and so fought the Civil War in clean air above the blood and passion on the ground. His dark blue eyes twinkled with charm, his skimpy fringe of mustache showed ginger against his swarthy skin, his manner was that of a man with a job to do and no time for peevish recriminations. He took immediately to Wilson, an easy-mannered man with a tough approach to the job.

"Wilson was very *simpático*," he said. "I had a feeling from the start we'd get on well." That was good; they were to have grueling months working side by side.

Then Montel went to see the Spanish authorities in the region. He found the people "totally confused. Even the mayors were all mixed up."

The order about the crops had led to fears that all fresh food was dangerous. People not only refused to eat the beans and the tomatoes that had been harvested before the accident, they threw away the eggs and the milk. The storekeeper, Antonio Martínez Saez, reported a run on canned goods the like of which he'd never seen. Martínez also owned the movie. He was a *Madrileño*, brought to the isolated province as a child in flight from the war in the capital, and although he stayed on in the village, he never came to feel himself a villager. He didn't mind talking about the villagers, a thing the others hesitated to do with a stranger. They were frightened, he said, and they didn't even comprehend the enormity of the danger. The schoolteacher, Pedro Sánchez Gea, reported that more than half the children were being kept away from school. Those who came were not allowed to chatter during classes, but they talked of nothing but the danger and the missing bomb during recess. Each relayed the latest story, the latest hint of trouble he had heard at home. Sánchez Gea did not insist that families meet the obligation of sending him their children for lessons. He sent his own wife and children away, "for some quiet," he explained uncomfortably afterward. "Their nerves were delicate from the shock. They stayed in a peaceful farmhouse at La Jauca. I went every Saturday to visit them and I came back on Sunday night. I looked after myself and made my own meals during the week." That hadn't been difficult. He had a can opener.

The fear had spread much farther than the contamination. The Palomares farmers who still tried to sell their produce in the towns were turned away in horror. Emilio Mulero, a lawyer, son of a lawyer, grandson of a lawyer, and thus a pillar of community in Cuevas, did not try to persuade his wife to serve tomatoes no matter where they had been grown. He ate meat in the cafés, but he did not argue with

her decision to serve their children and herself nothing that
had not come from outside the region in a box or tin. Nor
would people eat what came fresh from the sea. The price of
shrimp plummeted to less than a third. Not only in the
nearby towns but even in Almería, even in Madrid, there was
no market. The fishermen spent their days sipping beer or
brandy at the dockside stalls. What was the use of putting out
to sea if no one would buy the catch?

The fear of radiation spilled over and merged with the
fear of hopeless loss. When they began to clear the fields, the
Americans said they would pay for the crops they destroyed.
The promise helped. But what, people asked, of the tomatoes
spoiling in the warehouse? Of the milk thrown away? Of the
fish? And of themselves?

General Montel reduced it all to a brisk list of priorities.
He numbered them in order in the report he sent:

1. There is a psychosis. The people must be calmed.
2. Find the zero line so the rest of the fields can be
   reopened.
3. Settle the formula for decontamination so it is
   clear which crops must be destroyed and which
   can be saved.
4. Restore the market and the normal level of produce sales.

That was the order or need as he saw it. It wasn't exactly
the order in which things were done, since many measures
had been launched and could be pressed simultaneously;
some things were harder than others to achieve.

Montel's idea of how to ease the local populace was to
call a meeting of all the heads of families and explain the
situation. The men of Palomares and Villaricos were invited.
Women, even though they might have been left without a
man to rule their household, were kept out. It was the
Spanish way.

Five men, all more important, more learned, more
influential than any who had ever seen or even heard of
Palomares before the accident, addressed the solemn session
that was held in the movie house. There was no other
building where the people might gather. General Montel
spoke of the great service which the Americans were performing in defending the free world against the Communists,

a service which made it necessary for them to fly day and night even at the risk of losing men and planes in accidents. The civilian governor and the military governor of Almería province spoke in the same vein. General Wilson described his command at Torrejón and the job his men at Palomares were performing "toward taking the necessary precautionary measures associated with an aircraft accident of this type." He thanked the people for their help. "It is miraculous indeed," he said, "that considerable aircraft debris fell around Palomares and not one individual was injured. I know that the hand of God was protecting this community." Again he expressed appreciation of the support his troops received, and said, "I hope that our work will likewise gain your respect and confidence that we are doing everything possible toward eliminating any possible danger and making compensation for damages suffered. . . . As comrades in arms in the defense against communism, I know that the mutual admiration and high respect existing between the people of our two countries will continue in the future as in the past."

Dr. Iranzo lectured on the importance of washing and the total unlikelihood of even the slightest risk as a result of the accident if that simple precaution were observed. The meeting was then thrown open for questions. Señor Mulero, the lawyer from Cuevas, rose to speak. There were no questions, he said. The heads of families were all there to serve their country and to help in every way. The audience applauded heartily. They found the speeches serious and stirring. Then they left. Only gradually did they realize once again that the pompous officialese was almost empty of information.

Some of the women had pressed an ear to the keyholes at the locked movie doors. When the Guardia Civil noticed, they were chased away. They complained shrilly and were as shrilly told to mind their own business. Manolo González, the mayor's son, attended as head of his newly founded family. His wife did not ask him what had happened when he came home. She had learned not to ask. "I never tell her anything," Manolo said later with a warm laugh. He spoke some months after the accident. She smiled when he said it and cooed at her baby, born some weeks after the bombs fell. The baby, a girl, was flourishing and the mother had felt no ill effects. That, she indicated with a smile, was enough.

Meager as it was, the meeting helped. It did not explain much, but it was reassuring. There were other things. Most important: days went by and nobody died. Old Doña Antonia complained of terrible backaches, but she had complained before. A shepherdess said her sheep had suddenly succumbed on the hillside. But she had no carcasses to show. The wild dogs had eaten them all, she explained, but the Americans should pay for them nonetheless. The Spanish physicists examined Puig and told him the "burn" on his knee was a spot of dirt and would go away with a wash. It did. His urinalysis sample showed a lower plutonium content than that of Ambassador Duke and some of the other Americans. The architect still complained of terrible nervous headaches and knots in his stomach, but he had suffered from nerves before the accident and showed no other symptoms. Captain Calín, the police chief, lining up cheerfully on the side of authority, told people not to be frightened ninnies about a little thing like plutonium when the experts said there was no danger. "I brush my teeth with plutonium, and I can still keep things in order here," he said with a sly grin. And the people laughed. The only death in the area during the whole time the Americans were there was the Madre Política of the mayor of Cuevas. She was a great-grandmother and she had been ill for some time. She occupied a certain position, of course, enhanced enough to be spared the distasteful title of mother-in-law and to be called by the more delicate phrase "political mother." But it was accepted that ladies of the greatest authority came to the end of their time, bombs or no bombs, and her demise brought ceremonial regrets of the familiar kind. It was almost a secret consolation. Babies came and the aged were taken away as it had always been.

The passage of day after day without new disaster worked its balm. And yet there was always some little thing to freshen the sting of bewilderment, the hurt of fathers having to admit ignorance to their women and their sons. One morning Sabiote went out to fetch his cow which he had left contentedly at pasture the night before. The animal was horribly bloated, bleeding from the nose, obviously in acute pain. In a few hours she died. He saw no cause. Like everything else surprising, it must be due to the radioactivity, he reasoned. The Spanish and the American doctors examined the cow. They concluded that she had somehow gotten into the stocks of dried beans and filled her stomach. Then she had satisfied her thirst. The swelling beans pressed on her insides until her stomach burst. They told Sabiote what they found, but he had never lost an animal that way before. He shook his head. He had already heard too many things that turned out to be untrue, or not quite true. The one thing he knew for certain was that radioactivity had come and the cow had died.

The beekeeper came excitedly one day to tell the doctors that all the bees in three large hives had suddenly, mysteriously, succumbed. The JEN people collected the dead insects and sent them to Madrid for examination. For laboratory control, they also had to catch a stock of live bees. They had no gloves or masks. It was one of the bad moments for them. There was no evidence, the tests showed, that the bees had died of cancer as they suspected. That could not be completely ruled out, but the doctors found that the alfalfa fields where the bees fed had been sprayed with oil to help keep down the dust. They thought the oil a likelier cause of death.

Father Navarrete, the young priest from Cuevas, changed his schedule and went every day to Palomares. As never before, except on special feasts and holidays, the church was filled day after day, and not only with the women. His very presence was a help. Despite the curiosity that raged throughout the region and always drove people in throngs to have a look at every innovation, every little incident, the neighbors of Palomares stayed away. It was like being quarantined in an epidemic. The visit of people they knew brought a certain relief to the villagers. And Navarrete, fresh from the seminary, preached all the hopeful and consoling words he knew.

"God is helping us," he said. "God is saving us. We have to have confidence and put ourselves in the Father's hand, as children take the hand of their father when they have trouble they don't know how to face. As the Americans put their camp on the beach to look after Palomares and see no harm is done, so Christ put His permanent camp on earth to protect us."

The Americans began to nourish the hunger for confidence in a concrete and necessary way. When the great invasion of troops released him from the frantic job of searching, Captain Ramirez turned his attention to his real job, collecting and investigating claims. He quickly found he needn't wander through the fields to seek the owner of a crop marked for destruction. The men at the bar always knew and in a minute the farmer would be at his elbow. They plied him with coffee and brandy, always refusing to let him pay. "You are the guest," the men said proudly, and then they spoke of business. For a few days the legal people set up office in the little room above the bar. Later, they moved to a tent in Camp Wilson and there was always a long line of visitors. At one point there was a legal staff of 22 men. People brought in fish they couldn't sell, and the Americans bought it. The Americans went to the warehouse and bought 7,000 pounds of tomatoes which could no longer be exported. "Doc" Norcross was sent up to test them, pronounced them perfectly safe, and their price was added to the Palomares bill as supplies, not damages. From then on, as ostentatiously as possible, the airmen were fed great quantities of tomatoes at every meal until a Spanish newspaper asked, "Is the Palomares tomato the new American secret weapon?" When there were people to watch, Dr. Iranzo, General Montel, General Wilson, and other officers made a point of picking a tomato in a field, dusting it with a tissue, washing it, and eating it.

Some people had slaughtered their animals in fear. Norcross tried to persuade them that the meat was perfectly safe. He knew the details of the many experiments Langham had performed which showed that after a much larger dose of plutonium than Palomares pigs and chickens might have had, there was a small amount of contamination only in the liver. "And for a human being to absorb any of it, you'd have to eat contaminated liver three times a day for weeks and weeks," he said. "The only part of the animal that might present the slightest danger is the intestines," Norcross told them. "Nobody eats them."

"Well," said the people, "they're used for sausages."

"But you wash the guts first. And that takes care of it."

"No. Why should they be washed? You just squeeze them out and fill them up with sausage meat."

After that Norcross quit eating the sausage he had been enjoying. It wasn't the thought of contamination that made him squeamish.

The detailed Air Force procedures for handling claims, complete with forms, questionnaires, sub-sub-paragraphs of regulation, worked well enough in buying up harvested crops at the going market price. But fixing the value of a crop not yet quite ready to be picked was another thing. With the Mayor's help, a "committee of neighbors" was organized to go from field to field and make appraisals. It soon became clear that that was going to take time. Then the Air Force learned that the Spanish government had its own legal procedures. Another committee of experts was appointed by the provincial court in Almería. But people needed money to live on, especially since they no longer dared to eat what they had grown.

The chief of the legal office in Torrejón came down to organize what promised to be a complicated operation. He was Lieut. Col. Joseph G. Stulb, Jr., a New Orleans lawyer with a long, pale face and an air of scholarly isolation. It was days before the other Americans found out what the colonel with the blue Air Force attaché case was doing as he prowled around Palomares. Then they nicknamed him "The Bagman." He had brought $10,000 in peseta notes, a thick stack from which he peeled a few bills to hand to one after another of the claimants as an emergency advance against the future settlement. There was no place to keep the money, so he carried it in the case which never left his side until at last a safe arrived. Many people refused to accept a check. They had never been in a bank. From time to time the supply shuttle from Torrejón sent down more big bundles of pesetas.

General Montel quietly advised the Spanish government that direct action was needed to revive the produce market for the entire region. The buyers were rejecting the crop, partly because they did not want to visit the province of Almería and neighboring Murcia after what they'd heard, partly because they feared they would never be able to export the food. Even in Madrid, housewives were cautiously asking the marketwomen at their stalls whether their rich red tomatoes were from Palomares. Many decided to do without fresh vegetables for a while. At Montel's suggestion, the government stepped in and bought large quantities of produce for about ten days. Some was probably resold in normal commerce, some was used for the army, and for hospitals. It served to break the fall in prices and made the food commerce seem to have bounced back to normal. The trick worked. Within a fortnight the immediate threat of economic disaster for the whole region was averted.

The bulk of the airmen at Camp Wilson were assigned to the increasingly desperate search operation. Although there were more men in the tents on the beach than in all of Palomares, pairs of hands were still needed. Colonel White thought to hire some of the idle farmers to help haul the debris to the junk pile. He enlisted ten. On the first day only five showed up. The others were frightened. But as the bills came out of the blue bag at the end of a day's work and nobody saw ill effects, the chance to work was welcomed as another move in the direction of normalcy. White offered a messenger job to a withered old man with a harelip, a man the rest of Palomares treated with affectionate disregard as a sort of village idiot who could never be of any use to anyone. After that, whenever White drove by in his jeep, the messenger would jump to the roadside and perform a joyously exaggerated salute. It was something they both remembered long afterward. Such little things nibbled gradually at the edges of the fear.

One day when Captain Ramirez was jeeping through the fields with the Mayor to fix some questions of land ownership for the processing of claims, a tattered woman stopped them with a stream of shrill abuse. Ramirez climbed out to listen. She was so excited, so rambling, that he found it hard to understand. The Mayor said she was from Villaricos. It was the first he had heard of the fishing village, and gradually he realized that the people there were threatened with starvation because they were not allowed to fish their usual grounds. He visited the ragged little port and it was arranged that the idle fishermen would be offered work helping to clean up Camp Wilson and doing other Air Force chores.

The question of pay was a problem. There was no going rate and no possible way of saying exactly what the fishermen would have earned if they could have put to sea each day. The figure finally settled was 150 pesetas ($2.50) a day, well above the usual for casual labor, and almost all the Villaricos men accepted jobs. But it was also necessary to compensate those who did not work for closing off their fishing grounds. The rate was fixed at 125 pesetas a day. That meant that the men who hauled garbage and dug ditches for the Air Force wound up with only a few cents more than those who sat on the sea rocks or the stoop of the grocery, gossiping and waiting for the lost bomb to be found. The women bawled at the injustice whenever they saw the Americans. "I learned in Villaricos just what the old saying about screaming like a fishwife means," Colonel White said later. There was no warmth of feeling wasted between the Americans and the people of the fishing village. Like the residents of Palomares and Vera and Cuevas, the Americans came to look down their noses at Villaricos, and the fishing folk responded to them with the same clannish peeve they felt against their farming neighbors, all authority, and people who prospered.

Pride came along with Air Force pesetas to push aside a portion of the shadow. As the villagers began to realize they held the attention of the world, they held themselves with more self-conscious stature. They had always been curious, excitable, stubborn in their ways. But they were never whiners, never beneath concern to present an honest, self-respecting face when someone was looking. Many had children working in Belgium, Switzerland, Germany, and France, who sent home anxious letters and wildly imaginative stories clipped from newspapers. The mail brought several copies of a photograph, published first in an Italian paper and then republished in other parts of Europe, of the crumbling mine smelter, abandoned half a century before. The caption under the picture, achingly familiar to every European who had seen the ruins of war, said, "Destruction at Palomares." the villagers were infuriated at the misrepresentation of tumbledown bricks they had known all their lives as if they were bomb damage from the accident. "It looked like that when I was born," Doña Anna snorted. They were as contemptuous, and annoyed, at the appeals on the Communist broadcasts for Spaniards to demonstrate against the "American imperialist aggressors whose bases threaten Spain with the same inhuman misery as Vietnam." They could bring a certain slyness to the sale of a donkey or, as things went on, to the pressing of a claim. But the people of Palomares watched the Americans, and talked with some of them, and liked them. Above all, they were courteous and curious.

A villager studying the behavior of the Americans in camp happened to be standing next to Captain Calín, the Guardia Civil chief, and nudged him. "What rank is that man?" the villager asked, pointing to an officer who had just stooped to pick up a bit of trash.

Calín was proud that he had learned to read the American insignia. "He's a colonel," he whispered.

"That's an American colonel for you." They exchanged collusive winks. Neither one needed to point out what Calín said later when he repeated the incident. "You wouldn't find one of ours doing that."

So it seemed to the villagers that they were being presumptuously exploited, not defended, when they heard of the demonstration in Madrid.

The handbills had been circulated quietly at the university and in the workers' districts, but not so quietly that the Spanish police were caught unawares. The call was for a mass demonstration in front of the U.S. Embassy at "Seven-thirty in the afternoon" on February 4.

"Yankees and your bombs get out of Spain." "Spain, yes. Yankees, no," read the slogans. The text said that "vast zones of Almería province have been contaminated and hundreds of people are affected by radioactivity. . . . So long as there are American bases in Spain, another accident like the one in Almería can happen any day and the bombs can explode and wipe out millions of human beings."

The police told the Embassy what to expect and kept a discreet watch that evening. The estimates of how many people turned up ran from 500 to 2,000, depending on whether people milling around in the side streets were counted, too. It was a mixed crowd, some students and some work-worn old people, and they shouted such things as "Assassins," and "Get rid of the bases." After twenty minutes or so the police turned up to push them along. There were a few scuffles. No casualties were reported. It had worried Ambassador Duke and his staff, but after all, it blew over rather quietly. The Embassy had a worse scare when a brown-paper parcel arrived addressed to Duke. It was ticking loudly. He had had several anonymous phone calls threatening to blow up his family and himself because of the bomb. The Embassy's Marine Guard opened the package with delicate care. Inside was an alarm clock and a Coca-Cola bottle, empty except for a paper with the message, "Get out of Spain and Vietnam."

These weren't the sort of things that cause serious diplomatic strain, but they were signs of the way the incident was developing. As the first wave of terror receded in Palomares, a different fear pounded more and more insistently on the Americans. It was the fear of a lost bomb—of losing the bomb itself, and of the consequences of having to admit the loss before all the world. From the moment word had come of the accident, the search was a matter of urgency. As it dragged on, it was becoming a matter of desperation.

9

THE SEARCH

"All lost objects obey certain ancient natural laws," wrote Russell Baker, the *New York Times'* resident humorist. In a mordantly whimsical article offering help to the Air Force in its H-bomb dilemma, Baker said the thing to do was to pique the lost thing's pride by ignoring it, which would drive it to a neurotically violent reappearance the way a lost pair of pliers finally "hurls itself maniacally from garage rafter to skull. The ways in which an H-bomb might use nervous breakdown to achieve rediscovery are unforeseeable, but the Air Force reassures us that anything very violent is out of the question. Air Force safety techniques, it seems, are so efficient that the chances of a lost H-bomb's exploding are just as unlikely as the chances of an H-bomb's getting lost."

That was the way it looked to the world. It did not look even tragically funny to the Air Force, the U.S. government, and the thousands of people mobilized for the search. From the Monday of the accident through that Friday the human barricade of airmen moved across the rugged land, pinning their streamers to the cactus, and planting their flags. Somehow the bomb slipped through their ranks. Each night when the troops crawled into the tents after their dawn-to-dusk search, General Wilson and his aides plotted the ground that had been covered and made plans for the next day. A pattern of everything else that had been found after the accident indicated the limits of an area that had been trampled over and over without success. There were, as the military say, two possibilities, although they say it more coarsely. One was that the bomb was on the land, hiding underground or broken in so many pieces that it had not been recognized. The other was that the bomb was in the sea.

A Navy tug had turned up off Palomares the day after the accident, but it wasn't equipped to be helpful. Four days later two U.S. mine sweepers arrived from Barcelona and two more made their way from Rota through the Straits of Gibraltar. Their sounding gear made a large number of contacts just offshore, undoubtedly more pieces of wreckage, and their divers began bringing up all kinds of debris from the brief shelf before the bottom suddenly dipped to depths beyond their reach. The President's order had been to find the bombs quickly. Three were recovered in the first twenty-four hours. At the end of the first week Wilson had to admit that completion of the order was impossible. The realization dawned that one H-bomb, the length of a car and the width of a garbage can, packed with the explosive power of a million tons of TNT, was not just mislaid and proving hard to locate. It was thoroughly lost. Wilson called for urgent help, all that he could get to pursue both of the possibilities and refine them to a probability.

The collection of reports from witnesses was reviewed once more. Among them was the story told by Francisco Simo Orts and Bartolomé Roldán Martínez.

Capt. Joe Ramirez had driven alone to Aguilas the night after the accident to talk to the fishermen. He waited on the broad quay as the little boats rounded the breakwater and tied up. When the men jumped ashore, they all went into the port captain's office where a pile of debris was turned over to Ramirez. There were life rafts, survival kit, life preservers, and an assortment of bits. The fishermen had conscientiously salvaged everything they saw and they returned it all.

Simo's first words were a profuse apology for not having been able to save the aviator who went down at sea. All the Spaniards spoke earnestly of their sorrow for the men who died, and how glad they were to have rescued three of them.

"It was the human thing to do," Simo said, and the others nodded vigorous agreement. Roldán, the shy master of the second ship, spoke only when he was spoken to as a rule, but he added his word of gladness to have been of service and his regret that one of the parachutists had drowned.

Ramirez said nothing, although he knew there were no crewmen missing. Instead, he asked them in detail about the accident. Simo told about two chutes, a smaller brownish one that landed 25 yards on one side of his boat and a larger grayish one that crossed overhead and splashed down 100 yards on the other side. The first, he kept saying sadly, carried "half a man, with the insides trailing." The other carried "a dead man." Simo apologized again for not having recovered the body. But he was certain the man was dead, he said, because he was so rigid in the air and sank so fast, parachute and all. With his tanned, square-cut face and his honest manner, he impressed the Air Force lawyer as a man of utter sincerity. Clearly, from the look of him as well as the way he spoke, he was a hardened seaman, successful and self-confident, even dashing in his thick gray turtleneck sweater. He told all that he had seen of the accident, and Roldán confirmed each bit although his boat had been closer to shore and he was less clear about the "dead man's chute." They had seen a sixth parachute fall burning on the land. Everything fitted the details Ramirez already knew except the part about the two chutes that straddled Simo's boat. But Ramirez also knew that all personnel chutes were bright orange and white, that the only equipment with parachutes were bombs, and that bomb chutes were grayish-white.

It was late when he got back to his room above the gas station at Vera that night. The next morning he delivered the debris he had collected to the camp and reported his interview to General Wilson. Wilson ordered him to return to Aguilas with an Air Force weapons expert and talk to the fishermen once more. There was another long session on the dock that evening. The fishermen described the accident again, how they had seen the bomber move under the tanker and suddenly break up. Then the tanker shook wildly for a moment and exploded. The half man, Simo said, fell in profile to him. He could see the head and shoulders. The clothes, he said, were about the color of Ramirez' gray flight suit. From where he watched, the "other man" seemed strangely stiff. There was no movement of the arms or legs. Simo had started pulling in the nets the minute he saw the accident, but it was very deep where he had been trawling and he made slow progress through the heavy sea. The "dead man" sank within thirty seconds of hitting the water.

The questioning was precise and the fishermen answered everything. They gave the depth of the water where they had been at the time of the accident, the position of the sun, the wind conditions. It all went into the dossier, along with the

reports of dozens of other witnesses who told of being chased
by balls of flame, of parachutes popping out all over the sky,
of explosions from every direction. The first exhausting week
had used up what hopes the Americans had placed in a
hunt-and-sniff technique for finding the bomb. They had
arranged to unlock the cemetery gates and had gone inside to
peek under the roof of every one of the minuscule chapels
that lined its walls. They had infuriated a woman trying to
dry her laundry on a beach five miles away. One of the
helicopters had reported what might be parts of parachute on
the beach, and one team after another made its arduous way
to the coordinates given. The woman finally was so annoyed
with Americans picking at her washing all morning long that
she gathered up her sheets and towels and underwear and
took them home to iron wet.

The searchers had sent airmen crawling down the mud
tunnels that spiraled around the mountain, the remains of a
smelter which had used gravity and the steady wind to draw
the metal off from cooling slag. Someone suggested that the
bomb might have fallen into a tunnel at the top and slithered
part way down. They had lowered airmen down some of the
mine shafts that gaped suddenly in the fields.

One day the Mayor of Las Herrerías came to Camp
Wilson. Herrerías was a poorer, smaller village than Palomares,
tucked into the hills a mile farther inland. Many of its people
lived in caves. They threshed their grain by standing on a
wooden sled which a donkey pulled in endless circles over
the threshing floor. The Mayor had come to say that the
barkeeper in Herrerías had a brother who was a shepherd.
The shepherd had been in the mountains on the morning of
the accident and he had seen a white parachute fall in the
fields. With excitement, Captain Ramirez and Colonel Young
prepared to interview the man.

"There's a problem," the Mayor said with hesitance. "He
doesn't speak or hear. He's a very big man, we call him
Tarzan. He's, well, a little primitive. But his brother can talk
to him. Come and see them both at the bar. I will arrange it."

The barman translated the deaf-mute's sign language to
the two Americans. The description sounded like a weapon.
Young and Ramirez persuaded the shepherd to show them
the place where he had seen the chute land. They sent for a
helicopter. It was a terrible moment for the man who had

lived all his life alone with his animals in the barren hills. But he finally agreed to enter the contraption. They flew up into the mountains, then down along the line of sight that the shepherd drew with wild gesticulations. Finally, with his arms, his head, with all the expressiveness of his huge body, he pointed out his spot. It was Number One site, the place where the first bomb had been found the night of the accident.

There was still no clue to Number Four. So the searchers turned to technology and the textbook method, although they had to write the textbooks as they went along because it had never been done before. Wilson's call for help put two intricate machines in motion. One was the U.S. Navy. The other was the Sandia Corporation in Albuquerque, already involved but so far more as observers than as strategic planners on the search staff.

When the message came in, W. J. Howard, then Assistant to the Secretary of Defense for Atomic Energy, put through a call to Alan Pope, director of aero-projects at Sandia.

"Have you seen *Thunderball*?" Howard asked.

Pope said yes.

"Good. I want you to work on it."

Pope was not really perplexed. The spectacular film about James Bond's retrieval of an H-bomb that had been stolen by a super-gang out to pull the biggest blackmail coup in history no longer seemed so fictional. That is, the first part about a missing aircraft and a bomb theft had achieved a certain parallel in fact. But James Bond had not turned up this time to solve the case with daredeviltry and seduction, and there was no chance that he would arrive to keep the parallel going to the happy end. His replacement, at that stage, was to be Sandia's big computer. All the available information on plane speeds, wind speeds, altitude, coordinates, debris pattern, ballistics of the bomb without parachute and with its chutes in various stages of deployment, was fed into the less romantic but more meticulous electronic brain. A Sandia team worked from one-thirty Saturday afternoon until 2 A.M. on Sunday and produced some preliminary estimates on where the bomb might be. The trouble with the results was that the computer was not so good as Bond at winnowing out misinformation. Early in the second week of the accident, when it turned out that a lot of the facts fed to the computer had been wrong, two of Sandia's top ballistics men were rushed to Palomares to join the weapons experts and explosives experts already there.

The studies on the spot were cabled back to Albuquerque for a new computer calculation. They were put together by projecting all the evidence to the point in space where the accident occurred, and then retracing the way things fell and might have fallen. Only a computer could have held all the jumbled details together in its mind. Interviews with the survivors disclosed that Messinger, the copilot who had splashed down eight miles out to sea, had opened his chute manually at 28,000 feet. Wendorf, the pilot, and Rooney, the navigator, had waited for the automatic mechanism to function at 14,000 feet and reached the water near each other three miles from the shore. Figuring the ballistic trajectories of the men as though they were missiles helped to refine the data on drag and wind speeds at varying altitudes below the point of collision. Rooney's testimony of how he bounced around in the tumbling plane and was finally thrown out also helped to reconstruct the gravity forces when the B-52 broke up. That, in turn, enabled the experts to calculate the precise moment after the accident at which the bomb bay must have wrenched apart and released its package of four weapons. Technicians from Boeing, who made the plane, checked the wreckage to confirm the calculations. The pattern of debris and of the three bombs on the land convinced the experts that all four H-bombs had come out together, not one by one, as the shattered plane hurtled forward. The decrease of forward speed from the instant of the crash until the bombs broke loose was figured at 200 feet per second; the ground speed of the B-52 when it crashed was 615 feet per second, according to the calculations. Two weather stations, at Gibraltar and Palma de Mallorca, were asked to reconstruct their records of the winds.

An eyewitness in Garrucha who said he saw the accident verified the calculations on the point of collision. He stood in the spot where he had been that Monday and pointed his line of sight at 75 degrees above a lemon tree across a field. The experts questioned him closely. If he had heard the explosion and then looked up to see the accident, it would have taken thirty seconds for the sound to reach him and his sighting would have quite different implications.

But everything depended on the parachutes. The reconstruction indicated that the B-52 pitched sharply to the left, the left wing snapped off, and the bomb rack broke at a force of six times gravity. The bombs could have hit pieces of debris coming down that partly forced out the parachutes. They were held in the back of the cylinder by a tail plate with a small explosive charge which would have blown off to release the chutes at a predetermined moment if the bombs were armed for use in anger. An unexpected impact could have blown the tail plates off. Careful analysis showed that the chutes of the two broken bombs had never deployed. They had just been blasted out after the bombs hit the ground.

A lucky find brought the first solid clue. Part of a tail plate was found near the beach. It had a ring attached, and three tail-plate rings had already been recovered. Four rings were too many for three bombs. The serial number on the tail plate was still legible. An urgent cable to the Albuquerque files produced the exhilarating answer. This was definitely part of the missing weapon. A new series of possibilities was deduced. Perhaps Number Four had broken up so completely on impact that its parts were mistakenly lumped in with the scattered pieces of the other bombs.

Sam Moore, a broad-faced, sturdy, easygoing Sandia man, made a recheck of every bit of bomb that had been found. He had designed the bomb. He knew what everything in it had to look like and, like a mother, could not be fooled by twins. His assistant, Stuart Asselin, made sure all the serial numbers checked. They were an interesting pair, these American Dr. Strangeloves, Moore with his white hair and pale blue eyes and big, relaxed outdoorsman frame; the younger Asselin with his short crew cut, his wan face and long, thin body already slightly bent at the shoulders to a laboratory stoop. There was nothing eccentric about them and nothing escaped them. One piece of badly damaged debris was found 1,000 feet from Number Three site. The distance aroused their suspicions. It was sent home for what they called the stolen-car treatment, an acid test to trace the obliterated markings. That was a false clue. It did turn out to be a part of bomb Number Three, not a remnant of the missing weapon as they had thought possible.

Another possibility was that whatever blew off the tail plate had also caused the high explosive in the nose of the bomb to go off in the air, leaving it to fall in pieces. There were some traces of radioactivity on an engine nacelle and on the tail section of the B-52. It could have been spray from the plutonium dust on the ground, or it could have indicated an aerial explosion. A huge crane was brought into Palomares to turn over the bomb bay so that radiation measurements could be taken and details ascertained of the way the structure failed. That showed nothing one way or the other about a breakup in the air.

So far the search had been made on the assumption that the weapon fell whole. The airmen marching fingertip to fingertip were looking for big craters. They were instructed to go back over the entire area and look for much smaller craters, the kind the uranium log or plutonium "melon" might have made if it hit and buried itself in the ground. There were questions about just how far under soft ground a piece of bomb might penetrate and the likeliest shape of the hole.

On February 13 Operation Sunday took place at White Sands, New Mexico, to find the answer. The fall of a major piece was simulated from a high-flying plane to see how it would hit the ground, and the information was cabled back.

The find of the tail plate proved one thing—that the missing bomb had behaved differently from the others. The difference could also have been that one or more of its parachutes deployed. The story of the Aguilas fishermen took on renewed interest.

Randall C. Maydew, an affable, sandy-haired, round-cheeked man with a dimple, was the chief ballistics expert sent hurrying from Sandia at the start of the second week after the accident. On February 3 he and Ramirez went up to the port for still another session with Simo and Roldán. Maydew listened to the now-familiar story, but he was looking for subtler points of confirmation. He asked Simo to draw a sketch of his position and of the things he saw. Although it was simply a few lines, it gave the relative distances of the parachutists from each other and the shore quite correctly. Then Maydew outlined a parachute and asked, "Did it look like this?"

Simo shook his head sharply. He corrected Maydew's sketch. The canopy was deeper, its greatest width was reached halfway from the top and not at the bottom of the shallow arc

Maydew had drawn. That was the "dead-man chute." It was solid, Simo said, and it had come down swinging, sort of tripping in the air. He drew the other one, the "half-man chute." Its crown was long and it was made of ribbons, not cloth. Simo described how much more smoothly it descended.

The big chute had floated down for six to eight minutes, Simo said. It was much larger than the orange-and-white chutes in the distance, and came down more slowly than the ribbon chute which fell closer to the shore and sank immediately.

Every point was vital. Maydew would not have believed any of the story if the fisherman put the ribbon chute five miles out to sea. His calculations showed it could not have gone that far. Nor would his doubts have been satisfied if the fisherman agreed with his suggestions. He had deliberately misdrawn the bomb's main 64-foot chute to test the accuracy of the fisherman's memory and observation. Simo's corrections were exact. And Maydew had said nothing about the small ribbon chute packed in the weapon casing to lower the bomb smoothly to the altitude set for main chute deployment. Maydew knew every detail of the chute pack. As for every heavy object to be dropped, there was a set of three. First there was a pilot wind-catcher to pull out the ribbon chute, which dangled the packing of the main canopy after full release. The "half man" was no doubt the sturdy sacking of the big parachute with its strings trailing. The "dead man," Maydew came to feel with full conviction, had to be the missing bomb.

Simo agreed to go down the coast to point out the spot where the things he saw had fallen. It was arranged for a helicopter to take him and Roldán from Aguilas to Garrucha early next morning. There was a tremendous crush of excitement when it landed on the quay beside the quiet line of boats, so Ramirez made his way to the open-air café at the dock to wait for the Navy captain who was to join them for the trip. He ordered coffee and chatted again with the fishermen while they watched the sun climb over the breakwater. The crew of the *Manuela Orts* was still grieving about the men who had gone to the bottom.

"It wasn't a man," Ramirez told them, "nor a half man. It was probably a projectile and the chute casing."

The fishermen were shocked and disbelieving.

"But all the bodies from both planes were recovered,"

Ramirez explained. "None was missing. I even asked the medics if there had been any corpses with the top half missing. There weren't."

That launched a commotion of argument. Simo spoke up. He was "El Catalán," the one who found it easiest to speak, and he was the master of one boat, the owner of two, a man of skill and substance. The others deferred.

"I swear it was a man," he said. "I saw him. He was a very heavy man, barrel-chested, not very tall."

Ramirez shook his head. "You only think so because that's what you expected to see."

It was days before Simo and the other fishermen finally accepted the idea that they had seen a tube of metal, not a body. But they were no less willing to help in the search. The helicopter took them to board a U.S. mine sweeper. When they were out at sea, Simo and Roldán squinted at the shore line. Roldán had been closer to the land; he was not quite so definite. But Simo studied the way the mountains ripped the edges of the western sky and named his spot. The Navy captain checked his radio direction finder for coordinates and marked it on his chart. A few days later, in different weather, the fishermen were brought out again. That time the helicopter wouldn't start when they tried to take off from the dock. Simo took the Americans to phone Camp Wilson and order a truck. They drank several rounds of beer while they waited. The Americans were his guests, he insisted, and he refused to let them pay for anything. After an hour the pilot did get the chopper going, and the trip to the sea off Palomares was repeated. Simo guided the mine sweeper confidently through the empty sea and stopped it at a spot only a few hundred yards from the one he named before. It was uncanny navigation, using only what the Navy called the Mark I eyeball. It was at least as hard for the electronic mariners to believe as it had been for Simo to believe he had not seen a dead man falling through the sky.

The folder of reports from witnesses was thick. Leafing through it carefully once more, Maydew found a reference to the pharmacist in Garrucha who had seen the accident. He decided to question the man about parachutes. It was 9 A.M. when the Camp Wilson team found the pharmacist, and they had to rout him out of bed. The Spaniard explained that he arose a little before ten every morning and took his coffee on the roof terrace of his house, a calm beginning to each day, devoted to the comfort of breakfast and the beauty of the Mediterranean scene stretching out before him. He was gazing at the lovely seascape when he saw the crash, and he watched as the parachutes tumbled from the sky. A big white one, he said, came down in the water on a line of sight just to the left of the palm tree across the street. Maydew had brought a compass to the interview and he noted the precise heading. It was 79° 15'. The pharmacist said his assistant, who opened the store in the morning, had seen the falling chutes, too. But not from the same place. Rodríguez, the assistant, had jumped on his scooter the moment after the explosion to see if his family a mile and a half away were safe from the falling debris. Maydew sought out the assistant and took him to the spot from where he saw the white chute hit the water. Rodríguez had been standing just in front of the gate of the Hotel Maricielo where Maydew was staying. The two white pillars of the gate had been Rodríguez' line of reference. The plotting Maydew made with his compass was 93° 16'. It lined up with the reading from the pharmacist's sighting and the two lines crossed about a quarter of a mile from the point Simo had indicated.

Maydew's team had drawn up three scenarios of what might have happened to the bomb: one if it fell intact; one if it broke in the air and part landed on shore, part in the sea; one if the high explosive detonated in the air. Each made a difference to the falling weight, and thus a key difference to the trajectory that should be plotted. All the information that had been collected, by Mark I eyeball and every device and test the experts had at their command, was fed into the Albuquerque computer for the last missing act of each scenario. When the results were cabled back to Camp Wilson, a great chart was drawn.

A circle 12,000 feet in diameter with its center on Simo's spot was marked Alpha I, the zone of highest probability. There was, the mathematicians said, a 66⅔ per cent chance of the bomb being in that area. The chance of its being in Alpha II, the area closer to shore where most of the debris had fallen, was rated one-third. But that was merely the likelihood. In addition, for later attention, there was zone Bravo reaching far out to sea where the survivor blown farthest from the shore had landed. Zone Charlie was an irregular blob mostly over the land that had been combed a dozen times and was to be combed again. The chart reduced the sea search area from 125 square miles to 27⅓ square miles. It was figured that it would take 341 days to cover the high probability area with a 95 per cent assurance that the bomb had not been missed. "I'll tell you how slippery the problem was," Maydew said later, "it was like trying to handle a bag of worms in a bucket of snakes in a barrel of eels. There were so many things we couldn't be sure about." The land and the water were divided in 1,000-yard-square patches on the charts, and the search continued through each one in turn.

The Navy began to arrive in force during the second week. The message for help from Palomares on January 22 went to the Secretary of the Navy, to the Chief of Naval Operations, to the Commander in Chief U.S. Naval Forces Europe, whose headquarters are in London. Rear Adm. William S. Guest got the telephone call at his home, near Naples, on Sunday morning, January 23. The order was to proceed to Torrejón Air Force base in Spain immediately, with no explanation. The Admiral's aide met him at the airport with a folder. It had some dispatches on the crash and some sketchy reports on the search so far. And it ordered a 6th Fleet Task Force to fish up the bomb which the Air Force had dropped, if it was in the sea. The Task Force was designated 65; Guest was named commander.

Admiral Guest was a Georgian, the son of a cavalry officer who badly wanted him to go to West Point. His stubborn streak (he had no nickname although subordinates often called him "Bulldog" behind his back) turned him instead to Annapolis where he was tempted by both the submarine service and the Navy Air Corps. But he gave in to his mother's fears about the perils of the depths. Soon after the United States entered World War II he was flying dive bombers off the *Yorktown* and he was credited with being the first carrier pilot to sink an enemy ship. Six months later his own ship was sunk under him. With flames billowing up onto the flight deck, he took off and landed his bomber on the *Enterprise*. Three carriers went down beneath him during the war. It only confirmed his opinion about his father's plans for him.

"I didn't want to be a mud-scrubber," he said when he

had become an admiral. "I want to die clean. I never envied the GI's and I remember the Army Air Force pilots coming in at Guadalcanal. The first thing they wanted was hot showers, clean clothes, and a bed with clean sheets."

Those things he never lacked in the Navy. He had had sea commands, always before to do with planes, however, and armchair commands. Task Force 65 was his first experience with salvage. Short, stubby, wih the square face and loose jowls of a bulldog as well as its approach to things, Guest was a man of intelligence who trusted his own mind and cared little for what was going on in others'. His own mind demanded order above all, such a tight, ship-shape, no-nonsense order that the discipline he imposed was not founded on respect alone. There was fear as well. He probably knew it, but the knowledge neither worried him nor muted the outbursts of his temper. His way, he felt, was the way to get things done. There could not be two commanders of a ship, a task force, an operation. There was always only one who must bear the full responsibility. There could, then, be only one way.

When Guest reached Camp Wilson only the two mine sweepers and their complements of divers had yet arrived to start the sea search. Helicopters were patrolling the shallows for sightings to guide the divers. That day they had picked up two Martin-Baker ejection seats from the B-52. He discussed it with General Wilson, but he did not wish to stay on shore. The divers took the Admiral out to the U.S.S. *Skill*, one of the mine sweepers, in a rubber boat. As more units arrived, he transferred to the larger ones until at last he raised his flag in comfort on a cruiser, the U.S.S. *Boston*. Within a few days there were a dozen ships on station off Palomares. At one period of the search there was a fleet of 18.

Unlike Wilson, Guest had no initial problems of isolation. His communications were in good order and the messages streamed in from special command center that had been set up in Washington.

Rear Adm. Leroy Vincent Swanson, Director of Fleet Operations on the staff of the Chief of Naval Operations, was called to his chief's office on Saturday, January 23. There was a terrible snowstorm. It wasn't easy to get through the thickly covered streets and across the river to the Pentagon.

"It looks," said Adm. Horacio Rivero, Vice Chief of Naval Operations and Swanson's immediate superior, "like the bomb is in the sea. We can't leave a single stone unturned to find it."

Swanson was put in charge of coordinating the operation. He telephoned the area commander in London and said, "This job has the highest national interest. Get what you've got and we'll send on what's needed, top priority." Then he assembled a team to study the problem, list and collect every kind of equipment both military and civilian, operational or experimental, that might conceivably be thrown into the search. By that night calls had gone out across the country to every station, institution, company, that had expertise in the ways of the silent land beneath the seas. Other calls began to come in as word spread that the Navy was looking for pioneers on the near but so largely unexplored frontier. The suggestions ranged from ingenious to idiotic. Someone said put down a huge magnet and drag the ocean. But the bomb casing was aluminum. Someone said drop a net and drag for it. But the terrain was unknown, the bomb might be broken, and in any case an H-bomb could hardly be treated like a hunk of scrap. Jacques Cousteau sent word through the French government that he would make his deep-sea equipment available if needed. But it lacked mobility, it was made for research, not search.

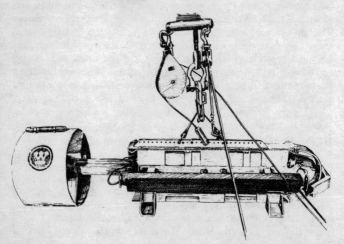

Westinghouse OBSS

"I didn't know how to pronounce oceanography when this came up," Swanson said later. "Now I'm overwhelmed with how little we know about such a huge subject, how little capability we have to pursue it."

"I never heard of a lot of the things they offered to send," Guest recalled. "I had to message back and ask what they were, what they could do, before I had a notion of whether we could use them."

The first of the long series of strange equipment that arrived were two deep jeeps, flown from the naval research station at Pasadena. They were clumsy vehicles, good for scrambling down in not very deep water to see what it was that made an interesting ping on surface sonar. But their motors were not powerful enough to hold them on a target against the strong current. Westinghouse sent five "acoustic fish," officially called Ocean Bottom Scanning Sonar, electronic ears that can be towed above the bottom to hear pings off objects that cannot be noticed from the surface. But they had no way of skimming a rugged terrain. Three bumped into underwater peaks and ridges and two of the expensive "fish" were permanently lost. The Navy hydrographic ship *Dutton* reached Palomares early in the second week after the accident and began to chart the unknown bottom. The Navy research ship *Mizar*, undergoing conversion in the Philadelphia shipyard, cut short the work and sailed for the Mediterranean to tow underwater television sleds. The divers from *Sealab II*, a Navy research operation conducted the year before, were sent to probe the depths that frogmen and hard-hat divers could not reach. Experts who had searched for the *Thresher*, the nuclear submarine that burst 8,400 feet below the Atlantic on April 10, 1963, were sent with their equipment. A Decca radio navigation system was installed on shore to enable precise charting as the search progressed. Under good conditions, the eye or the camera cannot see more than a distance of 20 feet below the depth of sunlight penetration under water. It was essential to have a navigation system that would pinpoint positions to an accuracy of at least 10 feet if there was to be any assurance that the search pattern which looked so orderly on the charts was not in reality a crazy quilt of overlapping lines and empty spaces.

The sea was parceled out to the people who could cope with it. Up to 130-foot depths, Navy frogmen searched swimming shoulder to shoulder. Up to 400 feet, the hard-hat divers worked. They held knotted lines to keep a constant distance from each other, or followed lines laid down on the ocean floor (a request for paint to mark squares on the bottom brought a snort from Washington). They brought up things ranging from the size of an orange to the size of a limousine. The surface searchers, the underwater sonar, and the television worked the deeper areas, marking each electronic response on the new charts which took six weeks to complete. At the end of a week of sea search there were 66 contacts noted. Each had to be identified and, if of any value in itself or as a clue, recovered. Both the Sandia calculations and the search in the shallows showed, however, that the main job had to be in deeper water than the Navy was equipped to send its men.

Three peculiar little submarines were among the special equipment mobilized on the snowy Saturday night when the Navy moved into action. The *Cubmarine*, a two-man submersible developed by Perry Ocean Systems, Inc., was flown from Florida. It operated at depths between 200 and 400 feet. The *Aluminaut*, a Reynolds Aluminum Co. development, was an orange monster of 81 tons displacement, an average speed of 2.5 knots, and a maximum dive capacity of thirty-two hours. It could carry six men and go down to 15,000 feet, but lacked what might be called elevator capability. The depth of each dive had to be determined beforehand, and once the *Aluminaut* started up it could not change its mind and go back down again. The *Alvin*, designed by the Woods Hole Oceanographic Institution, was a white 22-foot-long toy, made to hold three men in a cramped sphere, cruise at two knots, and dive for eight hours. Its midget size and its unusual ballast system enabled it to squiggle through bad terrain at the same depths where the *Aluminaut* could only float. But it took nearly a month after the accident to get the little submarines into operation.

Heavy seas kept forcing suspension of the search. Guest sent the U.S.S. *Pinnacle*, towing the "acoustic fish," to look for contacts in the area that Simo's two trips to sea had suggested. Nothing of interest was noted. Someone pointed out that nobody really knew what kind of reflection an H-bomb made on sonar. Perhaps they were not attending to the right echoes. A mock-up of a bomb was made, correct in size and shape, and dropped overboard at a carefully marked point. The sonar found it. The test only showed that the men had not overlooked vital clues.

The men worked at night planning and reporting, and all through daylight searching. The lights of the bomb fleet danced brilliantly on the sea, a gay display that mocked the growing nervous tension. From Mojácar, the hilltop Moorish village down the coast, it was a beautiful sight. The people of Mojácar had always felt quite separate from Palomares. They did not share its fears. An old peasant woman remembered the time of the bomb with pleasure when she spoke of it.

"I've never seen anything so pretty in my life," she said later. "Why should we be afraid? Nothing fell on us. We sat on the wall by the square every night and watched the lights on the sea."

The sea was crowded. Both for security and for safety it was felt necessary to keep the fishermen away. The Spanish government barred all vessels from a zone that stretched from Garrucha to Punta del Ruso, a lighthouse two and one-half miles the other side of Villaricos, and went ten miles out to sea. It was a somewhat delicate matter that a large part of the search area was in international waters, but no one made a point of it. When a Soviet trawler turned up on the horizon in February, Guest sent two destroyers out to shield the fleet from its approach. Presumably it watched and listened with its advanced equipment, but the trawler did not try to intrude. If it had, there might have been another incident because the United States really had no right to close off a corner of the high seas. Guest was not given contingency orders on what to do if a foreign vessel, such as the trawler, showed an aggressive curiosity. The Task Force oiler, a fast ship with a saucy master, went out to inspect the trawler and wheeled taunting circles around it. The Russians pretended not to notice. Guest watched the trawler come in about two miles from the search area in the daytime, recede some 30 miles out to sea at night. And he made his own plan. He had a fleet tug ready.

"If the Russians attempted harassment," he said later, "I would have put the tug between the Soviet vessel and ourselves. If they kept coming, I would have just pushed them away." But the trawler chugged off after ten uneasy days. Patrol planes followed it south until it was well clear of the area.

Spanish navy vessels patrolled the inshore areas of the

closed zone to ward off fishermen who tried to sneak in despite the ban. Before the ban was decreed, one of the Aguilas boats had caught something heavy in its nets, too heavy to raise. They dragged it to shallower waters and notified the U.S. Navy, setting the net to a buoy. The next day, the fishermen said, they came back to find the net broken and nothing in it. A rumor flew that the bomb had been secretly found. But when it was obvious that the search continued, the Aguilas fishermen became convinced that they had snared the "black box" they'd heard so much about. They believed the Navy had slyly retrieved it in the night. Later, U.S. officials insisted there had been only a concrete buoy anchor in the nets. The fishermen never accepted that story. "The Navy knew we had something," they said, "but they didn't want us to know. They kept asking us to show where the parachute fell, but they didn't want to admit we found anything. They wanted all the credit." It hadn't helped that every question put to the authorities at the time was answered only with "No comment." Colonel Young, the spokesman on the beach, was under strict orders to say nothing else. The Spaniards took to calling him "Señor No Comment," and a British newspaperman went further when Young persistently refused to confirm or deny a story that the Combat Mission Folder with its top secrets still had not been found.

"Well, Colonel," the Englishman said when his temper finally outran his vocabulary, "I guess we better start swinging." He hitched up his sleeves and clenched his fists.

"You'll have to start," Young answered. "I'm not allowed to swing first."

That was more official information than had been released since the admission that the bomber carried nuclear weapons and that the Air Force and Navy were looking for "wreckage." Perhaps the surprise, perhaps the fact that Young and a companion officer outweighed the newsman by a good deal, ended the episode peaceably. Under the circumstances, the restraint on both sides was remarkable. Tension was nearing the snapping point.

10

THE WAIT

The people of Palomares settled into a frightened resignation. Many still refused to eat fresh food. Anna, the wife of Navarro Portillo, stayed with her daughter in the middle of the village, unwilling to return to her house next to Number Three site half a mile away. But life went on and the urgent subject for the villagers came to be the question of claims. As a kind of calm descended upon Palomares once more the Spanish government and the Americans faced a mounting strain. They were frightened for quite different reasons from the villagers, but they had perhaps even better cause. Trouble was growing each day of the search.

The French tabloid *Paris-Jour* ran a two-page spectacular complete with bikini girls headlined "Atomic Super-Alarm! The A-Bombs 'Missed' in Spain Have Not Yet Been Recovered." The American TV comic Henry Morgan quipped that "I understand everything is all right, but personally, I'll miss Spain." The Manila *Times* said that the crash "should serve as a warning to the Philippines. It was one of the tragedies of people who play host to military bases of an alien power....Are Filipino authorities going to act only after an air accident over Manila has resulted in jettisoning one or two atomic bombs upon this populous metropolis?" An Italian TV ad urged people to holiday in Italy because Spain was radioactive. Embassy officials in Madrid stayed late in their offices trying to figure out what nasty tricks the Communists might play so they could be ready with the answers. What if, someone pointed out unhappily, the Russians were to pull up a fish, sprinkle a bit of plutonium dust on it secretly, and then proclaim to the world it proved that the United States had made the Mediterranean radioactive? Radio Moscow did say that "weeks have gone by and the bomb is still in the sea, irradiating the water and the fish." A British Member of Parliament asked the Secretary of State for Foreign Affairs at question time in the House of Commons what advice should be given British tourists planning Spanish vacations "in regard to radiation danger from the U.S. nuclear bomb recently located in those coastal waters." Mr. Walter Padley replied for the British Government, "I am advised that there is no indication that [the accident]... resulted in any present or prospective risk to holiday makers." In Mexico City 400 anti-Franco Spanish exiles held a meeting to denounce the existence of foreign bases in Spain and sent a protest to the United Nations demanding its "intervention in this affair." Spanish workers demonstrated in front of the American consulate in Frankfurt, Germany.

On February 16 the Soviet Ministry of Foreign Affairs formally summoned U.S. Ambassador Foy Kohler. He hurried through the frozen streets to be handed a heated memorandum. The Russians said the United States had broken its commitments under the 1963 nuclear test-ban treaty. "It is common knowledge," the note said, "that the most important purpose of this treaty was to prevent radioactive contamination of the atmosphere, outer space, and water of our planet. However, the southern coast of Spain and also the sea expanses washing it are now subjected to radioactive contamination from U.S. nuclear weapons.... U.S. statesmen have more than once mentioned the danger of outbreak of war as a result of miscalculation or incident, but flights by U.S. bombers carrying nuclear weapons are fraught with just such a danger. The Soviet government has more than once warned the United States against the hazards connected with flights of bombers carrying nuclear weapons." The note demanded an immediate end of all such flights "beyond the boundaries of national frontiers." It was a demand that not only would put SAC out of the air-alert business, but disrupt Nato's defenses and disorganize a large part of the U.S. atomic defense program. American planes do carry bombs as a precaution against surprise attack. They also ferry all kinds of nuclear weapons ranging from missiles to short-range atomic artillery, to allies and U.S. forces stationed abroad.

The next day Soviet Ambassador Semyon Tsarapkin arose in the gold-and-sepia ceilinged Council Chamber where the Disarmament Conference was wrangling in Geneva and read out the main points of the Russian memorandum. He added solemnly that "a densely populated Mediterranean area is now in grave danger." The Polish delegate stood to voice "full support" for the Soviet demand that the entire conference issue an "urgent appeal" for an end to such flights and the elimination of all foreign bases. The American delegate, William C. Foster, answered that the charges were false and the Russians were simply making a propaganda play by introducing the subject at Geneva without waiting for the United States reply to their note. On February 25 Kohler went back to the Soviet Ministry with an American note pointing out that "no nuclear weapon test, no nuclear explosion of any kind, and no radioactive pollution of the sea were involved in the unfortunate accident over the coast of Spain. Consequently, there is no question of a 'violation' or of 'actions in conflict with' the test-ban or other treaties." The United States found it "not surprising that the government of the U.S.S.R. is opposed to military security measures undertaken in defense against the threat of its armed power, or that it should attempt to limit or reduce such defense. It is, however, a matter of deep regret that the Soviet Union should be willing to distort the meaning of international treaties to suit the purpose of a propaganda campaign to that end. . . ."

They were the crocodile tears of horny diplomatic custom on both sides. But the propaganda was having its effect. Further, Washington and Moscow were eyeing each other with particular unease at the time because of the escalating war in Vietnam. Every clue to Russian intentions about relations with the United States was being carefully analyzed. There was no telling whether serious new trouble lay ahead, and no telling what might be used as an excuse for the opening of a new East-West crisis. If the queazy détente in Soviet-American relations were going to harden back into cold war, a lost H-bomb in Europe would obviously be a handy weapon for Moscow. The State Department watched and waited nervously.

It wasn't only what people said. Columnist Art Buchwald had another version of what might soon be happening at the Geneva conference. He satirized a certain real danger. According to his transcript of the awesome moment, four surfers walked into the grand chamber and told the Russian delegate, "Move over, Charlie. We're a major power."

"'What is the meaning of this?' the chairman says. 'Who are you people?'

"'We're members of the Black Feet Surfing and Nuclear Club. You can't ignore us any more. We've got the bomb.'...

"'Ya, see,' one of the kids says, 'Morty and I were out skin diving off the coast of Spain two weeks ago and we found the hydrogen bomb that was lost. Morty was for setting it off right away just to see what kind of bang it would make, but I said the bomb really belongs to the club and we should all decide what to do with it.'"

Buchwald's surfers had a lot of super notions, but they finally decided that instead of popping off the people who bugged them, they would take their bomb to Geneva and make a deal. The argument went on endlessly. But when the pointed threat was made that "You either take us in the club or we join France and Red China and go it alone," both the American and Russian ambassadors scurried off to consult their governments about concessions.

"'Well, don't take too long,' one of the kids says. 'This Geneva hangup is a drag.'"

It wasn't quite surfers that State and the Pentagon and the AEC worried about, but the prospect of any other country's finding the bomb became more of a nightmare and less of a gag as the search dragged on. It would be bad enough if the bomb stayed lost. There was a bundle of horrors conceivable if anyone else ever found it. It was of very recent design. The experts of a nuclear power, such as the Soviet Union, could learn a great deal that the United States wanted to keep secret for the most urgent reasons of national security if they could inspect it. "I can tell you I would love to get my hands on a Russian weapon," one of the American experts said by way of explaining cautiously what it might be worth. The experts of a non-nuclear power could learn even more, although, as the AEC's Dr. Gordon Dunning put it, they would have to go about dissecting it "the way porcupines make love, very tenderly," if they found the bomb and wanted to use it as a model. The plutonium itself was of great value, much harder to acquire now than the knowledge of how to make an unsophisticated bomb. Plutonium, Dunning cracked, "can't be made out of strawberry jam." The point had been reached in the world where not secrecy but the difficulty and cost of producing the new element were the main barriers to emergence of new atomic powers. It no longer seemed so hilariously absurd that some version of the Buchwald-*Thunderball* notion of nuclear blackmail might be practiced or, perhaps worse, that some small country under an uncontrollably impulsive leader might get hold of 1,000,000 tons of firepower and try to finish off a long-standing quarrel with its neighbor at one blast.

As the difficulties became increasingly, titanically clear, it also became clear that at the least the United States had to be absolutely certain no one else could find the bomb if it failed. And yet, the consequences of failure would be a painful national setback. The Spaniards began to receive evidence that the consequences of failure could be a national disaster.

Paris-Jour presented another bomb sensation to its public. Under the headline, "Yes, the bomb in Spain could have exploded and THIS IS WHAT WOULD HAVE HAPPENED," the tabloid carried a map. It showed in concentric circles the area of total destruction, fire and partial destruction, and fatal radioactivity covering southeastern Spain and part of Morocco. The area of "great radioactive danger" was shown to include all of Spain, most of southern France, and a large chunk of Africa. Beyond that, the map read, there was a danger of contamination in all directions. Sub-headlines highlighted articles about "A Terrifying Disaster" and "24,000 Years of Mortal Danger from the 'Strayed' Plutonium." The paper also thoughtfully provided "A Hope for Those Who Are Atomized" in an article saying that the Curie Institute in Paris was the one European center capable of treating victims of nuclear accidents.

The information was accurate enough. If there had been a thermonuclear explosion, heat, blast, and radioactivity probably would have killed tens of thousands of people—depending on the altitude of the bomb burst and where the people happened to be at the moment that it happened. The cave dwellers in the region would have been the most protected, but they would have been exposed to disease and slower death from contamination of their food and water even if they escaped the period of maximum fall-out in the air. Depending on the winds and whether or not rain fell while contaminated clouds were passing by, people in a much larger area, including a large arc of Western Europe, might have received radiation doses sufficient to cause cancer. And quite probably, although again it was a matter of the altitude of explosion and how much dirt was drawn up into the fireball, the contamination level of the whole atmosphere would have been increased as it has been after every atmospheric bomb test.

There was no nuclear explosion, and therefore no fall-out of radioactive fission products whose characteristics are more lethal than those of plutonium and uranium. But for many people the distinction was blurred, and the apocalypse seemed to have struck next door, or to have come so near to striking that the effects were almost the same.

The Madrid government got hold of a handbill that was starting to be widely circulated in Paris. It read, "WATCH OUT! The soil in Spain is radioactive! No Spanish fruits or vegetables on your table! No vacations in Spain!" There was no signature, no identification of who was responsible for the alarm, but the Spanish Ministry of Tourism received an avalanche of notices from tourist agencies that people were canceling their summer reservations in Spain. Just under half of the 14,000,000 tourists who had gone to Spain the previous year were French. West Germany, Britain, and Portugal, where the scare was also spreading, had sent a million each. Spain had earned a billion dollars from its tourist industry in 1965, and that and exports of fruit and vegetables to northern Europe accounted for almost all its foreign exchange earnings. Those two items were the nourishment that was reviving a Spanish economy stricken in the Civil War and moribund for a generation. And it was economic revival that held the main promise of gradual Spanish emergence from isolation, of gradual transition to a modern and perhaps democratic state. The United States had accepted a certain responsibility for Spain in the base agreements, and it was a lost American bomb that seemed to threaten all the country's hopes.

The small item that crystallized for Ambassador Duke the imminence of an economic-political blow was a secret telegram from American Ambassador George McGhee in Bonn. McGhee reported that German customs inspectors had tested shipments of vegetables arriving from Spain and had found no trace of radioactivity. Duke read word that these unusual checks were being made as a warning that nothing said so far had succeeded in reversing the spread of fear. Manuel Fraga Iribarne, the Spanish Minister of Tourism, told the Ambassador he had dispatched his top assistant to Paris to see what could be done about reassuring tourists. Juan de

Arespacochaga y Felipe, a towering, gracious Basque who
headed the Directorate of Tourism, held a meeting with some
French journalists and the managers of the main travel agencies in Paris.

"Can you eat fish? Can you eat vegetables in Spain?"
they asked him. "How can people get to Málaga and
Torremolinos if they have to go through the danger zone?"

"I have nine children," he answered patiently. "I love
them. They depend on me. I was there in the area just
recently, working on our big new plans."

"Yes, we understand," one Frenchman said. "But what I
want to know is exactly how high is the degree of radioactivity?"

That was too much. "Exactly the same as in the Bois de
Boulogne," Arespacochaga snapped.

But the mission failed. The cancellation rate went on
increasing. Fraga was growing frantic. Something dramatic
and visible had to be done to prove there wasn't a real
danger. A new government-owned hotel, the Parador de los
Reyes Católicos, had just been completed on the beach below
Mojácar, a few miles down the coast from Palomares. The
chain of Paradors was part of the government's tourism drive,
a program of using public funds to lead the way for private
investment in areas that businessmen had proved slow to
develop on their own. Almería province was a scheduled
target for a general public development program which, the
government hoped, would break ground for a wide crop of
private projects. Fraga wanted to open the Mojácar Parador
with ceremonious fanfare that would give the program a good
publicity send-off. The tourist season would begin in April
and he was eager to have the Parador launched and running
by then, but the opening had been postponed repeatedly
because the American search fleet and the Air Force tent city
were just the kind of backdrop that could kill prospective
business. Fraga kept pressing Duke with the idea of going
ahead with the ceremony and hoping nobody would mention
what was going on next door. Duke kept answering that a
demonstrative première was a good way to show that the area
had returned to normal and tourists were warmly welcome,
but that it would boomerang if it were attempted before life
along the coast really was normal. The pressure for doing
something was irresistible. Both of them fished furiously for
ideas.

There was no denying that the Palomares zone was still overwhelmed by an operation unique in history. At Camp Wilson, the long hours, the isolation, the tedium of the search and its nervous urgency were beginning to wear on everybody. The Air Force did what it could to cheer itself up. By then the search groups had been organized to units of 25 men. They christened themselves—Hopper's Stoppers, Meredith's Marauders, Finkel's Farmers were some of the names they emblazoned on patrol banners—and they made rock mosaic porches to give their tents a faint air of home. One canard rustled around that a GI from Germany who was shipped in to help run the mobile laundry had found the bomb and hidden it under his bunk because he couldn't bear the thought of leaving the Palomares sunshine until the winter field exercises had ended in snowy, fogbound Germany.

A few of the officers who were allowed out of Camp Wilson had picked up "boinas," the black berets of the region, and the berets became a mad fad among the airmen. The complete boina stocks of shopkeepers in all the nearby towns were bought out, replenished, and bought out again. Someone bought one for General Wilson, pinned two stars on it, and thereby made the black beret official search headgear. A special patch was designed for men who had been in the Palomares Theater of Operations. It showed the red mountains, the white Air Force stars, the blue sky pierced by a yellow broken arrow, "the symbol of the condition that requires our presence," as the Air Force memo put it. All SAC generals have code names. Wilson's code was Warner, and the patch memorialized that, too, with the inscription "Warner's Warriors." Col. Carl Payne indulged his fancy for a few other morale boosters. One was a formal presentation of the "Order of the Optike" to Airman First Class Philip A. Durbin who found the KC-135 boom nozzle, a key bit of debris that had eluded days of intensive search. The order was a tin-can lid, and the accompanying citation said that Durbin had "brought great credit and distinction upon both Clean-Shaven and Stubble-Faced Searchers alike. He is hereby entitled to wear said medal for ever and ever and ever so that all may know of his great heroics. Certified unofficial as hell." Similar awards of a painted overcoat button and a plastic spoon were made for other useful achievements. Lieut. Charles A. Rajczi got the "Order of the Purple Knee." In Madrid the effort to keep up spirits found a different expression. Night-club singers popularized a hard-beat song called "La Bomba, yé yé."

Everybody was talking about the lost bomb. There was still no hard news about what had really happened. The first full disclosure came in a brilliant, highly accurate series of articles by Howard Simons in the Washington *Post*. They were cabled immediately to Madrid where Duke had been negotiating unhappily for weeks in an effort to get agreement on an offical Spanish-American statement about the whole accident. The Spanish government still refused to permit publication of any details on the grounds that information would only increase the danger of uncontrollable panic in the country. But the Spanish government was not so monolithic as it seemed. Duke had advised Washington that nothing could be said without Madrid's approval at the risk of causing further strains in Spanish-American relations. When Fraga read the Simons pieces, however, they were quietly passed to Dr. Otero of the JEN and ministers concerned with the economy. The Embassy was stupefied when, at the end of February, it read in all the Spanish papers an Otero interview explaining that there had been plutonium contamination, giving some details, and reporting that the cleanup operation was nearing completion. It seemed a mean trick to the American officials who had been fending off infuriated American correspondents in hopes of working out a joint statement with Spain. They did not realize until later that the only way Fraga, who was also Minister of Information, could get a declaration of public reassurance past the veto of the military leaders of his own government was to take everybody by surprise. What they thought was double-dealing by Madrid rankled the Embassy officials for a long time, but they sent urgent word to Washington that there was no longer any reason to wait on Spanish endorsement of a bilateral communiqué. On March 1 the Pentagon and the State Department finally issued the first official American summary of the Palomares incident. By then public strains and private tempers of officials had gone too far for it to be of real help in easing nerves. Behind scenes, civilians and military in each government snapped and fumed at each other; Air Force and Navy cooperated but had more and more trouble suppressing bitter flashes.

The hidden chips on official shoulders added to the delicacy of the task. The problem of public opinion and its effects on the Spanish economy had become simply unbearable. Fraga called Duke again and said Camp Wilson and Geiger counters or no, something had to be done at once to show the world that Palomares, and Almería province, and Spain were safe to visit. The Ambassador was still convinced that photographs and reports of the scene as it was at Palomares would hardly help. What was needed was a dramatic gesture. When he got the idea, he checked once more with the atomic energy people. Then he made the proposal to Fraga.

They set Tuesday, March 7, as the day. All the press was notified, with plenty of time for the photographers and TV technicians to get there with equipment. Duke flew down to the coast the night before with his vivacious blond wife Robin and his children Marilú and Dario. Fraga arranged to follow early the next morning with his family. The Minister planned to make a speech at the Parador and tour the immediate region, with a special visit to Palomares. Duke was not sure whether he planned to join in the day's main act, but the Ambassador decided to go ahead anyway.

At nine-thirty that morning he appeared on the beach in front of the Parador with the children in a new kind of diplomatic uniform—bathing suits. "Moose" Donovan had gotten into his trunks, too. So had Bill Walker, the Embassy's Minister Counselor who had a bad cold and had to admit people might say he had radiation sickness if he came down with pneumonia. A number of the newspapermen, as ready to shiver for their craft as Duke was for diplomacy, were also dressed for the great swim-in. Robin Duke appeared in an elegant woollen country suit. That was not faintheartedness, it had been decided the night before when a last-minute hitch nearly ruined the show. On the plane down from Madrid, General Donovan broke the bad news to the Ambassador.

"You won't like it," he said. "There's an American movie actress, Anne Baxter, on location somewhere in Almería. She wants to come over with a bunch of starlets and get in the picture. Apparently she got on to Fraga and he told her sure, the more the merrier."

That was perhaps the coldest moment of the plunge for Duke. The bathing-beauty act he was about to perform was a calculated risk, but it would obviously be ruined if it were taken over as an off-Hollywood publicity stunt. He considered calling the whole thing off. That night the Ambassador appealed to General Montel.

"Don't worry," the General said. "I'm in charge of who comes here and who doesn't." They agreed that no ladies, but absolutely no ladies, would be allowed to take part in the show. The actresses stayed down on the Spanish range where they were making a Western. That was good, because it was enough of a circus as it was.

Impressed by the presence of Very Important Persons, a waiter from the Parador dressed in white tie and tails and followed the guests down to the edge of the water. He carried a trayful of glasses and a good-sized bottle of cognac. Even in the south of Spain the March mornings are chilly and the water is downright cold. Then they all plunged in, Duke with a rubber cap of the sort Australian life-guards wear. Tim Towell, Duke's aide, worried when he saw the Ambassador thrashing well out to sea. He wasn't exactly keen on a long swim himself but he was, as usual, ruled by his sense of duty and hurried out to be alongside if needed. But nobody got cramps or a sudden paralysis. Duke bounced out of the water and gamely announced for television that he had gone for colder swims in Long Island Sound in July. It was sheer diplomacy. Everybody else was freezing, but they made all the pictures before they wrapped themselves in towels and raced back to the Parador for a hot bath and clothes to suit the weather.

The next thing on the day's program was the Fraga speech and the dashing tour of villages. The reception was hectic. Palomares villagers pressed around the official caval-cade with banners saying "We need tourism" and "Welcome Minister Fraga and Mr. Ambassador." All the local people seemed to have forgotten the bomb in the excitement of being recognized at last by the top echelons in Madrid who held the development purse strings. It turned out to be won-derfully gay. That perhaps inspired Fraga who had not shown up for the morning swim. Duke was horrified when, on arriving at Camp Wilson, he suddenly noticed the Spanish Minister running into General Montel's tent and running out a minute later in his bathing suit, headed straight for the water. The children were with him, but all their suits, still soaking, were back at the Parador. It wasn't exactly the Battle of the Bathers but it seemed to be a skirmish and the Ambassador was determined not to let the United States be dried out of its share of the only good dramatic notice the incident had yet produced. There were many frogmen on the beach. Towell tore down to the tent they used as a bathhouse.

"Any of you fellows got a swim suit?" he asked breathlessly. A diver yanked off the one he was wearing for the good name of the nation. Duke popped into a tent, stripped off his diplomatic dark blue worsted, and made it into the water while the Minister was still cavorting. They came out of the sea together, grinning.

The photographs were on front pages around the world next morning. Furthermore, although it was barbed with a certain amount of jest here and there, the point took. The *Sun*, in London, added to its report an underwater cartoon showing a pair of wiggling human legs and a shark saying to her mate, "Well, then, it's perfectly safe, dear. That's the American Ambassador." A Madrid paper ran alongside the ministerial cheesecake a cartoon showing a pair of chorus girls and an eager agent telling the Minister of Information's secretary, "I want to give the Minister some more ideas I have on the subject of bathing-suit pictures. . . ." The *Times* of London had some sober fun with it all. "The example set by the Ambassador and the rest ought to prove far more persuasive than any amount of written or spoken reassurances," it editorialized. "American diplomatists are used to demonstrating that American wines are drinkable by drinking them. It is a new extension of their duty to show that waters are safe by bathing in them. . . . Mr. Duke has set a precedent which some of his colleagues are likely to take a rather jaundiced look at. Supposing a bomb is reported missing off Norway? In the winter? Perhaps in such cases the job could be suitably left to the Naval Attaché." The Italian press said, "We think Lollobrigida would have looked better in the role."

When Dario Duke, aged eight, returned to school next day he played radioactive tag with his schoolmates. "I'll touch you and you'll get it," he shouted gleefully as he chased them around the yard. Marilú, a wide-eyed, pig-tailed, sweet-voiced eleven, told her classmates earnestly that of course she wouldn't be sick although the water had been cold. It was great fun, she confided, especially racing around the countryside in the parade of cars.

There was a giggle in it for almost everyone, and although the problem *was* serious, that helped. "It did relieve some of the tension and gloom," Duke said later. After that, there was much less of an air of catastrophe in public comments on the lost bomb. The Mayor of Palomares was relaxed enough to tell people that he was going to write the Minister not to bother about developing tourism for the area, "just get the Americans to build an air base here and we'll all do fine."

Official Washington, following the secret search reports day by day, saw no grounds for cheer. The cost of the operation was becoming astronomical. Nobody ever figured it out exactly; it depended whether the pay of airmen and sailors who had to be paid anyway was counted and how much of the special maintenance of equipment should be chalked up to the Broken Arrow. Some said that counting everything it was getting up to $70 million and worked out at about $1 million a day. The Air Force flew 900 sorties in support of the Palomares operation. In addition to the bomber, the tanker, the seven crewmen killed and the bombs, it had lost a C-124 transport and its entire crew. The plane crashed in the Sierra Nevada when it was ferrying buses to Camp Wilson to help speed up the land search. The Navy had some 3,000 men and a lot of ships tied up, and the dozen private contractors who supplied technicians and equipment were expensive.

While the rest of the world was chortling over the Ministerial-Ambassadorial swim-in, the U.S. government quietly assembled a committee from all the departments involved. It was called the Search Evaluation Team. Admiral Swanson was in charge. The experts from Navy, the Air Force, the AEC, and State were told to prepare their views on the cost and desirability of searching indefinitely versus the cost to the United States of calling off the search and admitting failure. Everybody knew it would be bad for the most advanced technology in the world to throw up its hands and say, "We know how to make H-bombs, but we don't know how to find them when we lose one." The question was how bad, and how long was it worth forestalling what might well be an inevitable admission anyway. The committee's first meeting was scheduled for March 16. It was going to be terribly depressing, but sooner or later the decision might have to be taken. The government considered it was as well to collect the facts and figure out the worst beforehand. Just as quietly, the Embassy began to prepare the Spanish government.

"How much longer do you think now?" a Spanish official asked Bill Walker. "The suspense is becoming unbearable."

"We can't tell," the diplomat answered. "It's terribly difficult."

"But of course you'll find it," the Spaniard said heartily. "Maybe it won't be before the tourist season starts, which will make a huge difference. But you're bound to get it soon. You've got the best equipment in the whole world."

"You should realize," Walker said, "that we may never get it. It could just stay there forever."

11

THE FIND

"It isn't like looking for a needle in a haystack," Admiral Guest said. "It's like looking for the eye of a needle in a field full of haystacks in the dark." Almost every day there were false clues and false alarms. The divers kept bringing up oddly shaped bits of debris, and the weapons experts, busily examining some crater or unusual furrow on a hilltop, were rushed to the beach by helicopter to see if it was part of the bomb. Once it was an engine starter. Once it was the urinal from the KC-135. The work progressed feverishly in the shallow water and the areas of deeper water where the remote-control cameras and echo sounders could operate without too much interference from terrain. But it was a month before the equipment and the men and the essential charts could be assembled to start a really organized search of the more rugged depths. Even then it was only possible because of an earlier disaster. It took the loss of the nuclear submarine *Thresher* in April, 1963, with 129 men aboard, to drive home the realization that the United States was venturing into an element where it had no capacity to work and only a scrap of knowledge. As a result, the Navy launched a Deep Sea Submergence Program. It was to run to 1971 at a total cost of $300 million, including design and production of *NR I,* a nuclear research sub able to operate far below the few hundred feet that is the limit for ordinary submarines, a rescue system for crews sunk in deep water, a salvage system for ships up to a thousand tons at depths up to a thousand feet, a salvage system for small objects at much greater depths, and a man-in-the-sea research program to enable men to work in the earth's hidden spaces as they are learning to do in outer space. Only because of the effort stimulated by the *Thresher* there were teams and experimental vehicles available for Palomares. But almost everything was new. Nothing had been tried in such conditions.

As Cdr. Noel Petree, a cruiser officer who looked like a long, cool drink of beer, put it, "There was no cook-book solution. Nobody could say this is the way you do it, we did it that way before." The novelty heightened the tensions. From the shore, the ships seemed to sit idly in the waves. But the navigation problem was harder than crossing a dozen seas. They had to steam constantly to anchor, turning their engines just fast enough to hold against sudden squalls and tides crossed by current, not so fast that they would overshoot, drag, smash valuable equipment, and possibly collide. One day a huge sea came up so unexpectedly that the U.S.S. *Albany* found it impossible to lift its boats from the water. The *Albany* was the cruiser which came to replace the *Boston* when its Mediterranean tour had ended and it was needed by another fleet. All the boats were down, filled with men huddling unprotected against the driving rain and hammering waves. The *Albany's* commander, Capt. Jack L. Wohler, ordered them to tie up astern in a long string like ducklings trailing an irate mother, and they had to ride out the night steaming constantly to their moorings so as not to be hurtled at each other. Packages of wide-awake pills, hot soups, and rain slickers were sent down the string on pulley lines. The boats were caught by the storm at three in the afternoon. It was eight-thirty the next morning before the sea had calmed enough for the exhausted men to pull themselves up a rope ladder from the *Albany's* stern. Keeping track of the people scuttling from one ship in the fleet to another was an intricate communications problem. Like the two Air Force Colonel Paynes, there were M and M—Lieut. Cdr. Dewitt "Red" Moody, who was in charge of all the divers, and Lieut. Cdr. J. B. Mooney, a submariner and former bathyscaphe pilot who had found the *Thresher* and was in charge of the special deep-sea equipment at Palomares. The radiomen in the flagship communications room learned to shudder when they had to reach one of the two with the Admiral glowering as they worked. The message kept going to the wrong "M" and Guest, as one of the seamen said, "would blow every time."

Once in a while part of a mine-sweeper crew would come to the cruiser for "liberty." Weeks went by without shore leave. The men were aboard longer in that spot just off the coast than they had ever been at sea at one stretch, and the chance to go to the big ship's PX, use its library, just stretch legs on its decks, took the place of a day off. And the cruiser had a barber, the one amenity which the rest of the fleet could envy the Air Force. On the beach, a barber from a nearby village had set up shop in Camp Wilson. Or, rather, he set up a crate at first and later had his barber's chair hauled down and installed on the sand. He worked all day with his hat on, giving a shave, a haircut, or shave and a haircuit, for 10 pesetas, 17 cents, because it was easier than having a price list. The men at sea griped some, but they had little time for it. There was too much work for anyone to get more than four hours' sleep at a time.

When it had become clear that the bomb simply would not discover itself by some simple device, the need for precise mapping of the bottom was the first urgency. A plaster model, made when the tedious task had been completed, showed a tortured terrain, as jagged and precipitous as the land. The dry Almanzora must indeed have been a great river once, its mouth made a great canyon far out to sea with steep ridges and gullies on all sides. In recent geological times the sea level had evidently been much lower and there were even indications of a drastic climate change. Once, apparently, the barren hills of Palomares had been a rain forest. Navy geologist Ray Smith flew from Port Hueneme, California, to make thorough checks of the underwater soil and determine how likely it might be that the bomb had penetrated and buried itself deep in silt. That was the good side of the bad news of the terrain. It was rocky in some places, spongy or muddy in others, but nowhere was it so yielding that a sunken bomb would sink down to oblivion. There was assurance that if only someone could get close enough to the right place, the bomb could be seen. But apart from the divers, whose heaviest equipment would not permit them to go below 300 feet, only the men in the three little submarines could go to see.

Cubmarine, the little yellow fish, picked out efficiently the objects that surface sonar contacted down to about 1,200 feet. Beyond that there was too little light. At 1,800 feet all trace of sunlight disappears and the dark becomes as complete as at the bottom of a deep coal mine. Its weak motors

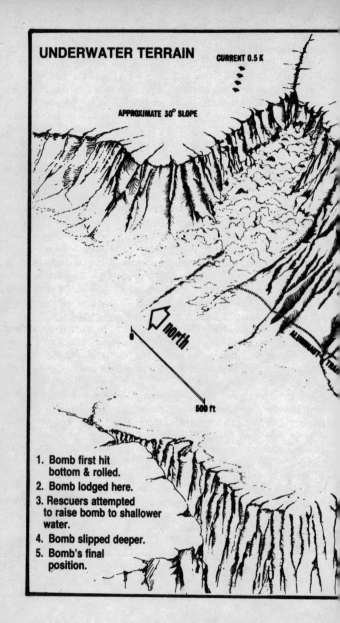

UNDERWATER TERRAIN

CURRENT 0.5 K

APPROXIMATE 30° SLOPE

north

500 ft

AIRCRAFT TRAIL

1. Bomb first hit bottom & rolled.
2. Bomb lodged here.
3. Rescuers attempted to raise bomb to shallower water.
4. Bomb slipped deeper.
5. Bomb's final position.

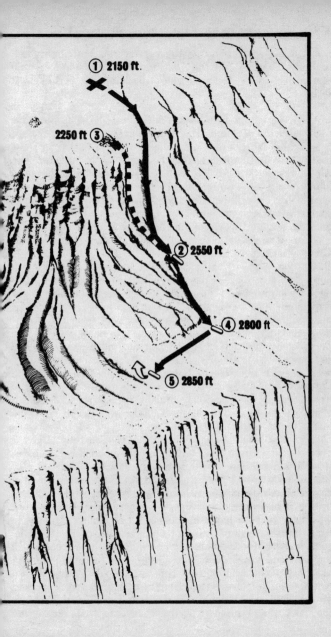

① 2150 ft.

2250 ft ③

② 2550 ft

④ 2800 ft

⑤ 2850 ft

could not give *Cubmarine* the capacity for both lights and mobility. That left only the *Alvin* and the *Aluminaut* for visual search in *Alpha I*, the area where the bomb seemed likeliest to be.

The directors had been notified on the first Saturday night after the accident. The *Aluminaut* was in Florida where it searched the deeps for minerals, wrecks, fossils, to show that wealth and knowledge can be found far underwater. The *Alvin* was at Otis Air Force base, Massachusetts, where it found haven in an unused hangar for winter repairs before its second big experimental mission. It was to be loaded on its special catamaran, a clumsy but marvelously equipped home for it at sea, and leave for the Bahamas on February 1.

Dr. Earl Hays, a comfortable, calm professor who was Chief Scientific Assistant at the Woods Hole Oceanographic Institution, was sitting in his garden staring at the gray sea and "having a nice drink of rum and cider" after an afternoon's weeding and lawn-mowing when the call came. It was a question, not a command, and he said he'd have to talk it over with his people, but he had no doubt from the beginning that the *Alvin* would have to go help search. The prospect was not cheering. A great deal of preparations had been made for the mission in the Tongue of the Ocean, a long, peculiar deep off the Bahamas, and the *Alvin* was still in the toddler stage of its life. It had made only one series of experiments, the previous summer, which showed that it could get to its design depth of 6,000 feet, that it could be maneuvered, and that its crew could survive. Besides, as its chief pilot William Rainnie pointed out when they talked it over next day, from the information they had the Palomares mission looked "like it will be fraught with no success at all." Bill Rainnie was a big, weathered, ex-Navy submariner, a handsome outdoorsman with deep-water eyes, who was quick to say "it gives me the creeps to be away from the sea," but who had come to have the same kind of feeling against the brass-button persnicketiness of a military way of life. What he considered important was engineering, absolute precision of his tools and instruments, the flair of ideas, and the integrity of a task, not regulations. He had left the Navy for an engineering job, chafed there at industrial bureaucracy, worked for the National Academy of Sciences in land-bound Washington, D.C., and jumped at the chance to help create the

Alvin. In a sense, he had been the little submarine's wet nurse, fondly and rigorously following every step of its growth, testing to his rigid specifications every bit of what went into it. He had his heart set on proving it in the Tongue of the Ocean.

Rainnie and his crew of two men began getting ready for Palomares the following day. There was, after all, no real choice of weather to answer the Navy's appeal, and the Air Force was ordered to fly them to Spain. The *Alvin* had to be dismantled to get it on the air freighter. Its batteries, its oxygen supplies, its air-purifying chemicals, its power van, all had to be sorted out and crated for shipment. The submarine, minus its conning tower and lift propellers, was boxed, bolted to a special skid built at the air base, and loaded. It took two planes to carry the men and all their essential equipment. On February 5 they started unpacking and putting everything back together again at the Navy base at Rota, Spain. Two days

ALVIN

later they thought they were ready for a test dive, but they never got below sea level. The plane ride had loosened the battery screws. Water got in and shorted the power. It took two more days to make repairs. The *Alvin* made its first dive in the Eastern Hemisphere on February 9, more than three weeks after the accident. They went only 40 feet down into the harbor, stayed submerged for an hour and twenty minutes, and came up pronouncing everything in order.

The *Aluminaut*, at 81 tons and 51 feet long, was too much for the Air Force. It had been raced across the Atlantic in the U.S.S. *Plymouth Rock*, throbbing all the way through the wintry ocean at 20 knots. They had just arrived in Rota when the *Alvin* was ready to go, a disappointment for Rainnie and his crew, who felt in competition with the only other deep-sea submarine in existence. Both vessels derived from studies made by Dr. Ed Wink of the Library of Congress. The Navy was going to pay for the *Aluminaut*, Reynolds Aluminum Co. was to build it, and Woods Hole was to operate it. But there had been red tape and angry arguments. Reynolds went ahead on its own. The Office of Naval Research finally decided to try a smaller project with Woods Hole, and that was the birth of the *Alvin*.

They rode through the Straits of Gibraltar together on the *Plymouth Rock* and joined Task Force 65 on February 10. They were to be transferred to the U.S.S. *Fort Snelling*, an LSD (Landing Ship Dock) whose tail gate enclosed a well where the fragile craft could be lifted in and out of the water with the ship's sturdy sides as protection. But they couldn't maneuver into the well that day. A storm whipped wind and seas so high that they had to wait overnight at moorings just to get back to the *Plymouth Rock*. The Decca navigation system on shore was blown down. It was a miserable night tossing about in the cramped steel sphere that was quarters inside the *Alvin*'s fiber-glass hull, with the rain beating down the conning tower. They had to stay there for twenty-one hours in shorts and T-shirts, freezing slowly. Nor did it help make the submariners feel welcome to Palomares when they reported in for instructions next day and were told that they had brought bad weather. The storm lasted four nail-biting days, with the whole fleet at anchor fighting the churning seas.

They used the time to repair the damage to the *Alvin*, replace the Decca without which the search was virtually in the dark on the surface as well as on the bottom, and to make plans. Admiral Guest had marked out his 1,000-yard squares on the Alpha One area. The Navy experts sent to help him explained what they knew of the *Alvin*'s and the *Aluminaut*'s capabilities. The little sub could maneuver into gullies, hop cliffs, skim ridges like a mountain goat, so it was assigned to the worst part of the area, to the south, starting from the point of impact fixed by the fisherman. The bigger one had a wider sweep of visibility with its six portholes, although they were only four inches across compared to the *Alvin*'s four five-inch holes which gave a little better depth perception. Also, the *Aluminaut* could carry six observers and more equipment. The *Alvin* barely had room for one extra man in addition to the two pilots. The area assigned to the *Aluminaut* was the north side of the circle where the bottom was a little smoother and shallower.

It was Valentine's Day, February 14, when the *Alvin* made its first search dive. Rainnie and Marvin McCamis went as pilots that day and they told copilot Valentine Wilson, who stayed above as their surface commander, that it was his duty to bring them luck on his name day. The sentimental Saint worked no miracle. It was the *Alvin*'s Dive 110, but a frustrating, seemingly pointless experience. "It looks like a long, dry summer," Rainnie said when he got out of the water. They floated down with their system of variable ballast, which moved oil from aluminum spheres, retaining almost as much weight empty as full to collapsible rubber balls which increased or decreased the submarine's specific gravity when filled or emptied. An important part of their job was to measure currents so that the computers could add, for the first time, the element of drag in the water to their calculations of where the bomb might have settled. They bumped the bottom, an unpleasant miscalculation which taught them immediately that the new charts were just not that accurate and that "the old eyeball," in Rainnie's words, was still ahead of electronics. For that matter, the whole operation was a demonstration that in a world whose poets mourned the conquest of man by machine, man was still the master of his own creatures. Rainnie and McCamis did not think of it that way, however. They were not the type to spend time worrying about the diminution of man in the world. They had always spent their lives energetically challenging an enormity of nature with machines they'd made and understood to help redress the balance. Surrounded by salt water they spoke roughly, but that was where they felt at home and alive with confidence.

"Mac" McCamis was also an ex-submariner whose distaste for the Navy way was even more intense than Rainnie's. He hadn't so much education but he had intuition, a passion for sound courage, an equal revulsion for sloppy or foolhardy pretense, and as much readiness to devote himself to what he respected as to rebel without thought of consequences where he felt contempt. He had sharp, clean features, a crew cut, and a sense of relief at useful toil on the sea that escaped him in the complex world of social pressures. He had grown up on an Indiana farm, joined the Navy before Pearl Harbor, and spent the rest of his life in submarines. He loved the sea, the machinery, the roaming, and he wasn't ashamed to express it.

"It's like a race," he said on one relaxed evening, "to make a beautiful piece of machinery run better. There's no end to it. You can always do it. That's why I don't have the military in me to take an order, I guess. If I don't think it's right, I can't do it."

They turned the lights on at 800 feet or so to have a look, and then turned them off again to save power until they neared the bottom. "It's so quiet then," McCamis recalled. "You just want to sit back and dream and watch the shapes and forms, the dim glows and the flashes. There are bright darts, like fireflies, and plankton all the colors of the rainbow."

They watched the "snow" falling upward, the plankton hovering almost stationary in the water which seemed to move up as they descended. It was familiar, a quicker way to judge their rate of descent than looking at the instruments. After the first time they learned to judge how to make a soft landing by looking at the edge of the 20-foot pool of brightness that their headlights cast instead of looking directly down, so that they could see the shadows of their own tail and the soil contours. They had gone all the way down before, but never in the Mediterranean. The creatures, to their surprise, were not so different from the western Atlantic. There were white and bright red lobsters, shrimps that swarmed like insects, bigger shrimps with beady black eyes and long blue tentacles that looked to Rainnie like "tiny old men sitting in a two-runner sleigh," brown luminescent pencil fish, chunky hatchet fish. They discovered each time they reached the bottom that they were in a cloud of fish and shrimp. The creatures seemed to have followed them down, perhaps out of curiosity. After a bit the marine life always swam away. They went down 1,800 feet that day and surfaced after six hours for their first return to the well of the *Fort Snelling*.

The *Alvin* had to come out of the water after each dive for inspection, battery recharge, and cleanup. The time it took for men and equipment to get ready for a dive had made the normal maximum schedule two days underwater out of three, and preferably only one dive every other day. For the first time in its life the *Alvin* at Palomares dived day after day without stop until maintenance absolutely required interruption. There was one series of eleven dives without a break. Only high seas that made a launch impossible and essential repairs kept it out of the water. When the sub came up, there were reports to make, charts to study, instructions for the next day's work that kept the men up most of the night. Both the *Alvin* and the *Aluminaut* crews finished about 2 A.M. and were up again at five thirty to get into the water at dawn day after day.

Guest controlled each day's operation, assigning them to points where echo sounders had made contacts that he wanted to have identified. The Admiral always knew what he wanted. Along with his Chief of Staff Captain Horace Page, he kept a tight control on everything, feeling strongly that efficiency required absolute centralization of command and security required telling no one what anyone else was doing. He did not often see the submarine crews, but when he did, he did his best to make sure they understood that civilians or not, they were under his command. They did not like it. They felt they knew better than he what the underwater work demanded and were certainly no less eager than he to achieve success. Guest leaned heavily for advice on Ray Pitts, the representative of Ocean Systems Inc., which had contracted for *Cubmarine* and as consultant for the research. Pitts was an old friend of several ranking admirals and he was also named representative of the Navy's director of salvage to help coordinate the operation. His two hats, as spokesman for a contractor and for the salvage bureau, were never clearly described to the other civilian advisers and they came to resent his interference. Some felt that his influence served as a buffer between the underwater technicians and the Admiral, instead of bringing the commanding officer closer to the problems of the strange new equipment and the men who operated it. They did not understand that Pitts had an official responsibility as well as the contract obligation. It was another factor for confusion and bruised feelings.

In any case, the surface-to-bottom navigation was chancy at best. The submarines were never altogether certain of their position. That was one of the technical needs which the operation illuminated. Since Palomares, work has been done on trying to improve a way of fixing points in the trackless dark beneath the seas.

One day the *Aluminaut* wandered out of the square that Guest had set for it, following what seemed to be a promising picture on its underwater sonar. Its captain Arthur Markel was called to the flagship that night for a dressing-down. Like the *Alvin* men, Markel was ex-Navy and sensitive about it. He was a husky pioneer, proud of his competence, and having troubles as it was because he had no spare crew members to give anyone a rest, and no permission from the Admiral to give them a day ashore. A member of the *Aluminaut* crew, a twenty-two-year-old sailor, jumped ship. The Guardia Civil picked him up quickly. Guest fumed, and ordered Markel to see him off on a plane that would take him back to the United States as a forfeiter. Markel took Guest's "Will you see him off?" as a question and decided it would be more useful to pilot his submarine that day, what with one crewman gone already. That got them off to a stiff start. When Markel came, with some satisfaction, to report a find outside the square he had been assigned to control, it went from bad to worse.

"You disobeyed orders," the Admiral raged, his square face going red and his fist pounding. "You went outside the area."

"We didn't go," Markel said through lips held thin to restrain the words that pressed upon his tongue. "We strayed off course, and we found something." It was an important clue, a big piece of the B-52 fuselage. Sighting it in such deep water, so far out to sea, was the first concrete confirmation that heavy debris had indeed been strewn over a long path, that the bomb could well be even farther out.

"You disobeyed," the Admiral repeated. "You're unreliable. If you do it again, we'll have to send you home."

Guest's reaction was partly the effect of nerves on his own temperament, self-conscious, suspicious, assertive with vanity. Partly, it was the way he understood instructions from the high-level team following his work from Washington.

They had sent him a whole group of analysts to record the search each day, impressing on him the importance of keeping complete track of everything so that if the bomb were never found it would be possible to cite what had been done and say with scientific honesty, "We can prove to a 95 per cent certainty that the bomb is not there." When he gave orders, Guest asked for a 99 per cent certainty. Further, once each twenty-four hours, Guest as commander had to report to Washington the progress that had been made and the plans for the next twenty-four hours. "That was the daily moment of truth," one of his officers said later. "It didn't make you feel much good day after day to have to send the message full of where you'd been and what you'd done and then add, no results." The Admiral chose to seek the bomb with a precisely tallied method, eschewing luck and intuition. It seemed to some who watched him that he was operating almost more to prove it wasn't there than to find it. That was a delicate judgment of the subconscious, but it came through to some of the nonnautical civilians so strongly that one said afterward, "I think in his secret heart he was wishing it back on the land, on the Air Force."

In any case, the Admiral certainly strained himself no less than those about him. Once, on one of the few occasions that he went ashore, he brought himself to joke with General Wilson, "Let's trade jobs. You take the sea for two weeks and I'll take the land." Wilson laughed and sympathized. They both had problems.

The unproven, experimental equipment caused some of them. In a year the U.S.S. *Mizar* could have made a quite accurate contour map of the bottom in the search area. But in the meantime, operations had to rely on the less reliable sounders that could work more quickly. One day when the *Aluminaut* was loaded with the shot ballast for a dive to 1,200 feet, it hit hard at 600. The depth chart was that far off. The submarine was terribly heavy and had to slide down a hill, dragging the bottom as it went, to move toward the deeper water where it had been assigned. Dropping the ballast would have had to mean aborting the dive, and Markel was not about to waste a day's work because of somebody else's mistake even though it was hard on his vessel. But when they got down and jettisoned the shot, they found they had no lift. The sub refused to budge. The men's lives could be saved by blasting off the keel, the sub's last safety resort, Markel knew.

Then the sealed cabin, filled with air and crew and machinery, would be buoyant enough to rise although it would be surfacing uncontrolled. But there was no replacement keel in Palomares, and perhaps not even one available at the *Aluminaut*'s home in Richmond, Virginia. So pressing the safety button would have ended the sub's part in the operation. "Pappy" Reynolds, as the crew called the company's owner, had a temper at least as large as his fortune, and he had said, "You find that bomb."

The men did not want to die underwater but they did not want to abandon ship either until they were certain there was no alternative. There was no equipment on the surface that could have hauled them up. It was a time of terror for everybody, including Admiral Guest, who was given the urgent reports of the *Aluminaut*'s peril. Markel figured they were stuck in the mud. He ordered the crew to run in a pack from one end of the cabin to the other, desperately trying to rock the *Aluminaut* free. Finally it shook a little and slowly, very slowly, began to rise. It was a long, painful ascent. Not until they surfaced and hauled the sub out of the water did they discover the danger had been even more acute than they had thought. The downhill slide had scooped huge gobs of mud into the *Aluminaut*'s understructure making it far heavier than it should be for ascent. There would not, of course, have been any way to sluice off the mud underwater although some of it had perhaps fallen as the *Aluminaut* moved upward. It took two days on the deck of the *Fort Snelling* to pry off the sticky dirt and reduce the *Aluminaut* to design weight.

Apart from all the technical problems, the question of how much faith to put in Francisco Simo, the fisherman, kept cropping up. Simo had begun to speak up more and more as the search dragged on, arguing publicly that he could easily go and scoop the bomb up with his nets if only the Navy would permit it. He had a new nickname by then, Paco (short for Francisco) de la Bomba, and since no one else would talk to them, the reporters who flocked to the coast interviewed him one after another, put him on television, spread his words about the world, until the story did seem to resolve itself into The Fisherman and The Bomb. That did not improve Guest's temper. Nonetheless, he began to feel a certain desperation. Quietly, Guest asked Washington whether there would be approval for hiring several boatloads of Spanish fishermen who knew the area well enough to trawl

Guest declared brusquely. The search procedure he had established worked much better in the shallower areas. So he ordered them back each day to another square in the shallower part. It made him very unhappy when he had to tell Washington that the *Alvin* had spent the day revisiting a square with no results and nothing further to cross off on the chart. But sometimes that could not be helped. With only a 20-foot sweep of visibility and a 300-foot error margin for navigation, the *Alvin* could have searched the same square half-a-dozen times without knowing that it had overlooked a spot, perhaps the treasure spot.

Captain Ramirez vouched ardently for the Spaniard. He showed Maydew a 25-peseta coin, the size of a half dollar, and said Simo had often hauled up such elusive salvage from depths of 3,000 or 4,000 feet. The *Alvin* crew never met the fisherman, but they were all deeply impressed by the reports of his testimony and tried hard for permission to concentrate around the area he marked. After all, the Americans told each other, he's very successful as a fisherman. He's made enough to buy two boats. It must be because he knows his craft, his sea, his navigation better than most. Guest never tried to see him. It surprised the Admiral later to be asked why not. He relied on the Air Force interviews, the Maydew interviews, and the reports of his mine-sweeper captains who took Simo out time after time to mark the place once more. The Admiral stuck to his plan of squares and checking up on sonar contacts. It included the area that Simo had pinpointed in any case.

It was on the first of March that the *Alvin* saw the marks on the bottom. Rainnie was on the surface as contact that day. He was so long and bulky that his two copilots had persuaded him it was easier to work the long daily dives without having to worry about tripping over his legs. Wilson, they called him "Willie," was a stumpy man with grizzled hair and hot, dark eyes. He, too, had spent most of his life in Navy submarines. Capt. Frank Andrews, a retired Navy captain who had gone to Task Force 65 as consultant for the underwater operation, was aboard the *Alvin* as observer. He had already noticed that tracks on the bottom made by trawlers, by large fish, by avalanches were clearly distinguishable. It turned out to be a vital observation. Andrews was peering out one porthole, Wilson out the other as McCamis maneuvered.

"I see another track," Wilson said suddenly. "It looks very interesting." He moved aside for Andrews to have a look. They both began to get excited. This was much wider than the trawler tracks, about two feet across, deeper, and it was curved like the trail of a barrel sliding down a muddy hill. They followed it down the side of a cliff, reading off the direction, depth, and position to the surface. Rainnie noticed, when he checked, that they, too, had meandered out of their assigned search square. It was late in the day when they saw the track. A maneuver with currents, a skip around a precipice, threw the submarine off course for a moment and the track was lost. They were at 2,800 feet. The batteries were running low. There was nothing to do but surface and try to find the same spot the next day.

But the next day Admiral Guest sent them off in a different direction. He was not impressed with some scratches on the ground. It could be anything. The *Aluminaut* had seen some ancient cannon balls and pieces of a wrecked Spanish galleon. Centuries of fishing and debris had marked the bottom. The daily report to Washington should show another square covered, Guest felt, not another run over the same difficult, unproductive ground. That might sound inefficient, and the one thing he sought to make clear in every message was that he had tolerated nothing haphazard.

The *Alvin* crew grumbled and swore to each other, but they obeyed. Each night at the strategy meeting on the *Fort Snelling*, however, McCamis and Wilson argued their conviction that the track had been made by the bomb and they should follow it. Cdr. Rhodes Boykin, the operations officer assigned to the *Alvin* by the Office of Naval Research, and Cdr. Roy Springer, the operations officer for the search, were impressed. Each night they went from the *Fort Snelling* to the *Boston* to report on the day's work and to recommend that the *Alvin* look for the track once more the next day. But the Admiral kept reminding them sharply that the task of the submarines was to view and identify the contacts that surface electronics had made. The mine sweepers could move across the water picking up sonar targets much faster than the submarines could search, he said, so it was inefficient to let the subs maneuver on their own pattern. Furthermore, because of the top-to-bottom navigation errors, there was no certainty that what the *Alvin* and the *Aluminaut* crews saw in deep ravines and at the bottom of the cliffs was the same thing the sonar had picked out from the surface. That made it wasteful to wander around the deep parts on a visual search,

Guest declared brusquely. The search procedure he had established worked much better in the shallower areas. So he ordered them back each day to another square in the shallower part. It made him very unhappy when he had to tell Washington that the *Alvin* had spent the day revisiting a square with no results and nothing further to cross off on the chart. But sometimes that could not be helped. With only a 20-foot sweep of visibility and a 300-foot error margin for navigation, the *Alvin* could have searched the same square half-a-dozen times without knowing that it had overlooked a spot, perhaps the treasure spot.

Until the subs had gathered the experience of daily observation, no one had realized how much the underwater ravines could distort, even reverse, deep currents. John Bruce, the careful young oceanographer from Woods Hole who had made studies of the waves, the wind, the water temperatures, and salinity to help in search calculations, understood that assumptions about the currents might be quite wrong. He worked out plans for a dummy drop at the point marked by Simo, simulating the shape and weight of the bomb with parachute attached, to see where the currents would take it and how it might be dragged along the bottom.

The dimensions of the weapon, its exact shape, the kind of trail it might leave had been kept secret from the men who were searching for it. Now they were told, and interrogated, and they insisted that what they heard and what they had seen fitted together. Twelve days later the *Alvin* was transferred to the U.S.S. *Petrel* because ship-to-sub communications on the mine sweeper it was using as surface contact had broken down and the *Petrel* was equipped with underwater telephone. The transfer along with all the necessary supplies was arduous and no dive was scheduled for that day. Free of an assignment, the crew decided to go down anyway and look for the track once more. They found it after a long hunt. Once again it was too late to follow the scent because of dwindling battery power, but this time Commander Boykin was aboard as observer and he confirmed the peculiarity of the groove in the mud. It was quite different from the trawl marks; a bomb would fit it neatly. They went again the next day, cruising the cliff where they had seen it. At one point they saw signs of an avalanche and looked up to realize they were under a 100-foot overhang. The *Alvin* backed away smartly. That was a real danger. Poking around in loose soil could cause a slide that would bury the track, bury the bomb, and quite possibly bury the *Alvin*. They spent seven hours and eighteen minutes submerged, went down to 2,700 feet, and found nothing. But they had won their point that the track was worth keeping after and they were set to look for it again. The following day, March 14, the weather was too rough to get the *Alvin* into the water.

On March 15, two weeks after they had sighted the track for the first time, they made the *Alvin's* Dive 128, the nineteenth dive off Palomares. It was the birthday of McCamis' son Marvin, Jr., and Mac said as they went down, "I think it's going to be my lucky day." By then they knew the area well. Broken tin cans, eggshells, some kind of rag lying on the bottom had become familiar landmarks to show them they were approaching the point they sought. A tape recorder aboard caught all their conversation. The men were too busy driving their submarine, reading off their instruments, keeping watch outside to make a written log until they surfaced. This is how it went on the crucial moments of that day, omitting only the language that soldiers use anywhere but that submariners modestly insist must be reserved for salt water or salt air to echo emptily. McCamis and Wilson were piloting. The observer was Arthur Bartlett of Woods Hole, nicknamed "Mag." The bleeps of the sonar, the shrill purr of the blower circulating air inside the sub, the scratch of the tape, made a rough and sometimes overwhelming background noise as the men spoke. The first words were to Rainnie on the surface:

"This is *Alvin* diving."

"Goodo. Take good care of Mag and don't nit-pick him too much."

Not long after they reached the bottom Wilson spoke to his copilot.

"This looks damned familiar, man... I guess it's just a cliff. Now, look out the window, Mac. Not there, there's nothing over there."

"What the hell is that?"

"You've got it right in front of you now. That's the track. That's it. That's the son of a bitch. I'm sure it is. It's the same one. Don't touch down and get it stirred up so we can't see."

"Yeah, that's it. Okay. I'm going in, willy-nilly."

Wilson was taking pictures with the camera mounted outside the sub. They had learned the danger of stirring up clouds of silt that made a fog too dense to see for more than a few feet, but they had also learned the danger of not sticking closely enough to the track to be sure they wouldn't lose it.

"Better pitch 'em real fast."

"I'm clicking. I don't know what it is, Mac, but there's two tracks that come down here and converge."

"Okay, okay, snap pictures."

"If we hit the son of a bitch, we'll be in great shape. I want to make sure this is it. It sure looks like it."

"That's it, that's it all right."

"Get the hell out of here—060 is the course. Let's get out of here and report. See that groove up there?"

"Okay, I'm steering the thing up."

"Echo, this is *Alvin*. We have found our track. We are reversing course from 060 and going out and set down below it. Over."

There was no answer for several minutes. Perhaps the surface, code name Echo, had not heard.

"Did you read my last?"

This time the answer came. "Roger."

"You got us in reverse now. We're trying to get away from this thing without stirring it up. This is a very steep slope."

McCamis had decided, without discussing it, that there might be a better chance of keeping the track by going backward, watching it out of the front of the *Alvin*. Twice they had tried to follow it forward and failed. The trouble, he felt, was that they couldn't look directly beneath themselves and they overshot, blanking out their own vision.

"I told you I saw the SOB as soon as I saw the bottom."

"That's right."

The voices were taut, almost shrill, a completely different pitch from the sonorous, official voices they used on the telephone to the surface.

"Goddamn it's steep. I'm trying to turn around."

"Okay, you're about 75, 78."

"They told me it was a 10-degree slope!"

"Okay, you're about 90."

There was a burst of laughter as the light on the underwater communication blinked urgently.

"You just tell him to wait. Tell him we're taking soundings. Wait!"

"Echo. We're taking soundings. Wait." And then, in a personal voice again, "He knows what we're trying to do. If we ever get a sight of that monster again..." There was a nervous chuckle.

"We're going down. We're going down fast. It's 100, 130 now."

A hard noise, like the grinding of a broken gear, drowned out the voices for a moment.

"We must have hit a level spot. What have you got?"

"140 feet."

"Okay, I'm going to dive down now. Hold on to your hat."

"I've got to move on this damned course now. Mac, let me know when I'm 060 again."

"150 . . . 120 . . . 075 . . . 070 . . ."

"That's good enough."

"068 . . . 066."

"I've got it now. Move very slowly."

"060 right now."

"Goddamn. I've lost the stinking bottom. Christ. What happened to the bottom?"

"Mark!" The command was a bark. "Mark!"

A very tired voice asked, "What's the depth?"

"2,450." The answer held the tone of exhaustion.

"Echo. This is *Alvin*. The depth is 2,450."

"Roger."

(Twenty minutes later)

"I see something. Oh, it's a reflection on the glass. I can't see through this damned thing no more. . . . Okay, I got the track over on the left again."

"The track?"

"Eyup. That's the baby."

"5-4-3-2-1. Mark!"

There were bleeps, burps, honks, toots on the record at that point. The navigation was not close enough to be reliable. The men checked it by checking the speed of sound on the underwater telephone against their stop watches.

"I'm talking about that gully we . . ."

"5-4-3-2-1. Mark!"

"Christ, this monster bastard!"

"Ouch!"

"I can see the track! I can still see the track. It's swinging to the left. It's heading south now. The track is . . ."

"I can't come too far. I'm running right into the flipping slope here."

"You just made a 90-degree turn."

"I did? . . . Yeah, I'm spinning around 180. . . . Sharp turn to the left now."

"You want me to sonar or anything?"

"Okay, I'll try to come down again."

"We're still awful damn high."

"You meet something different every goddamn day."

"You're coming right into a deep hole."

"Yeah, I know, that ain't the one we want."

"Got to do something about this rudder. . . ."

"I see a slot down there. . . ."

"I'm still in the slot, Mac."

A grave voice intoned, "7-5."

"7-0-0-7-5," answered a husky voice.

There was a long silence. Then, tensely, "We're going higher. We're drifting away from it. . . . I can still see it but I won't be able to much longer if you keep on the way you're going. . . . Better hurry up. I'm losing it."

"How am I doing now?"

"It's on the right-hand side now. . . . Crossed over? . . . No, no, no. You've got to back straight up to get on it. . . . Back up like an SOB. Right rudder down some. . . . Okay, now drive down. . . ."

"I see what looks like a track. It's on that side now."

"I can't be sure."

"I tell you I can see it."

"Echo, this is *Alvin*. Turn down your transmitter gauge slightly." The heavy tones of tedium had crept into the strained voices.

"Coming down . . . coming down."

"About two inches you're going to hit!"

"That looks like a parachute! . . . A chute that's partly billowing."

"Could be!"

"Open up with the pictures."

"Wrong way, Mac."

"If you laid your tail (on the bottom) we could look out the front window."

"It's right underneath me."

"What is it? Can you identify?"

"You know what it looks like? It looks like . . . Get that flipping squid out of the way. You're spitting all over me. I can't see a thing. . . . You can back away, get a better view."

"That's it!"

"That's it! I've seen a lot of parachutes and this is a big SOB!"

"What a big bastard!"

There was a great burst of laughter.

"Let's get some pictures."

"Stand by."

"Start shooting!"

"Right rudder and back down, Mac. I'm going to lose sight of it."

"Am I coming right?"

"Yup. You've got to go down now, Mac. You're too high."

"I'm right at the tip of the flipping parachute. Can you see it yet?"

"That's where the stinking bomb went! Down this gully."

"No. It's going to be under the chute, I think. Let's go up and take a good look."

"I bet it's gone down the gully."

"No. Let's look under the chute first."

"Something sure as hell has fallen down into this gully."

"It's an awful big chute, isn't it."

"It sure is."

"I wish I could reach out this window and pick it up."

"We're on the straps, aren't we?"

"They're straps, yup."

"This is *Alvin*. Don't bother us now, Bill. We'll call you back."

"Take a good look at this one, over the edge. This is where I think the bomb is, right here, right here ahead of you."

"Can you see it?"

"There's something under there."

"See this wreckage right here?"

"Right here?"

"You know what that is, that's a fin! Mac, that's what a fin looks like on a bomb."

"Echo, this is *Alvin*. Bill, get as good a position on us as you possibly can. I think we got a big rusty nail down here. . . . We found a 60-foot parachute and we believe we have a fin of the bomb in sight. It's underneath the parachute."

"Ro-*ger!*"

The code fixed between the *Alvin* and the surface contact for discovery of the bomb was "Benthosaurus." Guest had insisted on using codes because any other vessel in the neighborhood with underwater listening devices could have overheard. But it was one of Dr. Earl Hays' little eccentricities always to carry an old nail in his pocket. He really kept it as a good-luck piece, but he had often told the *Alvin* pilots, "The thing is, you never know when a rusty nail will come in handy." Val Wilson and Rainnie had decided that that provided a better, more relevant code. The words they had agreed on were "Bent Nail." It was the excitement that made Wilson say "Rusty Nail" instead.

Five minutes, ten minutes went by in silence.

"See anything out the window?"

"The bottom, that's all."

"Swing back. Look out where your head is. Ow!"

"I don't know if that's the bomb or not. This is the gully. It must be right."

"We ought to get a bing-bing-bing on that metal bomb out there."

"I'm getting crud right on the front of the screen. I think it rises there and blocks you out."

"We can't stay in this steep SOB. We're *in* the gully and it's on the side of the gully, remember?"

"Depth is 2,550."

"Roger. Give me outside."

"That is the outside corrected reading. Inside reading is 2,500 feet."

"Say it again."

"Outside corrected reading, 2,550. Inside, 2,500."

"Roger."

"It ain't in this gully."

"We didn't drive that far down."

"This is Echo to *Alvin*. Your depth is 2,640, outside uncorrected. Repeat, uncorrected."

"You still think it's the right place?"

"Yeah, I think it is."

"We didn't drive that far down, Willie."

"Okay, you think it's the next gully over, huh, Mac?"

"I wish we had the big flipping light on."

"I wanted to put it on last night, but it wasn't connected so the wires would fit."

"Currents are taking you west, Mac."

"Can you see bottom?"

"What an eerie-looking thing it was when I first saw it! It could have been 18 miles long."

"Hey, what was that? . . . It must have been when you flipped a switch or something. Stop doing that. It's scaring me."

"The mud's mucked up now. I don't know where in hell I am."

"How in hell are we going to know if that's really the bomb?"

"I don't know. The best thing we can do is get a lot of pictures so they can analyze."

"They could come down and bring up the chute. But it'll start sliding again."

"The big drag could get it, though."

"But how in hell could we ever guide it down?"

Twenty minutes passed.

"Why don't you back up again and go straight down?"

"That piece of wreckage sticking out, it looked to me about this long and it had holes. What color was it?"

"I don't know, about the gray of a ship?"

"Jesus Christ. . . . Remember, we can't be *sure!*"

"This is *Alvin*. We have found a very large parachute. It appears to have some wreckage underneath it. I can't be sure exactly what it is. It's lying on a very, very steep gully. We can't get close enough to the chute to move it and see what's underneath. . . . However, part resembles a fin . . . a rib, really."

"This is Echo. Roger. Just stay there for a moment. Zero in on it."

"Good goddamn!"

"Current reading, position reading 22 knots east to west."

"Do you think you've got the bomb?"

"Affirmative! Affirmative!"

Twenty-five minutes passed.

"Where in hell is it? I see something. Ah, no, that's a disturbance."

"Ouch!"

"Oh. Pardon me."

"What can we do about going up on the SOB besides knock it off of there? What more are we going to accomplish?"

"We could get some more photographs."

"I *saw* it. Out the window."

"Yeah, but it's just a chute."

"I haven't the slightest idea now where the SOB is."

"All of us haven't seen it. I didn't see the fin, but you both did."

"Yeah. It's not so much a fin. It looked like a structure with holes in it."

Five minutes passed.

"It'll be bright as hell if you see it on sonar."

"I don't see it."

"You don't see the bottom now, do you?"

"No, you're going down though."

"It looks like an avalanche has been here."

"Yeah, I saw it, too."

"Take some pictures."

"Did you bump yourself when you hit?"

"There's some eggshells. See 'em again?"

"That ain't the track we're looking for."

"We're too deep—2,650."

"Echo. This is *Alvin.* Say again. Say again . . . Something is coming up over ahead of me. I've got the bastard again, I think."

"Yeah, you must have. I see a piece of wire."

"This is *Alvin.* We are now directly over the object. Over."

"Is that it right in front of us? Shoot it."

"I'm getting damn all on the sonar. I'm going to catch the SOB."

"Take pictures. Hard as you can. Take pictures."

"I'm moving lots of film through that camera, Mac."

"I can turn some more lights on."

"Uphill? Down?"

"It's going to be upward, 'cause we're pointing thisaway."

"I see some blue."

"I see something blue, too. I can't read it."

"It's a blue-and-gold insignia of some kind. The goddamn cloth is still crumpled."

"This might be the very flipping nose of the thing. You're going to set down on it in just a second."

"This goddamn track is going due north at 030."

"Look down there and see if you can read that insignia."

"I'd rather go up and see the other end of it."

"God. This muddling rudder."

"This has got to be the SOB. Twenty degrees to the right. A strong target there . . . we're losing it."

"Oh, damn it! We're going to murder it!" The anguished voice rose almost to a scream. "There's nothing I can do with this flipping rudder."

"Okay, park it... Christ... Ouch... Hold, hold, damn it."

"There's something wrong with this..."

"Glad we got out of there! Now it's easier. Are you ready to get more pictures?"

"I'm ready. I'm ready."

"Keep going straight up. We're going right beside the chute. Right straight up the side of the chute."

"Echo. This is *Alvin*..."

"Try it again. Try it again.... I can see the bomb nose. That's it right at the end. Yes, that's the button. No doubt about it. Look right up here..."

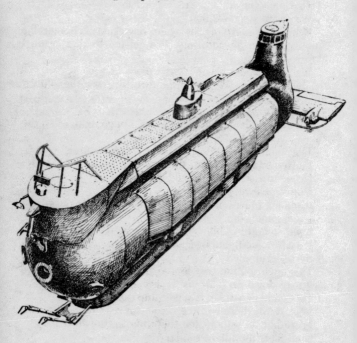

Aluminat

"Take a look at it before you shoot."

"I've got to get out of here before I tangle up in that stuff."

"Let me see if I can get a number off it or something. I know what numbers mean on the side of a ship. . . ."

"Let me get one more look."

"It's no doubt in my mind."

"Me either."

"I can see the flipping nose of it."

"Echo. This is *Alvin*." This time there was calm triumph in the voice, no more strain or excitement. "How do you read me?"

"I read you loud but not clear."

"I think we have enough identification. We'd like to skip clear of this area. There's several straps hanging down loose. There isn't any doubt in our minds about what we see. It's wrapped in the chute, but part of it shows. The thing is still lodged on a very steep slope. We got a good look at it. It's exactly the shape we've seen in the pictures."

"*Alvin*. This is an A-one job. Outstanding."

"Thank you."

The submarine was told to move to a position as close to the bomb as it could safely hold. It was to stay there and wait for the *Aluminaut* to come down as relief. That, too, would be a first. There had never before been a rendezvous of vessels in "inner space."

While they waited the *Alvin* crew all began to talk at once, to the surface and to each other. The code was entirely forgotten.

"Did you see the bomb up there? We saw it. We got enough info. I don't want to get buttoned in there. I can see the nose of the bastard now."

"Yeah, I did, too. No doubt in my mind."

"I don't know how we're going to salvage the bastard, do you? All we can do is roll it down the hill."

"That ain't a fin . . . that's part of the bomb-bay door or something."

"We'll have to pick it up by the chute."

"Yeah."

"It looks like a ghost down there now."

"I raised a big pile of muck with that move."

"You know, we were in a dangerous spot taking those pictures."

"I know it."

"We were right underneath that bastard."

"I know it."

"I hope your cameras were working."

"Whaat!"

There was a hearty laugh before he said it again. "I just hope your cameras are working."

"It looks like a big body in a shroud..."

It was 11:35 A.M. when the *Alvin* first sighted the bomb, but by the time the *Aluminaut* got down and they were allowed to surface, it turned out to be their longest dive. They were submerged for ten hours and twenty-three minutes, almost the extreme limits of the little submarine's power, life-support system, and crew endurance.

To stay in place without using up all the *Alvin's* power driving against current and drift, the pilots wedged the vessel in the mouth of a crevice, like a toothpick between two hunks of cheese. They sat in the dark waiting for eight hours, flicking on the lights from time to time but mostly with the lights off so as not to drain the batteries. When the black water to the south began to glow a brightening jade, it was a moment of almost as great excitement as finding the bomb.

What McCamis remembered most vividly about the whole day was the approach of the *Aluminaut*.

"It was beautiful, the most beautiful thing I ever saw. A great silvery-pink monster, it looked like, with great green phosphorescent eyes coming up silent through the water. I dreamed of seeing something like that, but I just thought it was a dream. I never thought I'd see it."

12

THE RECOVERY

The U.S.S. *Albany*, a guided-missile cruiser, set out from
Norfolk, Virginia, in early March and steamed straight across
the Atlantic, through Gibraltar and on to Palomares. The first
time it dropped anchor on the trip was when it drew up
alongside the U.S.S. *Boston*, Admiral Guest's flagship which
had to report for duty with another fleet. That was March 15.
Captain Wohler, the *Albany*'s commander who was to be
Guest's new host, was invited for a ceremonial lunch aboard
the *Boston* before the transfer of the flag. While the Admiral
was performing the ritual farewell an aide broke in on the
party with an urgent message. Guest read it and rose abruptly.

"Get my boat," he ordered. "I'm going to the *Mizar*."

He said something about the "instrument panel" and
explained nothing else as he hurried off. Wohler wondered
what kind of instrument panel could have made a man of
meticulous routine so defy tradition. But as the officers
saluted the tense Admiral to his barge, Wohler realized it had
to be some kind of code. Something important had been
found. That evening, when the Admiral moved aboard his
ship, he learned that "instrument panel" was Guest's code for
the target of the search.

Simo, now Paco de la Bomba, was making another trip
out to his spot that day. Each time he had gone out a bright
red buoy with a concrete anchor had been placed at the point
he marked. Sometimes the buoy stayed in place for two or
three days. One vanished after only half an hour as the
anchor waltzed down the cliff walls at the bottom and dragged
it below the sea. This time the mine sweeper was equipped
to make a Decca hi-fix. John Bruce, the Woods Hole oceanographer, was along. He had no Spanish and Simo no Eng-

lish, but they did better exchanging drawings of what had been seen than dealing through interpreters. Their lunch, too, was interrupted. The message that came through was that the *Alvin* had a "hot contact." Simo went up on the bridge to look at the area where the *Alvin* reported its find.

"Well, that could be it," he said. "It's not so very far from where I saw it sink." It turned out to be 1,000 yards away.

A buoy was planted some 300 yards from the spot that the *Alvin* had reported and that the *Aluminaut* had fixed accurately with a pinger, a device which sent bleeps to a special receiver on the *Mizar* and, with the Decca system, permitted much better position finding on the bottom. Installing the pinger was one of the tasks that delayed the *Aluminaut's* descent while the *Alvin* waited, but it was the key to history's first underwater rendezvous. After that, both the *Alvin* and the *Aluminaut* were guided back to the bomb by the pinger which had been developed because of the lessons learned during the *Thresher* search. It gave a margin of error of less than 120 feet in navigating, compared to anything from 300 to 900 feet with other instruments.

It was not only the need to keep the buoy's anchor out of the way of the submarines and make sure it did not plunk on the bomb that determined the marker point, as far away from the hidden spot underwater. There was a security decision as well. Admiral Guest wanted to be certain there would be no "premature disclosure" that the parachute and probably the bomb had been located. To ward off speculation, he also kept the rest of the search going as usual. Divers, mine sweepers, and *Cubmarine* went on with what had become their normal chores for several days. Even the Air Force kept poking down mine shafts and combing the hills until well after the reports leaked out that the *Alvin* had found an "unidentified object." But despite Guest's cautious orders, the men knew they were only going through motions. Within an hour or two of the *Alvin's* message the little boats that taxied from one ship to another with passengers and supplies had scudded all around the fleet to spread the word.

"We've found it! *Alvin* found it!" the sailors shouted up to the decks, and sometimes, when he heard, a man would raise his arms and clasp his hands in the champion's sign of victory.

While the *Alvin* waited quietly astride its canyon for the

Aluminaut, Guest paced the bridge of the *Mizar*. He listened to reports from the bottom, watched the second sub go down, and hurried to the *Fort Snelling* when at last the men who made the find had surfaced. The debriefing was at times excited and gay, at times irritated and gruff. Guest threw his arm around the shoulders of McCamis and gave the pilot a warm, appreciative thump. But then, as the men recounted what they saw, his square face hardened. The pictures were hastily developed. In black and white, they showed what looked like a giant cigar tightly veiled. McCamis and Wilson explained how the thing was perched on the side of the slope, practically sitting on its tail with the chute billowing so that they had to approach it from above to avoid entrapment. The cameras were mounted atop the *Alvin*. It had not been possible to maneuver the sub so that the lenses could see what the men saw out the porthole, a portion of silver-gray casing, insignia on the parachute, a sense of size that eyeball perspective gave. Nor did the camera catch the near transparency of the parachute, the colors and solidity that showed through the cloth. The pilots had tried to photograph the better view through the porthole with a Polaroid. But the glass had to protect them against 1,200 pounds of pressure per square inch at that depth, eighty-five times the pressure of atmosphere at sea level. It was thick and diffracted the light so much that the film showed only a blur. They explained and explained. The Admiral was adamant. Finally, there was an argument.

Guest's report to Washington late that night announced that a parachute had been seen and something was wrapped up in it that could not be identified. He refused even to guess that it was the bomb. The photographs were copied and flown to the Pentagon in great secrecy.

The *Alvin* pilots were convinced, and frustrated.

"After a ten-hour dive you don't like to be told you've found a parachute full of mud," McCamis said later.

But Guest repeated it. "How do you know it isn't a parachute full of mud?"

Later the Admiral said, "I was afraid to believe it was true that we located it. The possibility was so remote."

Guest's terse message reached the Pentagon about an hour before the first meeting of the Search Evaluation Board. Experts from several agencies had been convened to find a way out of the search. Still, it was only an encouraging, not an optimistic, message from the Admiral. They spent the day discussing the search so far, sketching the consequences of quitting and admitting failure. When they parted in the evening, the chairman said he would let them know when their next session would be held. It never was. When the photographs reached Washington, the experts arrived at the same conclusion as the *Alvin* pilots, the staff officers on Task Force 65, Generals Wilson and Montel. The search was successfully completed. The next task was recovery.

Guest's doubts, his nervous reluctance to believe that "the eye of the needle" had indeed been found, led to reimposition of the tightest security. In Madrid, Ambassador Duke began to realize what had happened only when, quite by chance, General Donovan's representative at the daily Embassy search meeting mentioned what he'd heard via the military grapevine. "They seem to think they've really got it," he said casually.

That evening, March 17, two days after *Alvin*'s Dive 128, Duke received a call from UPI correspondent Harry Stathos. Stathos had just returned from a trip to Germany. A funny thing happened on the plane, he told Duke. He was talking with a Pan-American pilot who said he'd been drinking with an Air Force colonel in a bar in Wiesbaden the night before, and the Colonel said with flat conviction that the bomb was found. Duke said what he had to say, "No comment." The correspondent was disappointed, but they were friends and Stathos told the Ambassador that he planned in that case to publish the news as an unofficial report, since his other efforts to check had convinced him it was true.

Duke sent word to the State Department that the secret was out. Soon other correspondents began flooding the wires with questions. The Ambassador was having a huge reception that night in his handsome residence, one of those diplomatic occasions where champagne, princely titles, ball gowns, and international politics are stirred gently, never shaken. When it was over, he decided, he would hold a press conference to announce that the long wait had ended. He told Washington what he planned to say and the newsmen were called to come to the Embassy at midnight for a big story. They stood in the lobby for more than an hour. Duke never appeared. Just before midnight State had called back and ordered the Ambassador to say nothing, nothing at all. The Embassy information officer, Bill Bell, finally had to meet the press and pull as straight a face as he could manage while he released another "No comment." Everyone was furious, no one was fooled.

The next day a frantic exchange of telegrams across the Atlantic led to an evasive compromise. The first official statement after the find said that, "With regard to the unidentified object and a parachute at a depth of some 2,500 feet about five miles offshore from Palomares, Rear Adm. William S. Guest, the Task Force commander, has advised that because of the extremely steep slope of the sea bottom on which the object and the parachute are resting, he proposes to attempt first to move them to a more favorable recovery area. If successful, this course of action will lessen the risk of having the object fall from its present precarious position into much deeper water. When the object is positively identified, an appropriate announcement will be made." The headlines everywhere proclaimed, "Bomb Found." But the statement served mainly to convince people that the U.S. government's worst problem was telling the truth.

Guest's obsessive fear of raising false hopes did not keep him from turning immediate attention to the huge problem of recovery. Nothing of significant size had ever been brought up from such a depth. And there was the terrain, a series of steep cliffs plunging another 1,000 feet. Above all, there was the uniquely fearsome nature of the "unidentified object." Tests of the water and the underwater soil in the vicinity of the bomb showed no trace of radioactive leakage. Still there was always the possibility that it had broken or would break if a rough jolt, a bounce, or a tumble set off the high explosive. Later, the weapons experts said they regretted having warned the Admiral perhaps too much of the need for careful handling. He was reaching a state of exhaustion; he took the warning with an air of solemn dread. His stomach ulcers were acting up again. There were times when a tray would be taken to his cabin and brought away untouched. Although he irritated others, he anguished every minute.

Recovery became an all-day, all-night operation. The *Aluminaut* "bomb-sat," as the crew described it, for twenty-two lonely hours, its nose burrowed in a mud bank for stability, while the *Alvin* recharged batteries and prepared to dive again. A mechanical arm with joints to give it elbow, wrist, and claw motion was fixed to the little sub. The *Alvin* was to take down a thin line, three-eighths of an inch of polypropylene 3,500 feet long, as a messenger for a heavy hauling cable. The claw could not hold more than 50 pounds and could not have managed a big line. But if the frail one could be anchored, a heavier line could slide down it. Then the *Alvin* could attach it to the parachute. While the *Aluminaut* was bomb watching, while the *Alvin* was charging batteries and awaiting adjustments, Jon Lindbergh of Ocean Systems Inc., which had contracted for *Cubmarine*, designed and supervised the manufacture of a special anchor. He was Charles A. Lindbergh's son and he had inherited his famous father's technical interest, sense of adventure, and shyness. It was appropriate that he was on the scene. The little submarines were, as Commander Boykin said, the Model T's of the underwater future, at the same stage in their development as aviation had been forty years before when Charles Lindbergh crossed the Atlantic in the *Spirit of St. Louis* and first proved that men could get from one continent to another in rickety, engine-driven crates. At Palomares they were proving that men could work in the depths. Lindbergh produced a spike with two folding flukes in the fleet machine shop. It took all night. By the time everything was ready for the *Alvin* to carry it down with the line, it was dusk of the next day.

The descent was to the *Alvin* pilot Val Wilson the most thrilling part of the operation. No one had ever carried a line to such a depth before, and it was even more difficult than expected. Every shift or eddy of the currents forced a change of course, a new calculation. When the *Alvin* went forward the slightest bit beyond the slack, the arm above the submarine's nose bent back above its shoulder from the pull. The pilots decided it would be better to turn around and dive tail first. That meant reading the compass, the dials, the gauges backward when there were already enough new problems demanding concentration. They backed down, squiggling and tugging, guided to the spot by the *Aluminaut*'s pinger. But the anchor was too light and the bottom too hard for it to catch. McCamis turned the *Alvin* into a hammer. With the point of the spike held out above their nose, they charged with full power at the cliff some 40 feet from the bomb. The little sub's propellers chugged until the claw was buried to its wrist. Then the mechanical fingers released and gave a gentle tug on the flukes. It held.

The *Aluminaut* had been down twenty-two hours. The *Alvin* had more work to do, but first it had to get out of the way so the *Aluminaut* could surface without accident and without blinding the *Alvin* in a fog of silt. The smaller sub scuttled off and waited, the pilots calculating they were off to one side above the *Aluminaut*. But the canyons and precipices were deceptive. Suddenly they realized they were under the tail of the bigger sub and it was heaving down on top of them, its nose still buried in the mud but its rear lowering like a boom. The *Alvin* ducked out of the way. Later, the crews discovered what had happened. Markel, the *Aluminaut*'s pilot, was a man of 230 pounds for all his lightness of manner. At that particular moment he had left his seat and walked to the head in the back of his cabin. His walk almost crushed the *Alvin*.

The *Alvin*'s next job when the *Aluminaut* had gone was to sidle up to the parachute and try to lift it away from the monster it embraced. The pilots had been briefed on where to look for serial numbers on the bomb, where to look for a series of blue dots. If the casing was broken, they were to tip it up and see if the "watermelon," the plutonium core, was still there. Soil samplers mounted on the *Alvin* scooped earth from as close to the weapon as possible for radioactive monitoring on the surface. The first pull on the parachute showed that it had never completely deployed, it kept coming out of the canister. When the end was taut, the *Alvin* tried to stream the chute along the bottom. But the bomb was so completely wrapped that it proved impossible. All they could do was pick up some folds and peek beneath the cloth. They saw a steel plug, the size of a half dollar, and got a better look at the fragment of the bomb rack which still appeared firmly attached to the weapon. They found numbers on the chute, but not on the visible part of the bomb, and they took another large batch of pictures. The dive lasted four hours and fifty-seven minutes but it had been almost forty-eight hours since the men had slept.

There was still a long, excited debriefing to go through and there were the strategy sessions for the next step in recovery. The steel plug was the clincher. There could no longer be any question of some other piece of outrageously bomblike debris having tangled itself in the chute while the bomb slipped away somewhere else. Guest stuck to what one of his officers called his "I'm-from-Missouri" attitude, but he reported about the plug. And he concentrated on plans. The *Alvin* men wanted to attach grapples to the holes in the bomb rack. Then the bomb could be lifted on a strong line played down the messenger. The Navy said there was too much risk the rack wouldn't hold. The Air Force said the rack held four bombs in the belly of a B-52, so why not? But of course no one could be sure what metal damage had been caused in the accident. The messenger line had been fixed to a buoy for the night. For more assurance, it was taken onto a mine sweeper the next day. That ended the argument. Either the mine sweeper moved on the surface, or the currents moved the line and the mine sweeper stayed too still. It was impossible to tell which, but the result was too much strain and the flukes broke, freeing the anchor.

There was all the next day for further planning, to everyone's disgust. The weather was too rough for the submarines to launch. From the shore, where crowds had gathered because of rumors of the find, it looked like another routine day of search. The fleet kept up appearances. The *Aluminaut* got down the following day, March 18, to see what had happened to the line but never found it. Meanwhile, equipment was readied for the second attempt. It was to use *Mizar's* towed underwater camera sled as both anchor and line. It was 9 P.M. by the time everything was ready for *Mizar* to drop the sled near the bomb. The *Alvin* was to accompany it down, pick up a series of 300-foot hooked lines when it had reached the bottom, and attach them firmly to the parachute shrouds. Catching the lines, carrying them through the bottom current, and twisting them into the chute were not the tasks the designers of the *Alvin's* claw had had in mind. It was, Val Wilson said later, "like a drunken Swede trying to eat spaghetti with chopsticks." The *Alvin's* pilots firmly recommended that the next version of the sub should have two claws and be able to skitter sideways like a crab. "There are limits to what you can do when you're a one-armed, two-fingered man," McCamis pointed out. Still, they managed to get some hooks in, working all through the night. A halt was called at four-twenty-five in the morning. The seas had swollen to the point that *Mizar* could no longer hold the absolutely accurate position required for lifting calculations. Nor could it properly control the sled, swinging then in a crazy circle at the end of its line. It was going too fast for the *Alvin* and there was the danger of collision which might have destroyed the little submarine. The *Alvin* quit and reached the top at five-thirty. The pilots reported that the bomb had toppled over and had slid about 15 feet down slope. The whole idea of using *Mizar*'s sled was abandoned. It might have worked in perfect weather, but nothing was perfect.

The storm enraged the water and paralyzed the operation for five days. There were 35-knot winds. Two mine sweepers lost their bottom-scanning sonar, which cost $7,000 each. The U.S.S. *Luiseno* parted its anchor cable and the U.S.S. *Nespelen*'s whaleboat was torn loose from its mooring astern. Even nature was tense.

It was Wednesday, March 23, eight days after the bomb was sighted, before the third recovery plan could be attempted. By then all the world knew that the long-sought "unidentified object" was there below the Task Force. "When?" everybody asked. Rumors circulated slowly and then dizzily. One story said that the United States had planted a dummy bomb and was making a great show of recovery to hide the fact that it had never found the real one but could not bear to go on hunting. There were more exchanges in Geneva. Moscow radio discussed with stolid irony the plight of the clumsy Americans and their imputed tricks. The daily flow of telegrams to Washington about the need for information to drown out the increasingly wild tales became a flood.

That day the *Alvin* had ballast trouble and had to start late again. The experts' ingenuity and the fleet's machine shops had been working through the storm making new equipment to carry out the new plan. They called their invention a poodl. It was a device with one free line and several coiled lines which the *Alvin* was to catch, play out, and attach to the shrouds. The poodl was mounted on a stout line above a heavy anchor which the *Mizar* managed to drop with marvelous accuracy just 80 feet from the bomb. That day the *Alvin* took down pingers to sew into the parachute so that the bomb would send its own SOS signals at last. The system guided the anchor electronically. When everything was in place, the *Alvin* went to fetch its burden from the poodl. The lines had fouled, after all. Shuttling and weaving, the sub carried one to the parachute and then, its batteries near exhaustion, it was forced to surface.

Weather was ominous again on Thursday, but the desperate eagerness to complete the job drove harder than the wind. Even at the bottom it was murky that day. The tangled coils on the poodl simply couldn't be unraveled. The *Alvin* shifted to attaching the free line. Six parachute risers had been secured when the *Alvin*'s strength once more began to fade. It had to surface. Admiral Guest surveyed the equipment, the risks, the extra safety he would have liked, and decided it was time to try anyway that night. The pilots, the oceanographers, the geologists, the weapons experts, reported in detail. There was no guarantee that the bomb was intack but no sign that it was broken and could not be hauled along the bottom. The cliff dropped to 3,000 feet and then, after a kind of terrace, went down to 3,600. The *Alvin* pilots thought the bomb should be pulled down current to swing it free, and then lifted. Guest weighed the advice and made his decision. It was his decision to make. He ordered the bomb pulled uphill toward the shallows where, if this try failed, the next one might be easier. That night the anchor line was taken to the *Mizar*'s winch and the lift began. They all watched tensely as the line tautened and slowly, gently wound around the drum. Sonar sought to follow what was happening on the bottom. The bomb was numbered Contact 261, the last contact. When it perched on the cliff, its contours had been hidden by the boulders and jagged outline of the terrain. Now, the echo was coming back reassuringly off the metallic surface. The suspense did not last long. The men on top figured they had the bomb about 100 feet clear of the bottom, maybe a bit more, when the line took a heavy strain and suddenly snapped. There was complete slack. The bomb had dropped again.

The hopes for an imminent announcement of recovery had to be abandoned. After another hasty exchange of telegrams, a statement was made at noon that Friday, March 25. It said, "Admiral William S. Guest, Commander of Task Force 65, advises that operations for the recovery of the object with attached parachute (previously located off the coast from Palomares, Spain) are proceeding satisfactorily. These operations must necessarily be accomplished slowly and cautiously due to the precarious position of the object on a steep submarine slope and the great depths involved. Adverse weather conditions with high winds and choppy seas continue periodically to hamper current efforts. The limited endurance of the submersibles being employed and the necessity to recharge their batteries after each dive are primary factors which, with weather, control the tempo of our activities. Everything possible is being done to expedite recovery and identification of the object under these circumstances."

It was even more of an understatement than the wily statement makers knew. The *Aluminaut* hurried down but could no longer find the parachute. The pingers that had been attached were lost in the fall. The *Alvin* was held up with ballast trouble again and went down at dusk, hunting all night long and finding nothing but tracks made by the *Aluminaut*. Once again the bomb was lost.

It seemed too much. After two months of hunting, ten days and three tries to bring it up, the Task Force had struck out. If they had believed in myths and magic, the men might have argued that the bomb had grown fins and swum away. But they were seamen and scientists. They didn't expect miracles and they wouldn't accept vanishing bombs. It had to be in the well-charted, clearly fixed area where *Mizar* had begun to pick it up. The line had broken in the 300-foot section between the anchor and the parachute, some 30 feet from the anchor. All human logic guaranteed that the bomb was not far from the point where the *Alvin* had first sighted it. But it was nowhere to be seen.

"I was sick," McCamis said later. "It was like losing someone close to me." It wasn't that he had special affection for the bomb, but he did have deep feeling for his vehicle, its capabilities, and the staggering work it had managed to perform, now gone for nothing. "If anything happened to little *Alvin*, it would happen to me," he said. It was a sentiment the underwater pioneers all shared about their craft and tools, although few were prepared to express it so plainly and chose either the language of scientific obfuscation or hearty salt to cloak their passion. Capt. Willard Searle, the Navy's director of salvage operations, expressed his gusto and devotion to the deep frontier with a question gleefully tossed to any unwary visitor. "Do you know what the diver said to the mermaid?" he would ask. "How?" And then, with a guffaw, "If you wander into this office, you've got to watch out. We're sea devils." The underwater men were somehow set apart, like the devotees of outer space, and that was one of the problems in working things out between them and an old sea dog like Guest. The vocabulary, the habits, the experience, the outlook just were not the same upon the sea and underneath it, even though the brine was shared.

The submarines went down the next day, and the following day, and the day after that. The *Alvin* planted a flashing light on the bottom as a beacon to pinpoint the new search pattern. The dives went on to the point of exhaustion, and the rest periods were only long enough to charge the batteries and prepare another launch. They found some tracks uphill that showed the weapon had been dragged and had not lifted off the surface so soon as calculated from the sonar. There was a jumble of other tracks, from the *Aluminaut*, from the *Alvin*, from the equipment that had been towed around. And there was the smooth, wide groove downhill that had led to the bomb in the first place.

Once again, as the fruitless days went by, an argument developed over the search pattern. This time the prime possibility circle was only 100 yards in radius. The question was whether the searchers should concentrate on the northern, uphill half or the southern, downhill half. The first reconnaissance proved nothing. With 20 feet of visibility, the bad conditions, the previous demonstration that sonar could sweep over the bomb without picking it out, it was clearly possible that the submarines had driven almost over the target more than once and still had failed to spot it. The issue was where to go on spending search time. Guest said north. That was the direction he had sought to pull the bomb, that was where he wanted it, and that was where it ought to have fallen if it had really lifted free of the water. The underwater experts and the submariners considered the tracks the most important clue. "Whoever heard of a thing falling *uphill*?" they argued, agonizing, and yet search after search disclosed to track downhill but the old one the *Alvin* had first spotted a full month before. The daily dives, the daily arguments, the daily disappointments continued for a week.

Public reaction was growing increasingly shrill and volatile. It had looked butterfingers enough for the United States to lose an H-bomb once. Now it had happened twice, and while that was not admitted, it was obvious to everyone that something had gone seriously wrong. The political and diplomatic problems were mounting once again. The Spanish government was embarrassed. The Russians began urging publicly that an international recovery supervision team be formed since, Moscow radio said, the United States could not be trusted to tell the truth about the operation.

More and more people began to wonder aloud whether they ought really to believe whatever claims might be made when something happened. Everybody was sure that something would have to happen, but with so much drama already, would it be what it seemed or just a gigantic, theatrical deception? United Nations Secretary General U Thant privately approached Arthur Goldberg, the American Ambassador to the United Nations, and suggested inviting the International Atomic Energy Commission in Vienna to verify the search and recovery when it was made.

The suggestion caused a minor panic. The Soviet Union was a member of the Commission and neither Spain nor the United States could bear the thought of a bevy of Russians, and maybe Poles and Bulgarians, poking about Palomares and the U.S. Navy. Apart from the question of security, there would inevitably be political disputes, minority reports, another propaganda explosion. U Thant was quietly told that neither of the two governments involved like the idea, and it was dropped. But his gesture served to underline the need for some kind of special plan to prove American good faith.

The delays in recovery led not only to sinister speculation about American intentions. A Spanish cartoon showed a sailor perched on the prow of a tremendous ship, equipped with all the most elaborate modern devices. He held a simple pole and line and explained to a Spanish fisherman huddled in a rowboat down below, "It's been located, identified, and confirmed. Now we're only waiting for it to bite the hook." The Americans and their terrifying bomb were being made to look silly.

Ambassador Duke turned his attention to the "credibility gap," as he called it. He proposed that representatives of the world press watch the recovery when it took place and see for themselves that a real H-bomb, *the* missing H-bomb, was in fact retrieved. Both Admiral Guest and General Wilson angrily rejected the plan. They were concerned with the operation itself. Mixing in a crowd of uncontrolled civilian strangers would only complicate everything and possibly result in a dangerous exposure of secrets.

They drew up a counterproposal. An official Navy photographer would record the recovery and take pictures of the bomb when it was safely aboard a ship. After proper editing of unpublishable details, the Navy would distribute the pictures to all corners. Duke's exasperation was as great as the military's had been with his plan. It was perfectly clear that such a keep-your-distance attitude would be met head on by a why-should-you-be-believed attitude from the nonmilitary world. The impasse heated tempers in Madrid, Washington, and Palomares. But the major problem remained to find the bomb again and bring it up.

On April 1, a week after the bomb had been lost the second time, Commander Boykin went down with the *Alvin* to gather firsthand reports for Guest. They examined and re-examined once again the tracks from the lift-off point. There were clods, like drippings, which did seem to indicate that the bomb had been pulled upward. But that day, for the first time, they noticed what Boykin called "a cookie-cutter effect, as if the bomb had stood on its tail and jammed down into the mud." That could mean that the upward track was not made by the bomb at all but by the anchor dragging above it, and that the bomb had bumped upward for a few feet and then rolled downhill when a rock, or perhaps the anchor fluke itself, had cut the line. They investigated downhill and still found nothing but the old track, although Val Wilson, peering closely, thought he saw some minor variations at the edges. It seemed inconceivable that the bomb could have gone down precisely in its own groove, like a child going down the same slide again. And yet, they suddenly realized, it was not impossible. By then they had to surface. That night there was another long strategy argument. This time Boykin and Springer added their voices to those of the *Alvin* pilots who wanted to look south. Guest kept reminding them they had gone that way before. There was no time to waste circling old haunts. But they had been the other way as well. Guest finally gave in.

The pilots invited the Admiral to come down and see for himself. Guest, the ex-airman, had gone for a dip with the scuba divers, but eight hours underwater was something else. He couldn't afford to be out of communication with the Task Force and with Washington for so long, he explained, although he took their "C'mon, Admiral, let's go," with warm amiability.

"Why don't you go, George?" Guest said to his chief reporting officer, Lieut. Cdr. George W. Martin. Martin had been assistant commander of the *Trieste* bathyscaphe on the *Thresher* search and had a keen, personal appreciation of what could and could not be done in deep water. But he had never been on a vehicle like the *Alvin*. He accepted with enthusiasm. The plan for the day's search had been to extend the radius of the circle, going farther south than before and following the contour of the bottom. They started at the outside edge of their area, 3,000 feet down, and made a pass to the east. Then they moved up to 2,950 and made a pass to the west. It continued that way up 50-foot steps. At eleven-thirty they found their first clue, some big clods that looked, Martin said, "as though somebody uphill had been throwing down hunks of dirt. Some were six inches across, some were two feet across. It wasn't normal."

They decided to cruise up toward the point from which the chunks had come. McCamis was piloting and looking out the forward porthole. After a minute or two he said offhandedly, "There it is."

Martin had his eye glued to the port window and Rainnie to starboard.

"What is it?" Rainnie asked, thinking perhaps some new track lay ahead. "What do you see?"

"There it is, right there," was all McCamis would answer.

"Well, what? What's there?"

Still sounding quite casual, McCamis said, "*It's* there."

Rainnie was getting impatient. "Do you see the chute?"

"Yeah. I just told you it's there. Don't you believe me? You ought to have faith."

The others were too excited to mind the tease. They peered over McCamis' shoulder, but the hole was too small for more than one to see out at a time. McCamis parked, leaving the *Alvin* to hover in the water, and moved aside to let Rainnie and Martin have a turn at the porthole. They were at the downhill edge of the chute, stretched out now over 60 feet. McCamis and Rainnie stopped to discuss the code word for the day. Mac remembered it and Rainnie sent the message to the surface.

"This is *Alvin*. Brontosaurus."

That meant they had found the parachute. They could not see whether the bomb was still attached, but they knew it couldn't be far away. Before they moved, however, they had to make sure that the surface had their position fixed correctly. It took about four hours. They spent the time celebrating with a lunch of soggy peanut-butter-and-jelly sandwiches and going over the last eight days of effort. Then they reconnoitered until the *Aluminaut* could get down. It was a quarter past seven when they trudged into the *Fort Snelling* wardroom for supper.

"We were really elated," Martin said later. "We knew the recovery was going to be hard, but the monkey was off our back. We signed a short snorter on a 100-peseta note, Rainnie, McCamis, and I, and the date, April 2, 1966."

The bomb was at 2,800 feet, some 120 yards south of where it had been found the first time. During the second search Admiral Guest had made a whole new canvass of recovery plans. The Naval Ordnance Test Station at Pasadena, California, had offered one of its newest developments, the *CURV*—Cable-controlled Underwater Research Vehicle. It had been designed to recover test-fired torpedoes and had a depth limit of 2,000 feet. The strange contraption of ballast tanks, lights, tubes, and claw would have appealed to Guest because of its great advantage of being controlled from the surface without exposing men to the depths. But he rejected the offer because 2,000 feet maximum depth made it useless to him. In a fever of determination to make a contribution to the Palomares operation nonetheless, the Pasadena designers had raced to modify *CURV* for deeper work. They tested it hurriedly in the Pacific, found it could now manage 3,000 feet, and renewed the bid. That time Guest accepted. It was flown to Spain and arrived at the end of March. It was to be the key to the fourth recovery plan. There were others. The *Aluminaut* wanted to use a jury rig attached to its claws. The fishing tracks in the area of the bomb showed that a simple trawl was a plausible, if risky, recovery device. Simo, the fisherman, kept saying he could haul up the bomb with ease. But the *CURV* offered control and constant visual supervision through its underwater television. As long as the bomb did not fall deeper, it had the best chance.

The *Alvin* began the fourth recovery attempt by attaching pingers and trying once again to move the parachute for a good look at the bomb. That did not work. Repairs and bad weather kept interrupting the schedule. On the third day of the new try *CURV* was driven down and maneuvered to attach a five-eighth-inch nylon line to the sturdy apex of the parachute. The plan was to put just enough pull on it to haul the chute clear of the weapon. Then *CURV* was to put a big clamp on the bomb itself so that it could be hoisted free of the parachute. Sailors were put out in a whaleboat to strain the line in the chute. But it would not unlock the bomb. The *Alvin* went down to keep an eye on the work and continue to try for another good look at the bomb. It had disappeared again—lost a third time. There were a few hours of anguish, but this time the *Alvin* found the track quickly and followed it. As before, the first sign of the target was the parachute. Suddenly Val Wilson saw a great mantle of cloth blanketing the porthole. They had almost driven into the billowing chute which could have trapped them as securely as it held the bomb. It was the gravest danger yet because if the chute had draped itself over the *Alvin* and caught in the conning tower, they could never have surfaced. The weight of the bomb would have become the *Alvin*'s fatal ballast. A quick reverse and turn saved the little submarine just as the great shroud reached out to envelop it. There was near panic on the ships above them.

Afterward Wilson said with deprecation of the peril, "Of course *Alvin* would be very dangerous with a cowboy driver. But we're not in a dangerous business because we know exactly what we're doing. We're not a bunch of daredevils."

All the same, it was a close thing. Guest shook with relief that the men were safe and was all the more determined to make the unmanned *CURV* complete the job. The *Alvin* reported that the attempt to pull away the chute had only managed to drag the bomb 300 feet west-southwest. If the direction had been a little more southerly, the bomb would have dropped beyond *CURV*'s reach. And it was still moving. The submariners noticed that every time a sizable fish brushed against the cliff there was a little avalanche. The danger of banging the side of the ravine with the equipment and burying everything added to the tension. There was a danger that the bomb might drop into the chasm at any moment, forcing a completely new start on the recovery operation with equipment not yet available, not tested, not quite clearly envisioned. Guest spent night after night on the U.S.S. *Petrel*, the mother ship of the *CURV*, snatching a few minutes' sleep stretched out on the deck when the wind and the high seas forced a halt in the operations. Nobody had been to bed for thirty hours.

On April 6 *CURV* secured a second line to the parachute shrouds. Work went on through the night to attach a third. But every time the surface operators manipulated the claw up to the edge of the chute, the moving water depressed the cloth and it slipped away. They would have to wait ten or fifteen minutes for the turbulence to subside and then try again. Silt fog left only gray blurs to guide them on the television screen. Then *CURV* refused to move forward or backward. The operators realized that what had threatened the *Alvin* had happened to the unmanned machine. The chute had entangled its motors. Their attempts to work it free only made things worse. It would not go up or down. The motor that worked the claw was stuck. At 3:15 A.M. they saw that *CURV* was completely ensnared. "It was a hopeless situation," Guest said later. "We thanked our lucky stars that *CURV* was an unmanned vehicle instead of a manned vehicle."

The scene on the *Petrel* was a nightmare of tension. Suddenly the man who knew the most about working *CURV* collapsed. It was Howard Talkington, the brilliant underwater technician from Pasadena who had adapted the machine for the job and was, a colleague said, "the one we all relied upon, the number one in that part of the operation." They thought he had a heart attack. He was put on the floor of the wardroom and doctors worked on him in the middle of the frenzy. After all, it turned out to be complete exhaustion. Practically everybody was on the verge of crumbling. Capt. Horace Page, Guest's smartly correct chief of staff, was almost unable to speak. Nervous strain made his mouth move oddly in his grizzled jaw, unshaven for days, and he was hard to understand.

Still, a decision had to be made. The order was given to put a strain on the two lines already secured in hopes that that would steady the chute enough to free *CURV,* or at least to enable it to attach one more line. The seas were running high, the wind was heavy, there was no assurance that the two lines would hold. Nothing was right. But the risk of everything going completely wrong was worse at that point. The sailors at the *Petrel*'s winch began to slow turn, straining every nerve to smooth the pull and give no sudden jerk to the lines. The heavy drag of the deep currents, the ship's heaving motion on the waves, the painstaking effort to haul gently, all combined to mask any feeling of the tautness of the line. The men had to rely entirely on calculation of how many turns would take up slack without dragging the bomb. One of the civilian experts thought he heard the man at the lines call out 2,400. He felt he, too, was succumbing to the daze.

"What did you just say?"

"Twenty-four hundred. There's 2,400 feet of line out."

"But that's impossible. The bottom is 2,800 feet. It's a mistake."

"No," said the sailor, and he showed the green mark that clearly signified the length.

The civilian reported to Guest's staff. The Admiral was watching the dials, the instruments, the television screen on *CURV*, but they showed nothing unusual. The check was made again. It seemed to be true. Without anybody's noticing, the bomb's whole weight had been transferred to the line and it was already 400 feet clear of the bottom. It was the most crucial moment of eighty days of effort. The lines were thin; three had been thought essential to carry the burden. And Guest knew that at 100 feet from the bottom and 100 feet from the surface the nylon was subject to vibration so severe that it reduced the strength of the line by 75 per cent. The first peril seemed to have been surmounted. But there was still a long pull.

Should the whole thing be sent back down? The depth sounders showed that the bomb had been swung out over the chasm. It would have dropped to 3,000 feet or farther. *CURV* would probably be lost with it. The only thing left was to keep on pulling, and praying, that it would all come up. And so, by another accident, shortly before dawn on Thursday, April 7, Number Four bomb began the ascent from its hiding place. For an hour and forty-five minutes the lift continued foot by foot. When *CURV* neared the surface, the picture on the screen grew clearer. The camera was manipulated to focus on the burden beneath the chute. There was still the unanswered question of whether the bomb was intact, and it mattered gravely to the final stage of recovery. Guest studied the screen closely.

"That was when I finally could believe," he said later, "it really was the bomb. We'd found it."

When the tip of the parachute broke the surface, he ordered the lifting stopped. It was a strange sight. Atop the big blotch of white on the water was a jumble of bumps and runners. The men on the *Petrel* looked through their glasses. It was *CURV*, riding up "like a sleigh on the snow," as one of them described it. "It had just been sitting there all the way up like a king being carried." There was still the danger of the lines breaking under the special strain of the last 100 feet. The Admiral sent scuba divers down to wrap wire straps around the weapon, attaching them to heavy lines from the *Petrel*. The parachute and *CURV* were cut away and recovered separately. That eased the strain for the last, delicate stage. At eight-forty-five on Holy Thursday morning the missing H-bomb was lowered tenderly on the *Petrel*'s deck.

13

THE AFTERMATH

The sailors called it the Easter egg hunt. In Madrid, Joe Smith had been saying nightly prayers that the bomb would be brought up very soon, or else not for several more days, in any case not that Sunday, Easter Sunday. It would have been too much to have the rest of the world proclaim the recovery America's day of grim resurrection.

The bomb experts had spent the night on board the *Petrel*, waiting forward so as not to interfere with the nerve-racking job of the lift from the poop deck. There was Sam Moore, the weapon designer, Air Force Sergeants Stanley Nowak and Charles Grimmett, weapons handlers whom General Wilson had sent to sea to look after the bomb when it appeared. As soon as the dripping tube was laid out safely on the ship, Admiral Guest summoned them one by one to look at it.

"Is this a real weapon?" the Admiral asked. "Are you sure the serial number checks?"

Moore couldn't help staring with surprise. It looked so much like the Number One bomb, intact, with a dent on almost the same place near its nose. For a moment he thought he was seeing the weapon he had seen before, not the one that had lain hidden at the bottom of the sea since the day of the accident. But imagination was playing no tricks. The serial number was clearly legible and it was the number of the missing bomb. Three different people who knew looked closely and told Guest yes, it was precisely what they had been looking for. Certain at last, the Admiral hurried to the radio room to send the triumphant message: mission successfully completed.

The experts worked for an hour and a half, opening the

217

bomb and disconnecting the intricate circuitry so that there could be no further danger of a high-explosive detonation. The render-safe procedure, as they called it, was in fact an almost total disassemblage so that when it was finished the bomb casing held a pile of components, not a workable weapon any longer. Plans were made to build a "coffin," a great metal cylinder that would be used to pack the bomb in sand for shipment.

It was a moment of supreme happiness when, at 10:14 A.M., the weapon was pronounced beyond all danger of further accident and the job was clearly done. Nobody cheered or jumped with excitement, they were all too exhausted. Instead, there was a long, joyous sigh of relief. "Thank God," the Admiral breathed.

In Washington, the message was quickly spread. Dr. John Craven, the Navy's oceanographer, was awakened a little before 5 A.M., Washington time. He heard a voice say, "We hit three cherries in the jackpot." At first he thought it was some boozing friend on a fling in Las Vegas. To stall while he tried to figure out who it was, he said, "You idiot, don't you know there aren't three cherries in the jackpot?" But the man insisted, and the voice was so cheerful, so sober, that as Craven shook himself awake he realized what it had to mean. They had been singing a dirge for weeks, "The bomb in Spain lies mainly in the drain." Now he added the line of glory, "You think we've got it? We've really got it?"

General Wilson was in Madrid. The land search had ended three weeks earlier and Camp Wilson had been reduced to a few dozen men for the last phase of the operation. The message he received was that "Admiral Guest has a broken leg and wants to see you." That was their private recovery code. He headed immediately back to Palomares.

Ambassador Duke knew that the bomb had been located a second time on the previous Saturday and that recovery might succeed any day, or not for a long time. He had canceled a planned spring holiday to ride up the Nile because he wanted to be at Palomares for the day of triumph. But the months had been an intense strain on him, too, and there was little he could do in his Madrid office now but wait. He arranged to have a friend invite him and Mrs. Duke for a cruise along Spain's eastern and southern coast. Only Tim Towell, Admiral Guest, and a few other officials knew the

Ambassador's yachting trip did not mean there would be no news on the Palomares front.

Towell had taken advantage of a rare night off duty, with the Ambassador out of town, for some giddy recreation on his own account. He was slumping at his desk, feeling the dismal effects, when a code clerk brought the message that Thursday. It said, "The item was put aboard the U.S.S. *Petrel* at 0845 this morning." That meant the compromise credibility plan for recovery, finally worked out of bitter argument between the military and the diplomats, had to be launched immediately. Not only Duke was away. Easter week is something of a national hibernation as far as workaday life is concerned in Spain. General Montel was off in the provinces with his family. General Donovan was incommunicado at a hunting lodge in Pampano de San Juan. The plan called for representatives of top Spanish authority to attend a bomb review, but General Franco was off yachting and all down the line of officialdom people had taken the traditional time off for their traditional pleasures. The Embassy called one after another to round up a cast for the show scheduled from the afterdeck of the *Albany*, moving down the list from stars to understudies. There were not very many Spanish officials willing to interrupt their fiesta to look at a bomb. It was exasperating after such a long, querulous preparation, but Towell had been in Spain enough years to understand it. "A man here may be starving," he said later, "but he's not going to work during fiesta. It's considered uncivilized." Finally, a group was collected and flown to the coast. Newspapermen and TV crews, considered outside fiesta civilization in any case, were alerted and told to make their way to Palomares by the morning of April 8. They understood. The official announcement was made at last.

An intricate system of communications to the Ambassador had been worked out with the Spanish navy, but there was nobody but a grumpy corporal of the guard left on duty in each of the installations involved. Towell abandoned trying to make it work and switched to intuition. The weather was bad, the itinerary of the yacht might have been changed. He called the naval base at Cartagena on the hunch that Duke had put in there for the night, and asked for the senior officer available. Another sleepy corporal came to the phone. They had to scream because of the bad connection. Then the line went dead. Towell sweated. Fifteen minutes later he heard Duke's voice through the scratchy line on another phone. The port captain had run to the end of the dock shouting and waving his arms just as the yacht was steaming out to sea. It turned back and got the message to call Madrid. It wasn't necessary for Duke and Towell to use a code. The call itself was enough. The aide said, "We're all set." The Ambassador asked about timing and decided to go on to Garrucha, the port off Palomares, on the boat.

The nautical parade on Good Friday became part of the year's Easter celebration. Everybody in the area went down to the shore to watch. Hundreds of newsmen from Madrid drove throught the night, spent a few hours somewhere in sleeping bags, and turned up on the Garrucha dock next morning to be taken to the *Albany*. Only those with certified credentials were allowed aboard. But the audience ashore amused itself in the festive atmosphere. The wife of one British correspondent caused more commotion than all the arriving and departing boats. She was an ample blond woman, endowed with vast quantities of creamy skin, and she had what the Spaniards called a "titi," a minute "spider" monkey, on a leash. The monkey hopped on her shoulder, then plunged down her neck and popped out the armhole of her dress. "I can't tell you," the Guardia Civil's Captain Calín said later with moist lips and an unabashed leer in his eyes, "what shocks and shivers it gave us all to watch the creature dive into those depths, skitter about those contours, leap about those peaks. It was the thing everybody remembered about the day they got the bomb. What a day!"

At sea, according to plan, the vistors were escorted to the broad afterdeck of the *Albany* which served as grandstand for the parade. The bomb, its serial and Mark numbers masked with white tape, sat on skids on the poop deck of the *Petrel*. The two halves of its open "coffin" stood nearby. Led by the *Petrel*, the search heroes filed past in the water, the *Mizar*, the *Alvin*, the *Aluminaut*, the *Cubmarine*, the mine sweepers, and their divers. It was the first time they were publicly displayed since the beginning of the operation. It was the first time the United States had ever put an H-bomb on show. After the steam-past, Guest returned from the *Petrel* to the *Albany* and held a mammoth press conference, reviewing the sea search from the beginning. The room was jammed and hot. The Admiral was near collapse from fatigue, but elation carried him through.

It had been something of a miracle that the accident caused no damage. It was something of a miracle that the bomb was found and retrieved.

Everybody who could headed back to Madrid that afternoon. The bomb was packed and transferred to the U.S.S. *Cascade* for return to America. It could not have been loaded on a plane in view of the Spanish ban on overflights of nuclear weapons, and in any case nobody wanted to risk another plane crash. The *Alvin* and the *Aluminaut* were lashed on ships for the trip to their home ports. The other ships pulled anchor at last and steamed off one by one to their normal stations. They left in such a hurry that nobody remembered to say good-by and thank you to the port captain at Garrucha, an omission that offended his Spanish sense of hospitality after more than two months of helping to look after distraught guests. The *Albany* stayed until all the rest of Task Force 65 had been dispersed. On Sunday Captain Wohler ordered sunrise services on the cruiser's afterdeck. At noon a priest from Garrucha came to say Easter mass, and that evening the ship's company had a barbecued steak cook-out in celebration of the end of a mission. On Easter Monday they sailed for Naples.

On Good Friday morning, as the bomb parade was sailing past the *Albany*, a special train of twenty-six boxcars rolled into the private station of the Atomic Energy Commission's Savannah River plant, at Aiken, South Carolina. The cars were shunted to a siding during the Easter holiday. The following Monday unloading began from a specially built ramp to the deep trenches 100 yards away. One by one the 4,827 blue steel drums of what the AEC called "the mildly radioactive Spanish soil" were lowered into the red Carolina dirt. The huge graves, 20 by 20 by 400 feet, had been dug well in advance, alongside other graves for low-level radioactive waste at the AEC's 80-acre burial ground set in the center of the well-guarded, wire-enclosed 200,000-acre plant. The land belonged to the Federal government, acquired in perpetuity for the disposal of material that would be giving off harmful energy for up to a billion years. Whether the records and charts of what each trench contained would last that long was another question, but they were carefully kept with instructions and warnings to future generations who might forget what lay beneath that soil. When the drums were all in place, the dirt was packed above them until all trace of the earth cut had disappeared. There was no monument, no marker, just a flat stretch of Carolina clay kept regularly cleared of growth so that no audacious weed might send down roots and one day poke its way through rusting steel to draw up minute particles of plutonium.

That was not likely with the Spanish dirt in any case. It was covered with 10 feet of earth. Usually the AEC buried waste of that type only three feet down, but this time the extra precaution was taken because of special insistence about the danger of contamination. It came from the Department of Agriculture, which was not worried in the least about plutonium or uranium, but had demanded absolute assurance that "no injurious foreign pests" could be imported with the American-contaminated foreign soil. The interdepartmental negotiations in Washington had produced a stiff set of alternatives from Agriculture to the AEC: either sterilize every drum before it reaches U.S. territory or seal and bury them all so deep that no fly or beetle larva can ever wriggle to the surface and become an insect immigrant. Department of Agriculture inspectors were at the dock at Charleston Navy Yard when the drums came off the ship, and again at Savannah River when they were laid to rest. There was one tense moment. The U.S.N.S. *Boyce* had brought 4,829 drums of dirt. Two were missing from the funeral, and Agriculture almost had conniptions. The other two, the inspectors discovered, were being sent to Los Alamos for special research. Another set of negotiations, almost more intricate than those between the AEC and the Spanish nuclear officials for a Palomares follow-up program, took place before the two-drum shipment was permitted. Including transportation from Charleston, the burial cost the AEC $70,000, a modest sum in its budget. Dr. Iranzo of the JEN watched the operation. It went smoothly. The only accident on the trip from Spain to the Carolina cemetery was on the dock when a stevedore caught his finger in a banging freight-car door. Nothing broke, nothing leaked.

The two drums of contaminated soil shipped to Los Alamos were for one of the experiments in the follow-up program worked out by the Junta de Energía Nuclear with the AEC's help. Wright Langham, the Los Alamos plutonium expert, had explained to the JEN the details of studies made at the laboratory to find whether plutonium oxide, as insoluble as sand in the human body, could be dissolved by plants with their fantastic ability to break rocks and penetrate stone.

But the Spaniards asked, "How do you know the soil you used is like our soil? Maybe in Palomares soil it will be different." So the agreement was made to take a small quantity of the Palomares earth, add an additional 10,000 count of plutonium oxide, and grow tomatoes on it in the laboratory. The Department of Agriculture was finally pacified when Langham showed the plans for the greenhouse, well sealed, and the concrete vats with all drainage leading into the Alamos radioactive-waste treatment plant. The argument that fruit flies simply would not survive the treatment any better than grains of plutonium eventually convinced the inspectors. When the tomatoes were harvested, Langham said, they would be carefully analyzed and "we'll send all the results to Madrid. We'll send the tomatoes, too, if they want them."

"Who would eat them?" he was asked.

"I will," he answered.

The JEN's Dr. Iranzo visited Los Alamos to discuss other studies to prove that the decision on decontamination levels at Palomares had been well beyond necessity. A four-point program was drawn up to keep track of the aftermath for as long as the most skeptical might be in doubt. The people, the air, the produce, the soil were all to be checked for at least a year, a complicated operation involving special equipment and careful organization.

Dr. Eric Fowler, the Los Alamos plant and soil expert who was going to grow the special greenhouse tomatoes, went to Spain to give advice on soil sampling. The trick was to move parts of the soil that had been plowed and cultivated from one place to another and then take samples to test whether agriculture, time, and mixture had led to any increased concentration of radioactivity. All produce going to market from Palomares was to be spot checked, with plans for tracing the source of contamination if any appeared. Four white boxes, like well-kept beehives on stilts, were set up in the village near the areas where contamination had been greatest. The JEN hired a villager to go each day and open the equipment inside the boxes, collect a thin square of paper, fold it, wrap it, and mail it to Madrid. The machines were samplers that extracted dust from the air. In Madrid each day's sampling was examined for radioactive count. Except for the uneasiness which continued attention of the scientists caused the villagers, all that was no more problem than the technique involved. Checking the people was going to be more difficult. Langham explained how to get a really accurate urine sample, making sure of no impurities from external sources. It could be done only by taking the people away from their homes for several days. As a result, only a few would be invited by the government to Madrid from time to time, but there was no way to avoid the odd impression that would make. It was, in any case, going to be necessary to bring some villagers to Madrid for the most sensitive and most important part of the study. It was arranged that the JEN would get a whole-body counter, a device Dr. Otero had longed to acquire for many years. It had been invented more or less simultaneously by Langham and the Argonne laboratories and was the only possible way of measuring with fine accuracy the total amount of radioactivity in an apparently quiet healthy man. The machine is so sensitive that it can measure slight amounts of soft X rays penetrating outward through the flesh. There were only two or three places in the world equipped with them, and they took very special installation. Because of the very low-level energy the machine can measure, it has to be completely shielded from normal background radiation to function effectively. Steel plates were found to provide the best shielding but not new steel plates. The experiments had shown that any steel produced after the first atomic bomb was dropped on Hiroshima was useless for the purpose. Fall-out, no matter where in the world, had contaminated supplies of iron ore to a point where the steel made from it had an infinitesimal radioactivity of its own. So only old steel plates could be used. The AEC arranged to help Otero buy some from scrap yards where old ships are broken up.

"I really don't think they'll find enough radiation to worry about in anybody from Palomares when they have the counter working," Langham said with confidence.

But the scientists on both sides were glad that further checks had been arranged to add to the body of precise knowledge on plutonium. The incident was not over for them, there was still much to be done. The plans were worked out smoothly, without further friction.

A Spanish humorist thought the whole affair had wound up too smoothly. After all, he wrote, all through history countries had defended every inch of their soil with their people's lives, and here was Spain losing 100,000 tons of its patrimony to foreign sovereignty without a whimper. Honor should have demanded a show of bellicosity at the time of conquest, "at least a symbolic war. Given the place of the deed, it might well have been a tomato war with the people of Palomares bombarding the Americans with their fruit while General Wilson's soldiers could have defended themselves with Coca-Cola bottles. That would have covered the requirements of ancient form. Of course, it would have covered them with squashed tomatoes, but at least..."

The relief that it was over provoked a spate of good humor among those who could go home. General Wilson lit a cigarette as he climbed into the last helicopter to leave the empty beach, only to stub it out after a few puffs. It was his ritual of conclusion. He had promised himself to quit smoking "if this thing ever ends," and he did. There was a moment of fright when he returned to Madrid that almost tempted him to break his resolution, but he overcame it. That was at a party given by General Montel to celebrate the end of the job. When Wilson entered Montel's home, the Spanish officer reminded him of their agreement to kill a bottle of whisky together "when this is finally over."

"Now you must keep your word," Montel said solemnly. "Let us sit down and begin." He produced a package of quality Scotch. The label said 40 ounces, an imperial quart. "Open it," Montel urged as Wilson bugged his eyes and gulped. He was not a drinking man, and the Spaniard knew it. "You agreed, General, as an officer and a gentleman. You can't back out now. We must finish the bottle." Wilson proceeded with caution, but he saw no way out. He ripped off the wrapping, opened the package, and reached in. His arm went down to the elbow before he came to the miniature which Montel had hidden inside. The Spaniard roared with laughter, his first laugh since he had gone to Palomares in January, and the two generals split the single drink.

In Albuquerque, "Doc" Norcross and Capt. Joe Pizzuto went to work on the standard sized bottles they had won from men who bet the bomb was on the land. After the first few days of the search they had both decided "it must be wet." Norcross said later, "It took the brains weeks to figure it out. I got there by idiot logic, but it was quick."

The Pentagon, the Strategic Air Command, the State Department, the AEC, all began drawing the lessons they had learned. SAC rewrote its disaster manual, developed a communications kit for quick shipment to accident sites, revised and much enlarged the list of personnel and equipment to be kept ready for quick reaction teams. The old *Black Book* form sheet for announcing nuclear accidents in foreign countries was thrown out, it had been ludicrously inappropriate, and a new list of instructions on information policy was drawn up. Reports went in recommending amendments to the U.S. Foreign Claims Act to make provision for atomic mishaps. Other reports recommended early recognition that the Spanish bases treaty could never be renewed as it stood.

Nobody assumed that Palomares was the last accident. As long as H-bombs were moved about, something unpleasant was likely to happen with them sometime, some place. Gen. H. C. Donnelly, Director of the Defense Atomic Support Agency, put it plainly. "You could make sure by stopping all transport of nuclear weapons. But that would mean abandoning all nuclear defense. Or you could send another emergency plane along with every plane that carries H-bombs so that you'd have everything you needed on the spot the minute something happened. That's the other extreme. The way things are, neither one is feasible. So our job is to figure out something in the middle, the way to cut the risk to the minimum and be as well prepared as possible when we have to face it." It was not a cheering conclusion, but the same could be said for the rest of the world's prospects in the nuclear age.

Spain, at least, had better grounds to expect that it would not see another Palomares. The overflights were canceled and were not likely to be renewed short of a world crises so desperate that the danger of unarmed H-bombs cascading on a village seemed the lesser evil. In mid-April Foreign Minister Castiella visited the United States. The official reason for the trip was to present as a gift of friendship to America the statue of Queen Isabella which had adorned the handsome Spanish pavilion at New York's World Fair. But when he got to Washington, he presented the warning he had come to give. In talks with Secretary of State Dean Rusk, Undersecretary George Ball, Secretary of Defense Robert McNamara, Castiella said bluntly that Palomares had "put the validity of our relationship to a very hard test."

It was not a complaint. It was the first use of the incident as a diplomatic lever and both sides understood there would be more. In the circuitous language of diplomacy, Castiella served notice that Madrid expected the United States to help it achieve NATO and Common Market membership or some kind of association as the price for keeping the Spanish bases going after 1968. Palomares had proved, he argued, that Spain was accepting risks for the common cause of Western defense as great as those of other allies. He said Spain wanted equal treatment in return.

In their pride and isolation the Spaniards no doubt overrated the United States' ability to pry open for them the door to European respectability as long as Franco remained Caudillo. But their diplomats said openly that Palomares had crystallized their will to drive a better bargain.

The Madrid government probably did not exaggerate at all the implications of Palomares in its own political future. At the demonstration in front of the United States Embassy three weeks after the accident, the people had shouted "Spain, *sí;* Yankees, *no,*" and "Yankees out of Spain." A week after the bomb had emerged from the sea and sailed home, Moscow radio broadcast to Spanish listeners that "the Americans spent $70 million on the search, but nobody still knows whether they really removed the nuclear bomb." And the clandestine radio in Prague was saying that "Spain has a government incapable of defending its interests or saying no to the Yankees. The present regime is not just bad, reactionary, dictatorial. It is a regime without authority and prestige, one completely lacking in dignity. We must strive to see that no Spaniard is unaware that the unconditional submission of the Franco government to United States policy has almost resulted in the explosion of four thermonuclear bombs on our country."

The Spanish people had seen the accident, watched the search, cheered the recovery with an extraordinary fortitude, resisting all insidious appeals to panic. The calm, the common sense, the biting but not bitter humor that are the wry Spanish approach to life had been remarkable.

"Imagine," one Embassy official said in the gloom of the incident, "what we'd have had to cope with if it had happened in France or Italy."

"Or Miami Beach," answered his colleague. "Probably mass hysteria . . ."

But the Palomares affair came when Spain was moving swiftly into a period of transition, a period of uncertainty;

from its rulers' point of view, a period of danger. All during the incident firm censorship had kept the H-bomb swathed in polite discretion in the Spanish press and radio. Soon after, the long-planned press law was put into effect, not exactly freeing speech but removing the clumsiest shackles. Reforms in the parliament, in the unions, in economic affairs were scheduled. It was evident that Generalissimo Franco was seeking to prepare gradually, cautiously, for his country's entry to a new era approaching representative government and that he hoped to accomplish that most delicate feat of politics in smooth and well-controlled stages. From time to time the government drew back in its reform program, then edged warily forward again. Dropping controls without careening into disaster is far more hazardous than maintaining authoritarianism, and no one could foretell with assurance whether Spain could make its entrance into modernity and the democratic world without terrible upheaval. No one could foretell with any confidence what Spanish politics would look like a few years later. The one sure thing was that the fright and the muddle of Palomares would be available to any group of future dissidents seeking a handy club against the Spanish government. At the time of the incident the austere position of the government and the solidity of the people prevented its being turned into a political holocaust. But the record and the memories of what had happened were left, and eventually might be used.

Still, the kindliness, the stoicism of the Spanish people and the help of the Spanish government had kept a terrible incident from turning into an unmitigated disaster. Ambassador Duke felt an obligation to show America's appreciation, and Francisco Simo, the fisherman whose keen eye had been so crucial, seemed a fitting recipient for symbolic thanks to all the nation. Duke sought to arrange a spectacular trip for Simo to the United States, somewhat like the tour of President Johnson's Pakistani camel driver. Washington preferred to forget the name of Palomares and anything that would bring reminders. Duke tried then to interest unions, private organizations, in inviting the Aguilas fisherman. The response was cool. So he settled for a flashy week in Madrid. Simo and his wife were invited to the capital as guests of the American Embassy, wined, dined, and bedded at the new Castellana Hilton, formally honored at an ambassadorial reception where Duke presented a scroll and an L.B.J. inauguration medallion. The citation read: "As a testimonial of admiration for the exceptional abilities and profound knowledge of the sea of Don Francisco Simo Orts which led to the discovery of the bomb which fell off the coast of Palomares, and as a symbol of gratitude on behalf of my country, I inscribe this document in Madrid, today, 15th of April of 1966. (Signed) Angier Biddle Duke, Ambassador of the United States of America."

The Spanish newspapers hailed Paco de la Bomba as their own hero, the parties were gay, and, in one small way, the United States had made an effort to say thank you. But the warm feeling soon soured. Simo told people proudly that he could easily have fished up the bomb in a week if the Navy had given permission. The United States, and especially the U.S. Navy, winced in irritation. Then, for reasons not quite clear, the Falangist newspaper *Arriba* launched a campaign for public subscription to buy Simo a new fishing boat as a reward since, it claimed, the United States had treated him so shabbily. A Mr. Raymond Sayre in Baltimore sent a check for one dollar to the fund, and a reproduction was prominently displayed on *Arriba*'s front page. The Navy had billed the Air Force $6 million for the operation, the paper noted acidly, but there was nothing for Simo except the generosity of private citizens. No doubt the campaign started as some hidden maneuver of internal Spanish politics, but it began to take odd turns. There were more anti-American cracks concerning Simo than there had been about the bomb itself. He had been paid something, a total of $6,600 for damage to his boat and consultant fees, but suddenly in August a Madrid lawyer announced a plan to sue the United States for $5 million to compensate the fisherman.

In Aguilas the captain of the other boat which had rescued two survivors held his wind-tousled head in his hands and said unhappily, "The other is going to be a millionaire. And me?" Bartolomé Roldán Martínez, the shy one, the silent one, had saved men's lives and gone along to point out where he saw the "dead-man" parachute and done all that he could without a thought of earning or reward. He hadn't even seen his name in the paper. The time his picture was published getting into a helicopter to help with the search, the caption mistakenly called him Simo. And he laughed, but later it all began to gnaw.

"Did I go to Madrid? There wasn't even the medal for lifesaving awarded me. Nothing. You do a favor and you don't ask for a recompense. I'd do it again, any time, for nothing. In one year I saved the crews of two boats. When you're a man, you owe that to other men, and you do it gladly. But it's unpleasant. Now one is getting all the reward and I have nothing. I was born here, the son of a fisherman. I don't have a boat of my own, only my arms to live by and support my wife and children. That's the way it always was, but now it's eating at me. El Catalán is getting a new boat. And me—nothing."

He did not say it with a whine, nor with even a drop of gall. It was the simple statement of a man's uneasy feeling, embarrassed by envy but honestly admitting it. Roldán sat at the open-air café on the dock that evening, sipping an orangeade which was all he wanted after the long, sweltering day at sea, and he turned his eyes to the horizon as he spoke. It was hard for him to have unkind thoughts, but he struggled to get them out because they were there and he could not prevent them. Then he fell silent, watching the sun drop behind the Aguilas sea wall in watery orange glory. When it was dark at last, and quiet, he absorbed the calm and spoke once more.

"If I'm to have something, God will send it to me. This has to be done for humanity, not for interest. If I'm to be poor all my life, I'll be poor. If I'm to be rich, I'll be rich. It's not up to me. I only do my job."

It had been an experience no one would forget, but life went on.

The four surviving airmen were back on duty, three of them still flying bombers from Seymour Johnson base, Mike Rooney transferred to fighters in Vietnam, as he had wanted.

Admiral Guest was awarded the Distinguished Service Medal for "exceptionally meritorious service." The citation said, "Through his dynamic leadership, organizational ability, and inspiring devotion to the fulfillment of an extremely important and difficult assignment, he contributed in large measure to the success of the task force..."

There were many heroes, men who improvised and invented and organized and drove themselves beyond the limits of their strength, and villagers who lived stoically through a test no peaceful people had been made to endure before. A ball of flame in the sky that brought two airplanes crashing down upon them had catapulted Palomares from the innocence of one age to the shared despairs and hopes of another. Some looked upon them and bemoaned the invasion of their ignorance. Some looked and hoped for greater future wisdom everywhere.

"I don't believe it's a tragedy to confront the realities of the nuclear age," Ambassador Duke said afterward. "We're all in this together. We partake of the same common danger. I don't think there should be privileged pockets of protection from the truth of our world."

When it was all over, Palomares reverted to its daily life. The movie started up again twice a week. There was still no telephone. The goats roamed the river bed and the cows chewed alfalfa in the sheds beside their owners' bedrooms. The corn and beans and tomatoes started to grow, some green and thick and some frail and sickly in neighboring patches, depending on the water. There were only a few things to show what had happened there, and they had to be sought out. But nothing was forgotten and it made a vital difference. Life looked the same, but its flavor was not as it used to be. There had been victims.

14

THE VILLAGE II

In late June the two fig trees down the hill from the cemetery were heavy with their purple fruit. The leaves were thick and large, the deep foresty green of flourishing maturity. On the ground below, the fallen figs lay split and rotting. Except for a few crackling weeds, there was no other living thing in sight. The long, fresh furrows stretched over the hilltops and the valleys in all directions, as though the ground had felt the bite of the plow the day before. But months had gone by since the last American left Palomares. Life had been certified back to normal. Still no one climbed the hill to sow the well-turned black soil. Not even the children dared to go for the fruit, but Manolo González, the Mayor's son, led the way for me. At the crest of a small hill he pointed to a slope several hundred yards away and said, "There. One of the bombs fell there. But it's not worth going any closer, the ground's too rough." And he trudged across the fields in the opposite direction, to show all the digging and plowing that had been done for decontamination.

Although the sun was approaching the western horizon, it was still glaring brightly. Everything was parched except the fig trees, which made them irresistible. Manolo shrugged when I asked why no one picked the ripe fruit and he took it as a hint, reaching out to pluck a handful of the fattest ones. I peeled and ate a couple. He watched me and did the same. They were very good. After a while we clambered back toward his Citroën pick-up.

"Aren't you afraid to be up here, to walk around and touch things?" he asked me then. I hadn't realized until that question what an act of courageous hospitality it had been for him to show me where the bomb fell. He did not say he had never been back there since the first excited, ignorant days after the accident. But it was clear enough then that none of the villagers went there unless they had to. A new irrigation pipe had been laid up the hill the previous winter, but it was not being used. No one wanted to cultivate those fields.

"Well, I may still plant one or two," the Mayor had said uncomfortably when I asked whether he was putting back to work his plots that had been certified radiation free. "But who knows, maybe the soil won't be so fertile? Maybe the things won't grow so well now." The muscles of his broad neck and shoulders worked out his embarrassment. "It would be a shame to waste the seed and fertilizer and the effort. I'm not afraid, you understand, some of the uneducated people are frightened. They just don't know a thing about radioactivity and they couldn't understand the explanations that the scientists gave us about how everything has been cleaned up. Some of them are superstitious." He chuckled indulgently, to show there was compassion in his sense of superiority. Then his brows tightened and he looked away, the shoulders moving again, and he added, "Still, who knows..."

That was the way it ended. There had been the terror and excitement of the crash, then a paralyzing fear seeping through the mists of official secrecy. After that, for quite some time, it had seemed that the most poisonous fall-out from the Palomares accident was envy. A committee of five farmers had estimated the value of the crops that the Americans destroyed. But the district judge in Almería had appointed other experts who set lower rates for compensation. Some thought it was because the Spanish government was not eager for too high a precedent in the generosity of authority when taxpayers put in claims. Some said it was because the villagers had connived with city businessmen to avoid the charge for the use of their own wells and springs which petty district overlords managed to impose elsewhere, and that the feudalists were getting even. Some said it was the fault of a bad-tempered sergeant or a hardhearted lieutenant. But almost everybody complained about the way the American money was distributed. When almost all the claims had been settled, the United States had paid out a little more than $500,000, a figure considered fair in the aggregate, but many felt their neighbors had received a good deal too much and themselves too little. One claim for $1 million was from a French company that said it had planned a tourist hotel nearby and ought to be paid the profits that it had anticipated. That was laughed off.

The movie owner was refused compensation for the money he lost when nobody wanted to see films any more and he had to cancel his shows, and Bienvenido Flores Gil was refused compensation for the crop he had intended to sow but didn't because the Americans were tramping about his land. But the settlements were slow, partly because of cumbersome United States government procedure, partly because the standard releases had to be renegotiated with the Spanish government. It was fair, the United States conceded, that the usual release abjuring all rights to future claims from the same accident should be revised since no one could guarantee that damage traced back to the spread of radioactivity would never appear at some later date. The amended certificates left open the possibility for new claims if new signs of injury developed. But still, some of the villagers refused to settle, arguing that the offer of less than their personal estimate of a fair award was an insult, impugning their honesty.

"The money is not the point," said the movie owner. "The difference is so little it means nothing to me. I would gladly give it to the United States. But it's the principle."

"I, too, know how to be a man," said Manuel Sabiote Flores, arguing that he should have been paid for his dead cow without being asked for autopsies and investigations. "The cow was buried and they kept sending commissions from America. I couldn't explain all that. I just tell the truth. And they wouldn't give me anything. They said get a lawyer. I said no, I'm not getting into a quarrel. I've lost a cow, I'm not going to risk losing another in a mix-up with lawyers. I'm a poor man, but I don't squabble."

"What do you expect?" said a JEN scientist from Madrid, who had come down to Palomares for another soil check. "The Americans wanted to be generous, but if this coffee cup is worth 5 pesetas and you say I'll give you 20, I'll sell it and go away grumbling and thinking it was probably worth 30 pesetas, that you knew something I didn't and made a fool of me."

The payments were the big topic for months, deciding not only who could realize the life-long dream of a motor scooter or plumbing or a complete new roof, since they came in cash and all at once, unlike usual earnings. They also became the new test of dignity. A man was asked to put a value on his property and he felt it diminished the value of his word if others received what they asked and his claim was reduced. The complaints and quarrels and eager justifications took on a whining tedium and Captain Calín, the police chief at Vera, grew disgusted. "I don't go there any more," he said. "I haven't been back to Palomares since it was all over. They've gotten greedy, they think if one got this much, another will get more if he tries hard enough. They should be ashamed." A committee of five villagers made the trip to Madrid to call on Ambassador Duke in his handsome office. They did not trust the Spanish authorities to hand on their views, they said. They wanted to deal directly.

But gradually, as the days lengthened into summer and the corn climbed and the memories of the American invasion dimmed, it became noticeable that it was not just money that had been left on the villagers' minds. That was what they talked about mostly, it was something they knew and understood, and all the words to deal with it were familiar. How could they discuss radioactivity? What was there to say but the one word, and the phrase that peppers every Spanish conversation with the stoic skepticism born of ages, "How do I know?"

A few things were left as visible reminders that a moment of tragedy in the sky had led to eighty overwhelming days of fear and strain and ingenuity and effort. The roofless old mine building on the beach that had served as Air Force mess hall and movie house was abandoned once again, but scrawls on the flaking walls recorded the passage of strangers. There was a sketch of a boat tossing on the waves, not U.S.S. anything but something like Noah's Ark, and a message to "Hurry in, Santana is coming." Someone had scribbled "Welcome to the Alamo."

J. P. Lee of Titusville, Pennsylvania, Willie Webb, Peter Stones, and the "Red Baron" had left their autographs on the plaster. Along the road leading from the village, white concrete fence posts strung with barbed wire and in some places whitewashed concrete retaining walls marked the places where the Americans had cut down the usual fence of tangled cactus. The dirt road built by the Air Force to connect Palomares to the Garrucha road was getting rutted and sagging in some places, but it was still better and much shorter than the winding hill road to Vera. In Villaricos a few of the skinny legged boys sported Air Force fatigue caps and one of the shanties had been partially reroofed with a length of plastic that must have covered some phenomenal piece of machinery when it arrived on the beach. Screws and shreds of cloth and bits of wire and molten metal still littered the broad hilltop where the burning tanker fell. The stones there were blackened on one side. There was nothing else to show for what had happened.

The whitewashed church, set by itself on the edge of the village, was empty again. Since no one came, it was locked on weekdays. In the evenings, the doors were opened and candles flickered, but only one or another of the old women dropped by on a saint's day or the anniversary of a death to kneel in prayer. On Sundays, the young priest from Cuevas came roaring in on his red motor scooter to say mass. There was room for all who continued to attend.

The men of the Air Force had chipped in and collected 70,000 pesetas for Palomares, 12,000 for Villaricos, to use in equipping a new church. Father Navarrete said the money for the church was to come later from the U.S. government, but the plans had already been drawn up. When it was built, he said, there would be a special chapel in it as a memorial to the seven dead airmen. Meanwhile, on July 17, six months from the day of the accident, he said a mass in Cuevas for Major Chapla whose widow had sent him the six dollars in Spanish money recovered from her husband's wallet. Navarrete showed the letter to Captain Calín when it came. The policeman's eyes twinkled at the pink stationery and he told the priest, "Oh, oh, it's from a woman. Someone's got it for you." Later, Captain Ramirez translated it for them. Ramirez was one of the few Americans everybody liked. Colonel White said later, "If Joe ran for mayor, he'd get every vote there." Few others left even a memory behind.

General Wilson's rule confining everyone to camp except on business had prevented the flowering of friendship or romance as well as the outbreak of brawls, and in any case the girls of the area were known for their sound, sober-mindedness. "All they want is to get married," Calín said of them with a wistful eye, "nothing else. They kept asking me when an officer came to town, 'Is that one married?' 'Did he say if he has a wife?' There was a lot of staring and strolling, of course, but the girls thought the officers probably all had families already so they didn't bother asking to be introduced."

The girls of Palomares went on about their work, threshing grain and carrying water and tending their mothers' babies as before. The few lipsticks and face creams in the small glass cabinet at the store were dusty and untouched. No Palomares woman used them. They would sit on the shelves until Christmas when the native girls who had gone off to work in northern Europe would come home for the holidays and try to keep up the new vanities they had learned abroad.

The Parador below Mojácar was something new, but that had been planned before the accident and no mementos were displayed of its hectic opening and the chilly ambassadorial swim. By summer, American and Dutch and German tourists had filled it. Bikinis began to brighten the long pink beach. In the evening, Roberto Puig sometimes came down from his house on the hill and drank with the foreigners at the terrace bar overlooking the sea. One American, planning to buy and convert an old house in Mojácar, consulted with Puig as his possible architect.

"I'll have to ask some questions before I can even think of doing it for you," the Spaniard said, adjusting the silk ascot in the neck of his sports shirt. "Tell me what you think of Johnson's Vietnam policy, what you think of segregation, what you think of modern art." The American mumbled a banality, acknowledging neither favor nor disapproval on any of the points, and little interest. "All right," Puig said, "now we can talk business." They did. The price was wrong and there was no agreement. Puig never mentioned his conviction that he had been burned by the H-bomb and that his life expectancy was short, he never brought up the accident. He had an exciting pile of new plans to talk about with people at the bar.

There was, as the officials had thought wisest, no monument or memorial of any kind to the event that had focused world attention on Palomares. There was, in South Carolina, what Calín called "a little Spanish field" buried beneath 10 feet of dirt, and there were the feelings of the villagers. That was all.

Bienvenido Flores Gil, a thirty-nine-year-old farmer, had decided to move with his wife and three children to Barcelona. "There's nothing else to do," he said. "I couldn't plant my crop because they gave me back my land too late. So what else can I do but go? I'll work in a factory or construction or something. Maybe one day I can sell the land here and the house, but no one wants to buy them now. People are afraid to buy here. I'm not frightened, but it doesn't make me happy to live here any more."

His daughter Juanita, a round-cheeked fifteen-year-old, bent her head demurely over her embroidery as her father talked. She giggled when he said his age—she had thought him younger. The prospect of the move to the city both excited and worried her. She, too, like everyone else in the family, would have to get a job and leave the relatives, the fields, the horizons they had known all their lives. It was going to be a momentous change.

"Who knows," the neighbors had said, "whether they would be moving or not if there hadn't been an accident? People have been moving away for years. There's nothing here, it's too poor. The water is getting worse every year. If only there would be rain, or the government would bring good water."

"I certainly wouldn't go if it hadn't been for the accident," Flores said. "First because of the accident, and second because of the way they treated me. They wouldn't admit my claim. How can I stay here when I'm treated like that?"

His aunt, a chubby woman all in black teetering on the wooden stool that was left when the stranger was offered the good chair with a woven straw seat, echoed what he said. The women in Palomares never hesitated to speak up. But they always spoke in support of their men, arguing their wisdom, their righteousness, their honesty. "And besides," she said, "there's the radioactivity. That's the basis of the principle. Some say there isn't any more, some say there is. I don't know. I think more there is than there isn't."

"Well," said Flores, "if there wasn't any danger, why didn't they just leave the bomb in the sea, like anything broken? They just don't say when there's danger. You can't be sure of anything they say."

"They don't tell the truth," said Juanita. "I don't say there is or there isn't any more. But what about the water? They tested the water at first and then they went away, they weren't here all the time. They just don't tell."

"Yes," said the aunt, "life is impossible here."

"It's all right now," said Flores, "everything looks the same now. But who knows how it will be tomorrow? And I have too little land. You have to have more land to make a living now." He was taut, with a blade of bitterness on his tongue, worried by the burdens of his decision to start anew. "I'll take the furniture and just leave the house and the land here. I've got to make my own way. From the moment I have a job everything will change. I'm not going to live on the government, I can make my own living without bothering anyone. I'll look after myself and my family." There was the sound of fierceness, almost anger in his voice, but it was probably only the fervent heat of hope.

The neighbors did not really approve of Flores' leaving. Going away for work was well enough for the young, and for the men when it was necessary, but uprooting the family was something else. Manuel Sabiote Flores, who lived in the house just across a hard-baked patch of dirt from Flores Gil, had thirteen children and eight of them were away at work in Germany and Switzerland. One had recently married a Palomares boy and Sabiote said proudly that he had bought them a house with the savings they had sent from the jobs abroad.

"It's amazing, you know," he said, "they send one German mark and I get 15 pesetas for it. You would think it would be one peseta, but it's 15. They earn so much. Tell me, how did the Germans get to be so rich after such a terrible war? Do they have a tremendous lot of gold? And is the war still going in Vietnam? Where do the arms come from? Don't you think it's the Russians?"

One of the daughters flashed a worried glance at the old man and then at the radio, an antique affair on a little shelf just below the ceiling. "We can't put on the news any more," she said, "because it makes my father cry."

"So many people are dying all over," he agreed, "I can't bear to hear it now. Now that we're just sitting here, waiting."

I asked about the farming, the plans for a new crop.

"Our land is up by the cemetery, on the hill near where the bomb fell," he said, as though that explained everything.

His wife Carmen caught the lack of understanding. "We can't plant up there any more. It's fatal. How can I send my children to work there?"

Bright-eyed Paquita, the girl with the long blond pigtails, nodded in frozen awe.

"It's not the fault of the Americans," Sabiote added hurriedly. "I don't think that. I think it's the fault of the Spanish tyranny we have here."

They all fell silent. It was a daring thing to say, but there was an air of desperation so heavy in the little room that nothing seemed to matter. It was hot and the flies buzzed thunderously, as though mere insect noises could revive the sound of hope. Tears gathered in the father's eyes. Something had to be said. I began to talk about the thriving fig trees, about the things the physicists had told me, the white air sample boxes and all the tests and checks still being made to be absolutely sure there was no danger.

"But why do they keep coming to test if nothing's wrong?" the wife asked.

But then slowly, reluctantly, she nodded acceptance of the possibility that such extra caution, such thoroughness of scientific work proved "they" really were determined to eliminate the most minute risk, that "they" really had removed the danger. "You think we should plant?" she asked, narrowing her eyes to judge the sincerity of the answer. "You really think it is safe? You went up there, and ate the figs?"

In any case, they couldn't move away. The father was too old, the young children were too small. The mother sighed. "Yes," she said, "I guess we'll have to sow the fields. We can't afford not to. There's nothing else."

It had been an emotional hour. The farewells were warm. At the door, the father drew himself very straight to say good-by. He was a little man, short and thin and lined with the years of his life, but he held his head high and puffed his chest as he had seen dignitaries do to mark the formal importance of an occasion. "I am poor but I am honorable," he said. He held out his hand for a vigorous shake and smiled broadly as he pronounced the words of tradition, "This is your house. In this house you have a friend eager to be of service whenever you come to Palomares."

At the end of the road Eduardo Navarro Portillo was hoeing in the field behind his house. The crater made by the bomb had been filled in, chunks of new topsoil had been spread to replace the dirt that was removed, and alfalfa was sprouting up there now. He had not hesitated to plant, but some of the plots were fallow.

"Nobody will come to share crop my land," he said, "not

even at half the usual rent. They're afraid of radioactivity in these fields. But I'm too old, I'm sixty-eight, I can't do it all without help. My wife Anna is sixty. How much can she do?"

Anna was plump and talkative, dressed in black as almost all the married women were, eager to tell and to hear.

"Ay," she said, "what will come of it? My husband has a picture they made of him with the Ambassador and General Wilson. They sent it from Madrid with thanks for good cooperation because he had the most damage, the most trouble. But what will happen now?"

"I wanted to have a blood test," the old man said. "If I don't have radioactivity, nobody here has it. But they said blood tests aren't any use."

"No," Anna pronounced, "it's not like that anyway. One can catch it and not another. You can't tell."

"I always had a man here helping me," the man said. "He was twenty miles away on the day the bomb fell. He never came back since. And they never sent me the results of the tests they made. How do I know how I am?"

It was suggested that he might write to ask.

"Well, they'll tell me if there's anything. What good is it to ask?"

The question had been a gaffe. He never admitted that he was not able to write, he simply ruled it out as futile. But when a neighbor came to the door, prompted no doubt by curiosity about the visitor, Anna answered with authority. The girl had asked her if she knew the time. "You know we don't have the time," the woman said, "we broke our alarm clock two years ago and you know we don't have a new one." Reproved, the intruder slunk away.

Anna returned to the conversation at hand. "It was a very quiet place here," she said, "nothing so quiet in all of Spain. We had pigs, all kinds of animals. We had to get rid of them because we couldn't feed them. Anyway, it's too dangerous to eat chickens, eggs, anything like that. My daughter sells frozen fish in her store and we eat that. Since they got the bomb out of the sea, sometimes we eat a little fresh fish from Garrucha." She sighed deeply. "But not with the same satisfaction as before. Before we ate with much relish. Not any more."

"Anna won't eat anything from our land," Eduardo said. "She buys the food from the other villages. But I work the land. What is there to do?"

Not everyone was so resigned, but they said it again and again, "Maybe it's all right and maybe it isn't. Who knows? You just don't feel so quiet here any more."

That was the view of the village looking back on its entry into the atomic age. The people of Palomares might have been speaking for the world that lives with H-bombs, all the wide, uneasy world. Little else had changed, but with that feeling nothing remained quite the same. There was no panic, no frenzy, just an unhappy question—the question of the age. Maybe it's all right and maybe it isn't. Who knows?

The name of the village was a name of peace—Palomares means the place of the doves. It was a forgotten speck in a crowded world, and it was being forgotten again. Because man's ultimate engine of war had fallen upon it, haphazardly, it had been the place of a unique operation, not warlike but not peaceful either. Three times as many Americans as there were villagers had been drawn there for a frenzied effort. It had cost almost $1 million a day for eighty days, far more than all the toil of all the people who ever lived there from prehistoric times to the end of time ahead would produce. There had been dazzling achievement on the frontiers of science and foolish human muddle, extraordinary organization and red-tape nonsense such as the Air Force bill for $3.45 sent to Wright Langham months afterward. It was for five meals he had eaten at Camp Wilson. Douglass Evans, the explosive expert from Los Alamos, said he was billed a dollar for each meal, 50 cents for food, and 50 cents for service which consisted of ladling out beans as the men queued. But the Air Force said there must have been a misunderstanding, it really had not charged for service.

The villagers had lived through it all. In a way, they had scarcely been a part of it. In a way whose consequences no one could foretell, it would always be a part of them. Certainly, for many years to come, anything odd in Palomares would be attributed to the bomb. The birth of a Mongoloid, a defective child, an animal freak, the unpredictable accidents of nature would be called the fruit of the bomb, and who could ever say if it were true or false?

There were a number of villagers with congenital defects before the accident. It might have been the diet, the water, the centuries of poverty, the isolation that had led to generation after generation of intermarriage. But there were no records. It would not even be possible to tell whether the proportion of abnormalities had increased. There would be foolish alarms, such as the "blue goats" in Nevada. There, after one atomic test, a farmer reported excitedly that fall-out had made his goats turn blue. An investigator was sent out, and in a few hours he telephoned Los Alamos to say in fright, "My gosh, his goats *are* blue." Then he went for further details. He noticed the goats were only blue on their sides, not on their backs where most fall-out ought to have settled. It turned out that the farmer had put up a new galvanized wire fence and that his goats had just discovered it was a good way to scratch their sides. The galvanizing rubbed off and colored their hair.

There might be serious illness. There would be fear, the silent, nagging fear that dulls the bright eye of innocence and shadows the smooth brow of simplicity, and once existing can never be made to vanish. Although they were primitive, the villagers had never been ignorant of the basic patterns of life. They knew as much as people anywhere could know of birth and death and love and hate and gaiety and labor, and they accepted it all with the stoical wisdom that keeps the patterns going. They accepted the bombs, too, because there was no choice. They were practical people and did not let their imaginations dwell on the specter of what could have happened if a bomb had exploded; they considered it a foolishness of those who did. Nor did they resent the inexplicable way that fears and angers in a world outside had led a foreign country to let slip its pent-up fury on their calm.

For the village, the legacy of the bomb was not anger, not disease or damage, but the insidious, consuming plague of uncertainty that had already swept much of the world and had reached out to infect a handful of people whose poverty had been a shield. They had been made to pay the price of modern ambitions in which they had no part. And that was what disturbed them most, for they knew that people elsewhere tortured each other and themselves, and they thought their modesty had kept them safe. They did not think of telling America or other countries what to do. They believed they left others alone and had been left alone. They did not know that the kind of danger that had been born in the world no longer left anyone alone.

It is trite now to say that nuclear bombs are very

dangerous, and that it is excruciatingly dangerous to swing them across the world above people's heads, no matter how silently they fly and how high. But Palomares had shown that the danger has not faded with familiarity, that it must not be forgotten or wished away lest it fall from a blue sky, on a day of peaceful harvest, who knows where?

INDEX

ABOUT THE AUTHOR

Winner of numerous journalism awards, FLORA LEWIS earned her graduate degree in journalism from the Columbia School of Journalism. Since then she has worked for the Associated Press, *The Washington Post*, *Time* magazine, *The London Observer*, *The Economist*, *France-Soir*, and has traveled all over the world in the course of her work.

In addition, many of her articles have appeared in magazines, including *The New York Times Magazine*, *The New Yorker*, *Saturday Review*, *Life*, *Saturday Evening Post*, *Holiday*, and the *Atlantic*. She is currently based in Paris, where she is Foreign Affairs Columnist for *The New York Times*.

Join the Allies on the Road to Victory
BANTAM WAR BOOKS

☐	25991	**WAR AS I KNEW IT** Patton, Jr.	$4.50
☐	25946	**CHILD OF HITLER** A. Heck	$3.50
☐	24297	**TO HELL AND BACK** Audie Murphy	$3.95
☐	24127	**NIGHT FIGHTER*** J. R. D. Braham	$2.95
☐	26762	**PIGBOATS** Theodore Roscoe	$4.50
☐	25894	**NEW FACE OF WAR** W. Brown	$3.95
☐	26505	**ONE SOLDIER** J. Shook	$3.95
☐	26316	**WITH THE OLD BREED** E. Sledge	$3.50

*Cannot be sold to Canadian Residents.

Prices and availability subject to change without notice.

Buy them at your local bookstore or use this handy coupon for ordering:

Bantam Books, Inc., Dept. WW2, 414 East Golf Road, Des Plaines, Ill. 60016

Please send me the books I have checked above. I am enclosing $_____
(please add $1.50 to cover postage and handling). Send check or money
order—no cash or C.O.D.'s please.

Mr/Ms _____

Address _____

City/State _____ Zip _____

WW2—4/87
Please allow four to six weeks for delivery. This offer expires 10/87.

William L. Shirer

A Memoir of a Life and the Times, Vol. 1 & 2

☐ 34204   TWENTIETH CENTURY $12.95
           JOURNEY, The Start 1904-1930
☐ 34179   THE NIGHTMARE YEARS, $12.95
           1930-1940
☐ 32335   WM. SHIRER BOXED SET $25.90

In Volume 1, Shirer recounts American/European history as seen through his eyes. In Volume 2, he provides an intensely personal vision of the crucible out of which the Nazi monster appeared.

Anthony Cave Brown

☐ 34016   BODYGUARD OF LIES, $12.95
The extraordinary, true story of the clandestine war of deception that hid the secrets of D-Day from Hitler and sealed the Allied victory.

Charles B. MacDonald

☐ 34226   A TIME FOR TRUMPETS, $11.95
The untold story of the Battle of the Bulge.

John Toland

☐ 34208   THE LAST 100 DAYS, $10.95
The searing true drama of men and women caught in the final struggles of the epic conflict, World War II.

Prices and availability subject to change without notice.

BANTAM VIETNAM WAR BOOKS